FORTS AND CASTLES

THE STORY OF DEFENCE WORKS FROM ANCIENT TIMES TO THE PRESENT

Terence Wise

ALMARK PUBLISHING CO LTD, LONDON

First published — December 1972

By the same author:
AMERICAN MILITARY CAMOUFLAGE
AND MARKINGS, 1939 – 1945

Printed in Great Britain by
Staples Printers Ltd, The Priory Press, St Albans, Herts
for the publishers, Almark Publishing Co Ltd
270 Burlington Road, New Malden
Surrey KT3 4NL, England

Introduction

THERE are many books about castles, and quite a few on the Roman occupation of Britain, but few of them deal exclusively with fortifications of these periods, while there are great gaps in the study of fortifications during other periods of British history, notably the Iron Age and Dark Ages. The series of invasions endured by the British Isles has resulted in the islands being particularly rich in the remains of fortifications and I have two aims in writing about them. Firstly, I have attempted to summarize for the layman the development of these fortifications from the earliest times right up to the defences erected during World War 2, and secondly to list the sites of these works so that readers might visit them personally. Such a book cannot hope to cover all known fortifications of the British Isles and the gazetteer forming the second part of this book should therefore be considered as only a selection of sites to visit.

The major considerations in making this selection have been to include fortifications which best illustrate the evolution of fortifications through the centuries, and to list only those which make an actual visit to the site worth while. All too often, especially in the case of works constructed prior to the Norman invasion, it is possible to wander over a site, searching for the remains, without seeing anything but a beautiful view of the surrounding countryside. Once I ate my packed lunch sitting within the overgrown ramparts of a small Iron Age camp, but only discovered these fortifications during a second search in the area several years later.

Some of the gazetteer entries may appear at first glance to be hardly worthy of a special excursion: this will be found to occur when there is a group of sites in the vicinity, or when there is an important site nearby, the insignificant entry having been offered as a secondary objective. More often than not such a complex of sites occurs near a major centre of civilization, where succeeding invaders have built on the fortifications of their predecessors. York is an example of this, for here the Roman remains are slight but the later defences extensive.

Almost all the Iron Age entries are likely to disappoint the visitor, the fortifications now consisting of only overgrown ditches and a few grassy mounds. Such sites are best studied from the air and the large number of line drawings in the relevant chapter is an attempt to provide the reader with aerial views. However, nothing can take the place of a visit. You may not think much of the remains but a little imagination can reconstruct them to their original state: a look around the land from the high ground, where these forts are invariably placed, will show the wisdom in the selection of site.

ACKNOWLEDGMENTS

Many of the line drawings of fortifications in this book are based on plans drawn up in the past. I am particularly indebted to A. H. Allcroft's *Earthwork of England* which, although published in 1908, is still the definitive work on the

3

subject. The following figures are based on those by A. H. Allcroft: 1–3, 5–10, 12 and 13, 18 and 19, 23–27, 33, 37, 43, 62–65.

Figures 17, 34, 36, 38, 45–52, 55–56, 62 are Crown Copyright and are reproduced by kind permission of the Controller of Her Majesty's Stationery Office. Other figures have been based on work in various publications, as listed here: Archaeologia Cambrensis, figures 4, 32, 35: Bayeux Tapestry, figure 26: J. Collingwood Bruce's *Handbook to the Roman Wall*, figures 21 and 22: the Hatfield Manuscript, figure 41: *Colchester Castle* by the Colchester Corporation, figure 27.

Of the photographs those on pages 60 and 84 were taken by Fred and Lyn Hughes, to whom my thanks for permission to reproduce them here. Those in Section 11 were drawn from the files of the Imperial War Museum. All other photographs are by the author. The colour illustrations are by Alan Kemp.

CONTENTS

1: Iron Age fortifications

THE beginning of the history of fortification in the British Isles coincides conveniently with the beginning of the Iron Age, indeed this age might almost be re-named the Age of Fortifications as far as these islands are concerned, but before launching into an account of these works it is perhaps wise to cast a glance backwards in time to discover the reason for this relatively abrupt development of a military art.

Stone and Bronze Age Man appears to have lived reasonably peacefully in small communities, his primitive homestead designed only to protect him from the weather or from bands of marauding wolves. Sometimes these communities might be encircled by a small earthwork and on Salisbury Plain especially there are many examples of stock enclosures in the form of low, usually circular earthworks. Similarly Avebury, Stonehenge and some other 'henge' constructions of these two ages are surrounded by earthworks, that at Avebury having a diameter of 400 yards (giving a circuit of over three-quarters of a mile) with the rampart still rising nearly 40 feet above the bottom of its ditch in places. So impressive was, and is, this earthwork that the Saxons built a settlement within it and even now the village of Avebury remains largely within its circle.

However, the Avebury earthwork is of a purely religious nature and although some other apparently strong earthworks like those mentioned briefly above have survived from the Stone and Bronze Ages, they are not fortifications in the strict military sense and we must wait for the Iron Age before the advent of military fortifications in these islands. There is one possible exception:

THE CRANNOG

The word comes from the Irish *crann*, tree or timber, and is applied to an artificial island (not necessarily made exclusively of timber despite the name) bearing on it a hut or collection of huts. The method of construction was to pile stones, logs, brushwood and clay on to the bed of a fairly shallow stretch of water until a firm foundation had been made. On this were built the huts with floors of logs and more clay. Often these 'islands' settled after a while and a new floor would have to be added.

The timbers of crannogs have been found in a lake in Glamorgan, in peat in Breconshire and other parts of Wales, but so far there has been no scientific excavation of the sites. More crannogs have been discovered in Ulster and in Lough Gur and on the shore of Lough Gara in Eire, but there are no particulars available for these sites. Fair Head crannog in Lough na Cranagh, Ballycastle, County Antrim, is a very fine example, measuring approximately 120 by 90 feet and still more than five feet above water level. A few examples have also been found in Yorkshire and Norfolk.

Although basically dwelling places their choice of position makes these 'islands' natural fortifications, the only access being by coracle or a narrow causeway, and they continued to be used as refuges from the late Bronze Age right through to the 16th and 17th centuries in Scotland and Ireland. The method was developed more fully in the lake dwellings of the Iron Age, discussed later.

HILL FORTS

The Iron Age in Britain is generally placed at around 500 BC when various Celt-speaking peoples migrated to Britain. That friction took place is aptly shown by a decrease in the monumental religious building, a sharp increase in the number of weapons found during archaeological excavations at occupied sites of this period, and the first appearance of the hill fort as opposed to the simple stock enclosure. From the 3rd century BC these hill forts became more numerous due to the martial nature of the Celts, which showed itself in inter-tribal warfare, and the insecurity caused by the arrival of even more migrants. At first these tribes were strongest on the eastern side of England, more scattered in the south, south-west and Scotland. But more Celts appeared in Cornwall and towards the end of the 2nd century BC Belgae tribes of Germanic origin began to arrive, creating kingdoms in south and south-east England which covered areas approximately equivalent to two or three of our modern Home Counties. Warfare and insecurity increased alarmingly. What had once been merely small enclosures to protect Man and his domesticated animals from the wolves developed into small forts. The Age of Fortification had arrived with a vengeance.

The reasons why the forts were inevitably placed on hills are threefold. Firstly, at this period the lowlands were mostly covered by thick forest and the sides of hills offered the land most easily cultivated. (Many forts are surrounded by terraces on the hill sides and these are believed to be almost certainly the result of such cultivation). Secondly, from these high spots it was possible to see an enemy while he was still miles away, giving ample time for men and animals to reach the shelter of the fort. The third reason is the sheer bulk of earth which had to be moved to make a ditch and rampart in an age when the population was far from numerous and tools still primitive.

Fig 1 illustrates the mechanics of ditch and rampart construction. To build a bank one foot high requires the digging of a ditch one foot deep, but to raise a rampart two feet high necessitates digging a ditch four feet deep, four times the work for only double the height. On the same principle a four-foot rampart

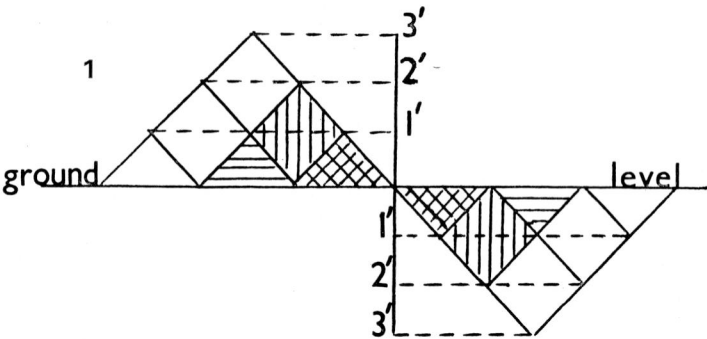

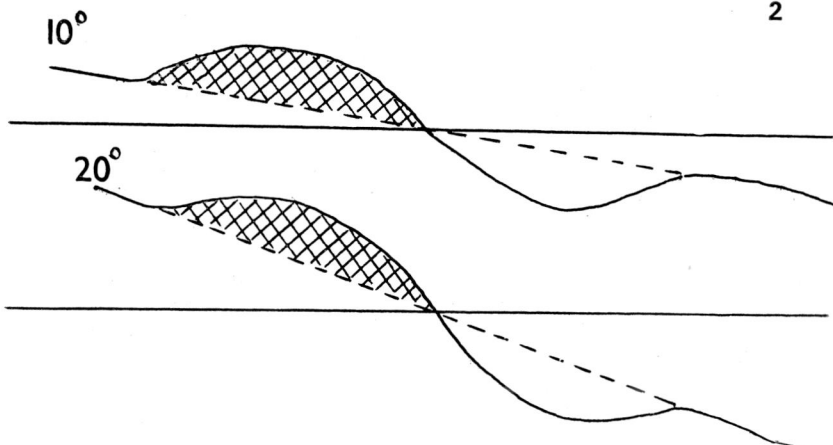

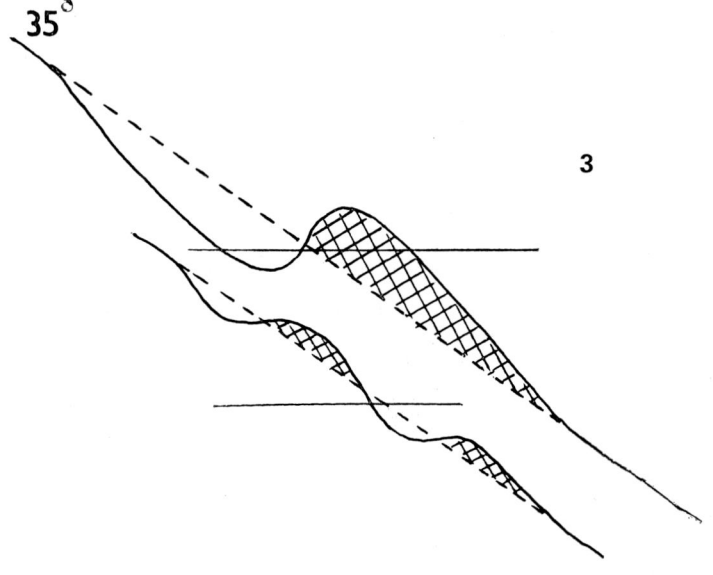

means moving sixteen times as much earth from the ditch and to erect a rampart of 20 feet no less than 400 times the labour is needed, not to mention the extra effort required to lift the earth to the greater height. At Cissbury no less than 60,000 tons of chalk had to be removed by hand from the eleven-foot ditch.

Iron Age Man may have had primitive tools but he had the wit to use the lay of the land to ease his labours. Fig 2 illustrates how the amount of earth to be shifted can be drastically reduced by building the rampart on a slope. At an angle of ten degrees a reasonable ditch and rampart can be constructed for a given amount of work, but on a slope of 20 degrees the same amount of work produces a much bigger obstacle. Obviously even better results for less work can be obtained on steeper slopes. In Fig 3 it is necessary only to throw the soil *down* the hill to form a rampart and a double ring of defences of this nature, as shown in the smaller diagram, would be very difficult to storm under fire. Hambledon Hill in Dorset, and Scratchbury and Battlesbury Camps near Warminster, were built by this method, as was the western face of Brent Knoll, Somerset, perhaps the best example of this type of earthwork. At Cissbury the north-west side is also constructed in this way. Occasionally a single ditch might provide the material for a rampart on one side and a counter-scarp on the outer side.

There does not seem to have been any common rule governing the height of the ramparts. Most often the inner rampart is the highest, though in many cases the outer, or middle if there are three ramparts, may be higher. In almost all cases the ramparts were topped by a stockade of timber, or a thorn fence, the original zareba which is more often associated with colonial troubles in the 19th century. This timber palisade was no small work, and it has been calculated that Cissbury required 10,000 timbers, each 15 feet long, to encircle the fort.

Ditches were normally outside the rampart, their purpose being to break the charge of any attacking force. Often a small rampart or parapet was built on the outer edge of the ditch to conceal the ditch from the attacker until the last minute. The attacker would know the ditch existed but not what lay within it, and sometimes there were some very nasty shocks for him. Caesar quotes sharpened stakes being used to line such ditches and on rocky sites slivers of stone would be planted in the ground to form *chevaux de frise*, that is a line of spikes projecting at all angles. The best examples to survive may be seen in Ireland, at Doocaher and Dun Aonghus on Inishmore in the Arran Islands. Another trick was to strew the bottom of the ditch with small rocks to break the rush of attackers.

The shape of the ditches varied greatly from fort to fort, some having steep sides meeting at an acute angle at the bottom, others having gradually sloping sides and a flat floor. The apparent anomaly of ramparts without ditches may be explained by the effect of the weather, slowly filling the ditch through the centuries. However, where ramparts were built on rocky soil, ditches were usually small or non existent, loose rock from the immediate area being used to provide extra bulk for a very high rampart in compensation. At Tre'r Ceiri (Fig 4) in Wales the dry stone walls stand 15 feet high in places and are 16 feet thick, but there is no ditch, the hill falling away steeply on all sides.

Where ramparts were built of stone various methods of construction were employed. The simplest method was to 'plant' large stones in the soil vertically and back them with smaller stones. The rampart of earth was then built against this stone face ; Fig 5. An alternative method, used to this day for small retaining walls, was to lay flat stones in rough courses with a slight batter, or slope, backwards. Often such walls would be double, the gap between them filled with rubble or earth. At Worlebury in Somerset is a good example of terraced walling, illustrated by Fig 6. Here the walls are up to 38 feet thick, consisting of a series of dry stone walls built against each other. Similar terraced walls occur at Dun Onaght, Doonconor and Dun Aonghus in the Arran Islands, and at Greenan Elly west of Londonderry. Those at Dun Aonghus are particularly fine, the inner walls still standing to a height of 18 feet with steps up to them at each side of the gates. The fort was restored in 1881 but it does enable the visitor to see what these forts must have looked like in their hey-day.

The half timbered walling method of the Gauls, which Caesar ran into on the Continent, has not been found in England but examples have been excavated

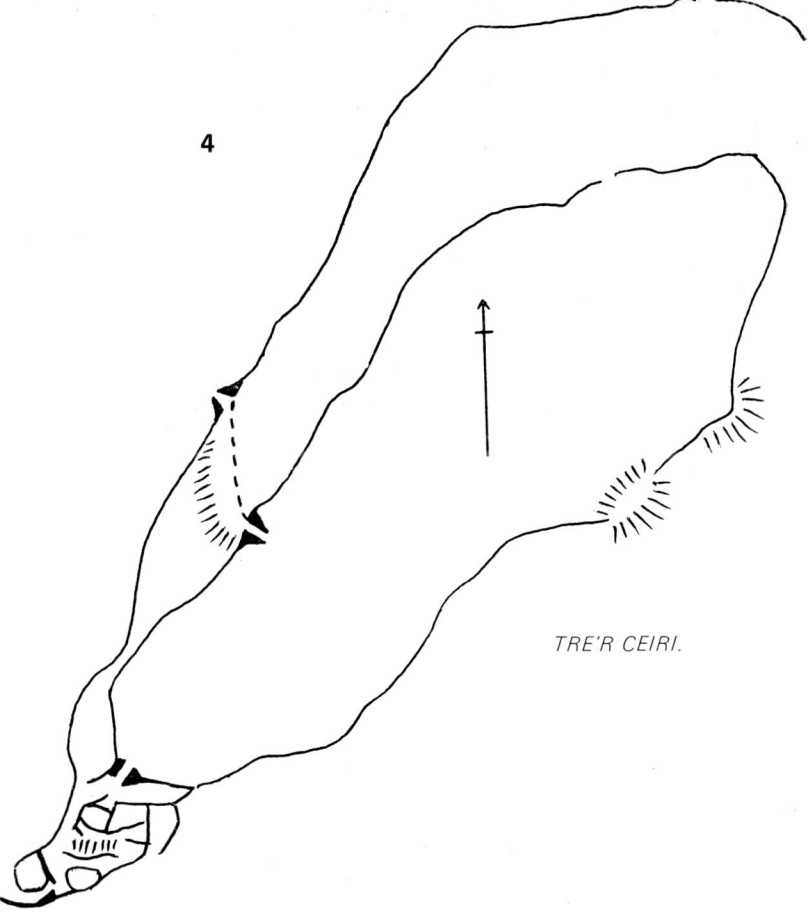

4

TRE'R CEIRI.

at Castle Law, Perthshire, and Burghead, Moray. In this method beams 40 feet long were placed on the ground at intervals of two feet, their inner ends braced by other timbers and their outer ends wedged between large boulders. This was covered with rammed earth and a second row of beams placed on top, staggered between those of the first row. The process was then repeated to the full height of the wall. Caesar states that neither fire nor ram could make any impression on walls built in this way.

All stone used in the ramparts of forts was in its natural rough state; squared or dressed stone and mortar is not encountered until the arrival of the Romans. Also these stone forts were rarely so complex or extensive as those of earth. On the other hand, the chalk-built forts of Dorset and Wiltshire are amongst the largest and most elaborate in design. Chalk, whilst being more easily worked than rock, is also a very enduring material and chalk-built forts have consequently survived the weathering of the centuries far better than most other earthworks of the same age.

When you see the defences now the ramparts often appear as innocuous grass-covered mounds perhaps 8 to 15 feet high, though some rise higher. Imagine these 2,000 years ago, before the centuries of weathering had broken down the ramparts and filled the ditches. Originally the ramparts may have been 40 feet high with a sheer vertical face, the ditch perhaps 30 feet wide

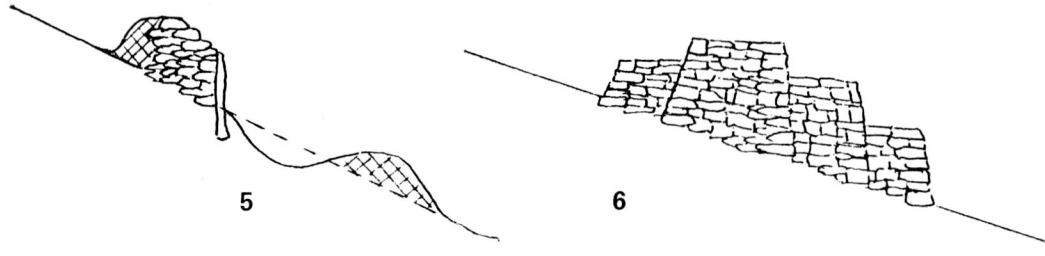

5   **6**

and 12 feet deep. Imagine trying to scale such fortifications, without the added complications of a timber palisade and the men behind it, busily engaged in discharging a hail of missiles at you. At this time the tribes knew nothing of siege craft and a successful assault on a fort was achieved by surprise and élan or treachery. This hit and run method also explains the absence of a water supply on most hills which have been fortified, a point which often puzzles those with a military turn of mind.

Hill forts vary considerably in size and complexity. During the generations and eventually centuries of continual occupation the defences naturally became more and more impressive. Larger groups of allied tribes replaced the original small groups of families with the result that some sites were abandoned or became of only minor importance, while others were adopted as the central fortress and were developed accordingly. But the arrival of a new race or tribe did not signal a change in methods of fortification, nor mean an increase in the size of an original stronghold. So long as the Iron Age endured, in Scotland, Wales and Ireland this meant right into the period of the Roman occupation and beyond, the same methods of fortification were employed regardless of race or tribe, and new tribes capturing old forts often occupied them as they found them, without any modification of the defences.

The defence systems of the earliest forts were very simple, usually just one rampart encircling a hill top with an accompanying ditch. Fugitives fleeing from the Roman advances into Gaul rebuilt many of these old forts, extending the number of ramparts and ditches. Where more than one line of defences were erected the ramparts had previously been kept as close together as the lay of the land permitted in order to save labour, but in these new forts a berm, or flat platform, was deliberately left between the lines of defences. This 'defence in depth' is associated with the widespread use of the sling, introduced from Brittany, as a long range weapon. On many of the later sites burnt clay sling bolts have been excavated: these were designed to be used red hot in attempts to set fire to the stockade and the huts within the fort. Finds of such bolts have been found at Ardoch, Mount Caburn and the lake village of Glastonbury, all pre-Roman. Both Caesar and Tacitus remark on the roofs of British huts being highly inflammable and should huts catch fire, perhaps stampeding the livestock, the rapidly spreading fire and resulting confusion could well have resulted in the fall of an otherwise impregnable position. The purpose of the berm and multiple ramparts in these later forts can therefore be directly linked to the necessity to not only keep the raiders out, but also to keep them at a good distance from the heart of the fort.

The number and size of the gateways into the hill forts varied but was normally governed by the size of the fort. The small ring-shaped forts usually had just one entrance, as did forts built on promontories. Larger forts had two, one being the main gateway, and the most complex systems had two, three or more, but with usually only one gateway into the innermost ring of defences.

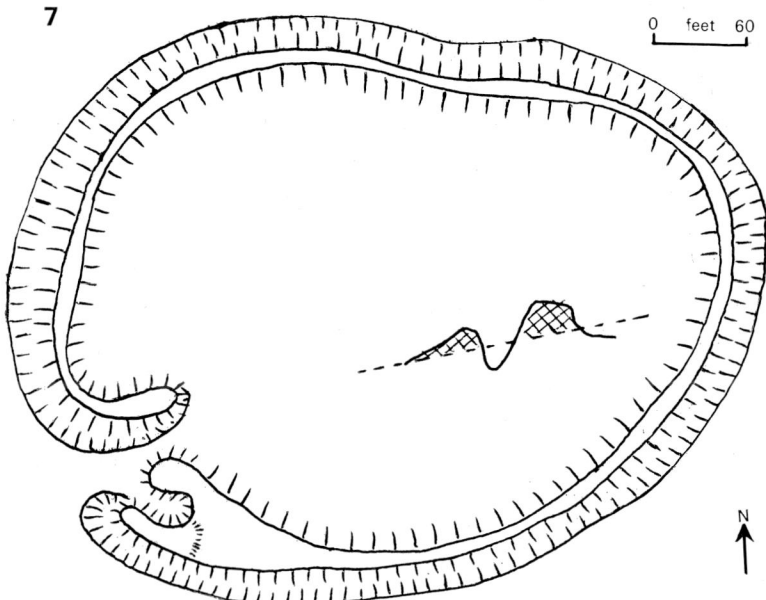

7

0   feet   60

N

Plan of Holne Chase hill fort with (inset) rampart cross-section relative to slope.

Defence of the gateways was mainly achieved by making the actual access route difficult. Often the gateway would be on the edge of a cliff in order to restrict the manoeuvring of the attacker, or masked by a succession of ramparts so that access was only via a narrow twisting path with the defenders confronting their attackers at every turn and often outflanking them at the same time. The ends of the ramparts at each side of the gateway were usually curved inwards or outwards so as to provide a flanking fire along the berm or ditch. Variations of these defence systems are best seen in the figures of the various forts mentioned below.

Some forts utilized the inward curve of the rampart to encompass a stone guard- or block-house, and in these more advanced examples, traces of wooden posts have been found which show that gates were also used. At Holne Chase Castle (Fig 7) one end of the rampart is curved inwards for twenty yards while the other rampart end is forked to allow a circular guard-house with a diameter of 22 feet to be built inside it. This forking is a common feature in many forts, perhaps for similar guard-houses, although the remains are mostly too ruinous to be distinguished as such.

At other forts the entrance is at an angle through the lines of ramparts so that an attacking force is enfiladed as it passes each line of defence. This occurs at Eggardon (Fig 8) and Hembury Fort (Fig 9). In the best examples this angle is slanted from left to right of the person entering so that his unshielded right side would be exposed.

One of the most ingenious of the many devices used by the builders to defend the gateways of their forts is that at Blackbury Castle (Fig 10) which reminds one of a medieval barbican, while at Maiden Castle (Fig 11) in Dorset there is literally a maze of passages in which any stranger could quite easily

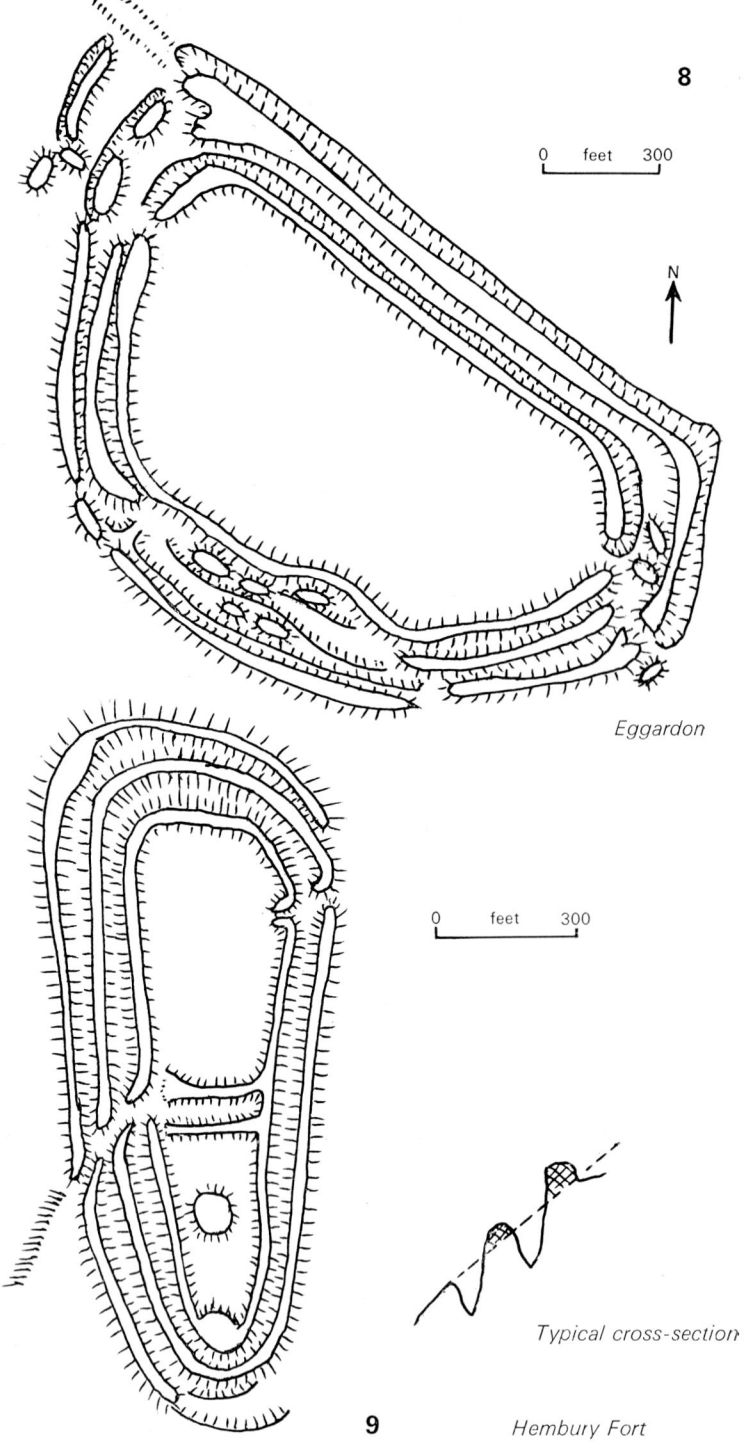

8

0 feet 300

N

Eggardon

0 feet 300

Typical cross-section

9 Hembury Fort

12

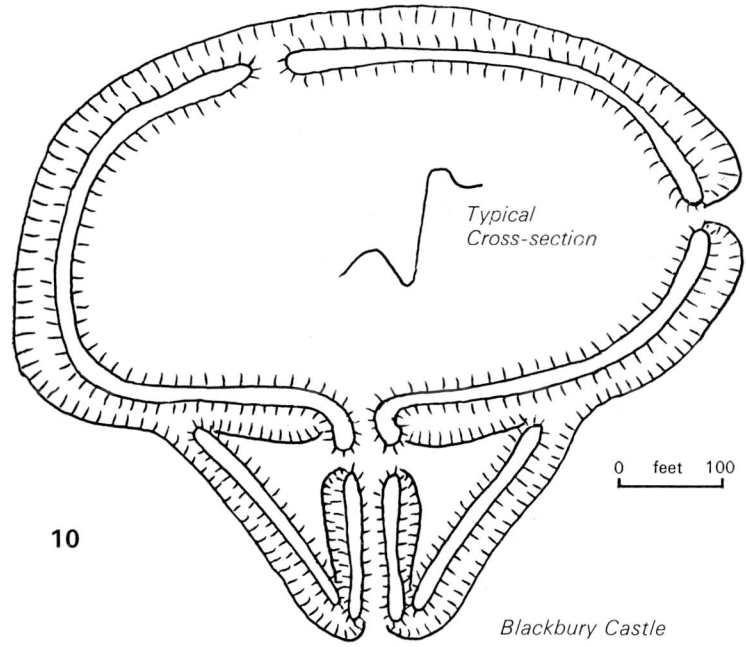

*Typical
Cross-section*

0   feet   100

10

Blackbury Castle

become lost and, taking the line of least resistance, become trapped in a
cul de sac. Hembury Fort can perhaps be said to be the ultimate in this sort of
scheming. Should any attackers penetrate the lines of defences at this fort
they would emerge not into the fort interior but instead find themselves con-
fronted by a further three openings. The centre one, the largest, would probably
lure them on, only for them to find themselves in a *cul de sac* overlooked by
two high ramparts. Should they have taken either of the smaller openings they
would have gained only half the fort and in order to take the other half would
have been forced to launch yet another assault at the double line of ramparts
across the narrow width of the camp. Here would be waiting the bulk of the
defenders, preparing for a counter attack or perhaps content to merely bombard
the attackers from the safety of their ramparts.

Platforms or small terraces can be seen at many forts, especially near the
gateways. They are very noticeable at Maiden Castle and Hembury Fort.
Bearing in mind the terraced walls of some stone-built forts, and that the
ramparts would be as steep for the defenders as for the attackers, there can be
little doubt that such platforms were merely the forerunners of the wall walk
or *allure* which ran behind the parapets of castles and town defences in later
centuries.

The question as to whether these forts were permanently occupied, in the
manner of the medieval walled towns and castles, or whether they were used
only in times of stress, is a difficult one to answer. A. H. Allcroft states '. . . built
originally to serve only as *asyla* for potential refugees they assuredly were not.
That is a pitch of political and military foresight to which we have not attained
even today.' He maintains that Man only goes to the trouble of building defences
when they are actually needed (as we have painfully experienced this century)
and that such defences are built to protect his possessions : therefore the great

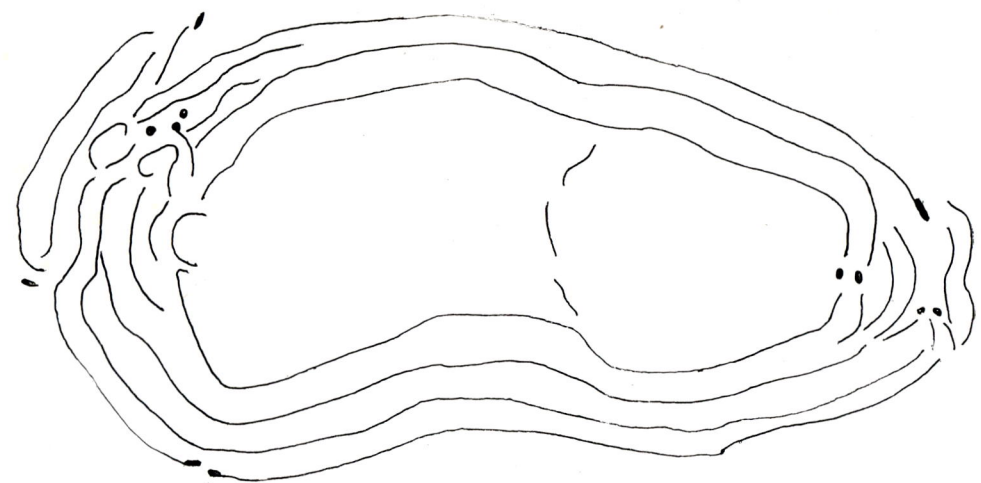

Maiden Castle

11

Iron Age camps were constructed around, or close to, the actual dwellings of the builders.

Whilst this is undoubtedly true of the great forts it does seem unlikely that this answer can be applied to all hill forts. However, it would appear that the term hill fort is itself suspect, and that perhaps these defence systems could be better described under three headings: hill forts, hill towns, and hill camps. The first is self-explanatory, referring to the great forts such as Maiden Castle and Old Oswestry (Fig 12). Maiden Castle is the supreme example of this type of fort, covering fifteen acres with five miles of earthworks in the form of triple ditches and ramparts and with extensive defences at the gateways. This fort had about 4,000 inhabitants and was a tribal centre which reached the height of its power in the centuries immediately preceding the Roman invasion.

Hill towns (villages would be a more appropriate term) were again permanently occupied, but their defences were such that they could not have withstood a determined assault and were perhaps designed only to cope with the casual raider. Good examples of such towns are Casterley Camp near Upavon, and Ogbury Camp near Durnford, both in Wiltshire. These were fairly compact towns, surrounded by a low earthwork, almost certainly topped by a timber palisade. Their interiors show the outlines of dwellings and even small fields or gardens. The fortifications were not strong enough for the defence of the town during a major tribal war or invasion, and the area enclosed was in any case too large (Casterley 68 acres, Ogbury 62 acres) for defence by the small community it contained.

The third classification, hill camps, might be called instead assembly camps. Figsbury (Fig 13), also in Wiltshire, is a good example here. It is a large earthwork, strongly sited in a commanding position on a ridge overlooking the Bourne valley, enclosing an area of about fifteen acres and with fortified entrances. Excavation in 1924 showed the site dated from the Early Iron Age. Few traces of habitation were found inside the defences, certainly not of permanent habitation, yet there were signs of a large population living all round the camp. Many of the ancient trackways also converge on Figsbury

12

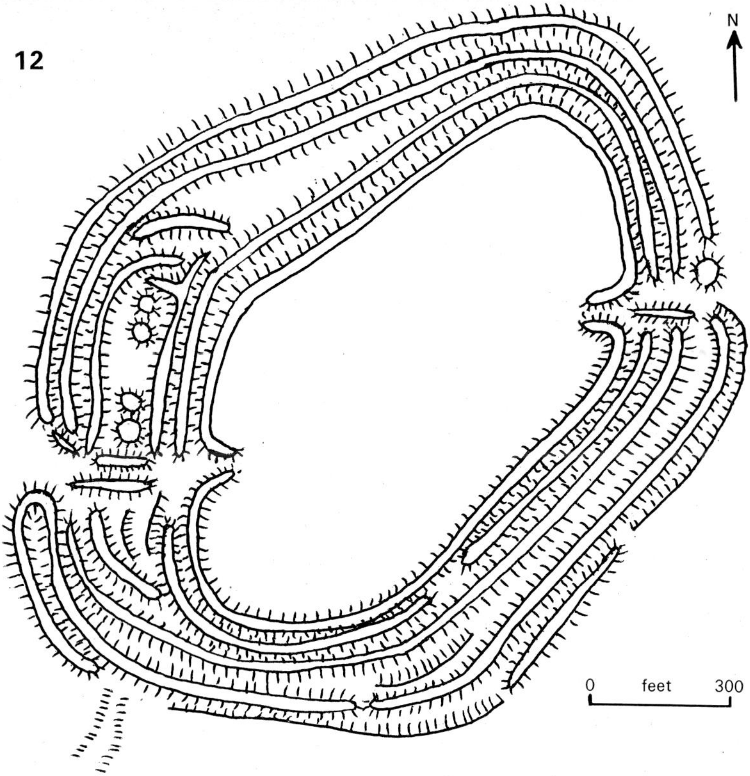

N

0   feet   300

Old Oswestry

13   *Finsbury*

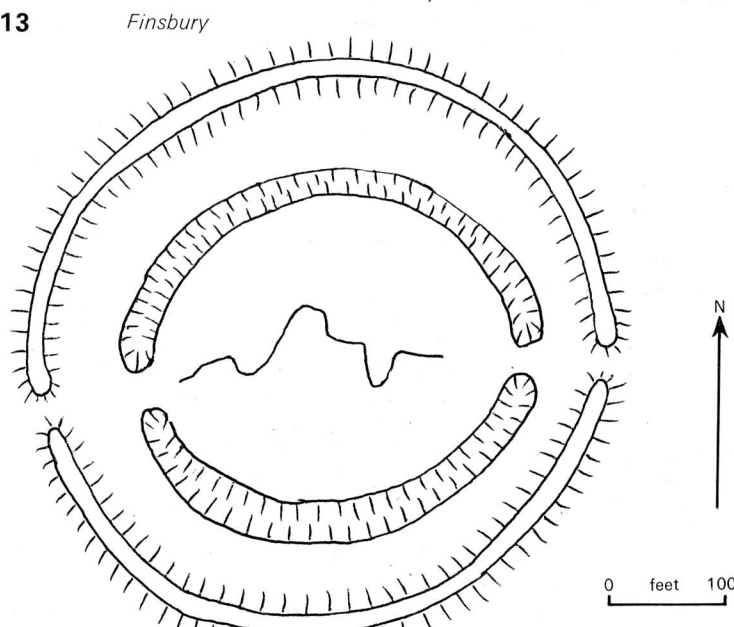

N

0   feet   100

15

and it would appear from the evidence that the earthworks in fact represent no more than an enclosure for livestock and for defence of them in case of a raid. It is worth quoting Caesar again here. 'What the British describe as a stronghold is any position in a thick forest which they have fortified with a rampart and trench and which they use as a place of refuge from invading enemy forces. We now started for this stronghold (that of Cassivellaunus, just north of the Thames, in 54 BC) and found that it was extremely well placed and extremely well fortified . . . We found a great quantity of cattle in the stronghold.' The fortress mentioned could well be Ambresbury Banks in Epping Forest.

IRISH HILL FORTS

These deserve a few words on their own owing to the extension of the Iron Age in Ireland until as late as about AD 500, there being no Roman invasion of Ireland.

Groups of Celts began crossing to Ireland from the middle of the 4th century BC yet the number of hill forts is comparatively small. Many can be dismissed as stock enclosures and the majority represent fortified farmhouses, a sign of the smaller and more scattered population. The remains of the latter usually consist of a rampart inside a ditch and enclosing an area about 100 feet in diameter, in which stood several buildings. However, the few genuine hill forts, allowed to evolve without Roman invasion or influence, represent the Iron Age hill fort at the peak of its development.

Amongst the best examples are Navan Fort, built on a site permanently inhabited since the 7th century BC although the date of the earthworks themselves are unknown; Tara, where there are extensive remains of a fort with three ramparts; Dun Ailinne which covers 20 acres, ringed by a massive rampart and ditch and with small ring forts or block-houses in the interior; and Greenan Elly in Derry, where three rings of defences surround a great inner citadel of dry stone, 77 feet in diameter and still standing to a height of $17\frac{1}{2}$ feet.

VITRIFIED FORTS

This name is applied to forts where parts of the stone walls have been fused into one mass by the action of fire. The forts occur chiefly in Scotland, where twelve definite examples exist, and in Ireland, though in the latter there has been no real evidence put forward. No examples have been found in England or Wales.

The amount of vitrification varies from fort to fort and even in different parts of the same fort. In some cases only the edges of the stones have been fused together, in others the stones are partially melted, and on rare occasions an entire section of wall has been welded into one solid mass. Various theories have been put forward in the past to explain how the walls became vitrified, most stating it happened accidentally, but these have now been discredited. It has been found now that where infusible stone has been used in the building of a vitrified fort, pieces of fusible rock have been transported from considerable distances to bridge the points where vitrification has then taken place.

It is currently believed that the firing was done deliberately in order to fuse together loose stone at particularly weak points in the defences. This welded section thus allowed the wall to be built firmly and to a greater height than was possible with the normal dry stone building, so making that section capable of resisting attempts by the enemy to pull it down. In Book XII of the *Iliad*

Homer tells how Sarpedon, King of Lycia, pulled down a section of stone wall built by the Achaeans to protect their huts and ships : 'Then Sarpedon got his mighty hands on the battlement. He gave a pull, and a whole length of the breastwork came away, exposing the top of the wall.' If this sounds facetious or an exaggerated account, take a closer look at broken sections of dry stone walling next time you get the opportunity. Although apparently very firm, the stones are easily dislodged by a man, and once the continuity is broken, whole sections begin to crumble easily.

LAKE DWELLINGS

This method of defensive building was brought to the British Isles about 300 BC by migrants from northern Gaul at what is known as the La Tène stage of civilization. The outstanding example in the British Isles is the lake village at Meare, near Glastonbury. Stone, gravel, clay, logs and brushwood were sunk to form a foundation in exactly the same manner as for the crannogs described earlier and a floor of more logs and clay was placed upon this; 65 dwellings were erected on such a floor at Meare, the floor measuring about 500 by 400 feet. The village was completely surrounded by a wooden stockade and the only approach, except by boat, was via two narrow causeways which ended abruptly about twelve feet short of the village. The gaps, where the water was about six feet deep, must have originally been spanned by a form of bridge, perhaps a drawbridge.

THE SCOTTISH BROCH

Fortifications in Scotland during this period tended to be much smaller, partly because of the restrictions of the terrain and climate and partly because the population was smaller in numbers and more scattered. This gave rise in some parts of Scotland, mainly in the north and west regions, including the Hebrides, Orkneys and Shetland, to the broch, a circular, tower-like structure of dry stones, peculiar to Iron Age Scotland.

The broch had no exterior windows, the only opening in the outer wall being a small doorway at ground level, and when this door was closed and barred the tower became impregnable to any assaults of which the men of those times were capable. (Mousa, the most famous of all brochs, successfully withstood a siege as late as 1155). The walls were made completely un-assailable by the upper courses being built to project outwards, so that in shape the broch resembles nothing so much as a modern cooling tower. The tower was open at the top and the interior was therefore simply a hollow cylinder. The open courtyard thus formed is believed to have been occupied by livestock during a siege.

The first eight feet or so of the tower walls were solid, except for an occasional chamber at ground level, but above this height the wall was hollow and this double walling provided the living accommodation. The hollow was divided into galleries running right round the tower by floors of flagstones and the galleries were gained by a spiral staircase which ascended from the ground to the very top. Light for the galleries came from windows left in the inner wall, one above the other so that they resembled a ladder and may indeed have been used in this role by some of the more active inhabitants.

Some 300 brochs survive out of an estimated original figure of 500. The best examples may be seen at Mousa (Fig 14), Dornadilla in Sutherland, and Carloway on Lewis. Almost all surviving brochs are to be found on low ground, usually on the shores of lochs or on islands laying close off shore. The first

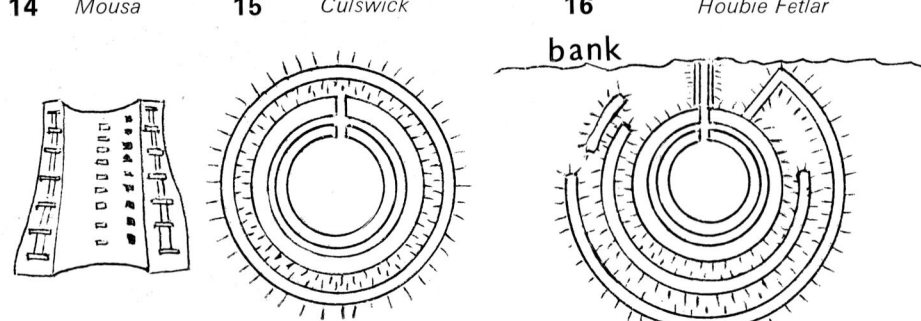

bank

are believed to have been built about the 1st century BC by migrants from south-west England and development of this type of fortification continued until the early 2nd century AD, though the brochs continued to be used as dwelling places for many centuries after that date and were in great use during the times of the Norse raids.

Dimensions of the various brochs vary considerably but the walls seem to have been an average of 13 feet thick with an internal courtyard of about 28 feet in diameter. The maximum height can only be guessed at nowadays for most of them are ruined and even the best specimen at Mousa lacks some of its upper courses. From its present height of just over 40 feet, Mousa may be said to have been 50 feet high, and from this it is fairly safe to assume that no broch would have been over 50 feet high.

On occasions the approach to a broch might be covered by outworks in the shape of the familiar rampart and ditch. Two good examples of this type are Culswick (Fig 15) and Houbie Fetlar (Fig 16). Water supply was of great importance in brochs, which is probably why they were built in lowlying areas, and in some cases there is a well within the broch, or in its immediate vicinity, when it was reached by a covered passageway. In some surviving examples the broch is surrounded by several dwelling places which are in turn encircled by a wall, suggesting that eventually the broch became the equivalent of the Norman keep and was only used as a last line of defence. In fact, much of the art of fortification as applied to the brochs of Scotland, and indeed the concentric ramparts and ditches of the hill forts, reminds one of the fortifications constructed over a thousand years later and brings to mind the familiar awareness that nothing is ever really new.

2: The Roman Occupation

THE first Roman fortifications in Britain were merely earthworks topped by timber palisades but like their Norman successors the Romans later rebuilt these in stone. However, unlike the Normans the Romans did not reduce Britain by a systematic conquest followed by suppressive tactics from regularly spaced fortresses. The Roman Army was never really strong in Britain; four legions, perhaps 20,000 men, with their auxiliary troops took part in the final invasion and one of those legions was withdrawn as early as AD 66. Conquest was achieved by treaties as much as by force and only in the north was there continual resistance, which led to the building of the Antonine Wall and Hadrian's Wall.

Hadrian's Wall has survived as well as can be expected but it is ironic that only fragments of the Antonine Wall, the great legionary fortresses and the civil settlements now remain while the simple earthworks of the Iron Age have survived in far better condition and in far greater numbers. To a certain extent the Saxons may be blamed for they destroyed every Roman town they discovered, but most of the blame must be attached to their descendants, our ancestors, who for centuries have removed stones from the Roman sites to help in the construction of their homes and public buildings. The effect of this stone-robbing is best illustrated by drawing attention to the Saxon shore fort at Brancaster in Norfolk. In 1600 the walls still stood some twelve feet high: today only portions of the fort can still be traced.

Although I have placed the types of fortification under various headings for convenience it is as well to remember that for the most part Roman fortifications were not individual strong points in the same way that the hill forts had been, but were rather part of an advancing network of military posts which gradually conquered and eventually defended Britain.

THE INVASION PORTS

The first invasions of 55 and 54 BC were merely punitive expeditions to stop the British aid to the Gauls and they left no permanent scars on the countryside but in AD 43 the legions established themselves at Dover, Lympne and Richborough. All three places were destined to be occupied as military depots for almost four centuries but of the fortifications at Lympne and Dover little remains to be seen. Within the castle walls at Dover there is the famous lighthouse, its lower 40 feet obviously Roman work, while at Lympne there are only a few pieces of broken wall, the sea long since receded from what was once a great Roman port. Richborough (Fig 17) has also been abandoned by the sea but here at least something remains and it is possible to piece

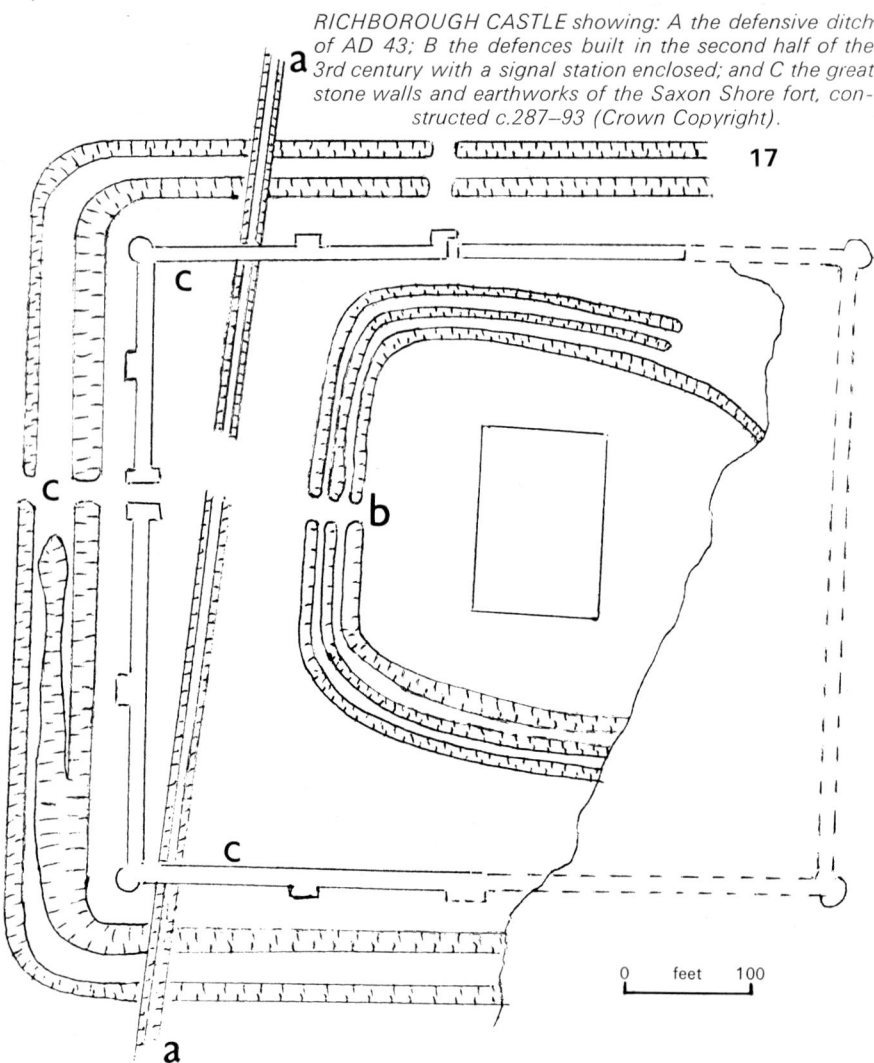

RICHBOROUGH CASTLE showing: A the defensive ditch of AD 43; B the defences built in the second half of the 3rd century with a signal station enclosed; and C the great stone walls and earthworks of the Saxon Shore fort, constructed c.287–93 (Crown Copyright).

17

together the long history. To defend their 'beach-head' the legions dug a double ditch which can still be traced for almost a mile. This must have proved largely unnecessary for Richborough very quickly became no more than a supply depot, full of granaries and a clutter of other buildings: it was not to revert to an active military role until the second half of the third century when it became one of the Saxon shore forts, dealt with later in this section.

MARCHING AND PRACTICE CAMPS

Most people are familiar with the regulation camp erected by a legion at each night stop when every legionary raised his portion of the rampart and planted his stakes at the top, and in accounts of ancient battles we often read how the Romans built just such a camp before advancing to do battle, yet this most common of all Roman fortifications was the least permanent and few examples have survived. Of the few examples in this country most may be classed as practice camps, constructed to keep the troops in training and out of mischief, rather like the warrens of slit trenches one is liable to fall into on modern training areas.

To the Romans such a camp was obviously a temporary structure, easily constructed by the large number of men involved but not built with any great care. Should the occasion arise it could be speedily converted into a more permanent work by the addition of another ditch, sharpened stakes planted on the outer face of the rampart, pit falls, thorn hedging and other such 'tricks of the trade'. Perhaps the only way to draw a firm line between camp and fort therefore is to say if there is masonry on the site it is a fort, a permanent work and not a camp.

These camps must have been built in large numbers during the early years of the invasion but after about AD 81 life became more settled in the south and midlands and most of the camps must have been gradually obliterated by cultivation of the land. Where an example does survive in this area it is usually in some uncultivatable position. However, Roman columns were still active in the north and it is therefore north of Hadrian's Wall that we find most of the surviving camps. Even so there is not a great deal to look at and the visitor would do well to remember that even the best examples were no more than unnamed, unrecorded, temporary camps of inferior construction.

The construction of all Roman camps and forts was dictated by rules and regulations. The length had to be one-third greater than the width, surrounded by a ditch and rampart, the latter with rounded corners, and with a gateway set at the centre of each of the four sides. Theoretically the rampart had to be six feet high and eight feet wide, the ditch five feet wide and three feet deep. Since three times as much earth was needed for the rampart as could be supplied from the ditch, stones, brushwood and timber were used to supply the extra bulk. The rampart was topped by a stout palisade of stakes. The ditch was most commonly 'V' shaped but some examples occur with flat floors and occasionally there is a berm between ditch and rampart. Fig 18 illustrates some variations to the standard. The gateways were sometimes protected by a short ditch or a curved extension of one side of the rampart, the aim being to force the attackers to advance on the gate at an angle and with their right (unshielded) sides exposed to the fire of the defenders, but these were not regulation.

Despite their reputation the Romans were only human and these regulations were not always obeyed to the letter. Coelbren in Breconshire is square in plan with two outer ditches separated by a 16-foot berm. Remains of sharpened oak stakes have been found in the ditches. The rampart, built on wet clay soil, was constructed from earth and brushwood, timber lacing being employed at the wettest spots and the corners. One of the earliest Roman fortifications in this area, Coelbren was occupied for about 30 years, probably being dismantled when abandoned.

The well-known practice camps at Cawthorn (Fig 19) in Yorkshire again show how sometimes the regulation plan was abandoned altogether, and for no apparent reason. Camp 1 has a double ditch and berm; Camp 2 is an unexplainable and peculiar shape; while all three have non-regulation gateways. The gateways of Camps 2 and 3 have outer works in the form of a curved spur. This same type of gateway may be seen at the practice camps at Y Pigwn in Merionethshire, but with the spur on the inside of the rampart instead of projecting. It is believed the spurs allowed two sets of gates to be erected. A still more complicated 'barbican' was used at a camp at Dealgin Ross (Fig 20).

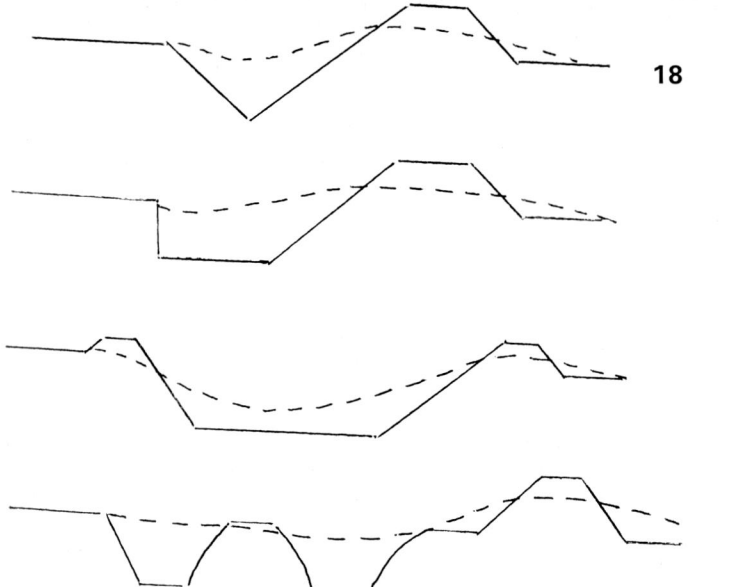

18

Variations in the standard ditches of Roman marching and practice camps. The dotted line shows the original lie of the land.

19 Three different types of practice camp at Cawthorn in Yorkshire.

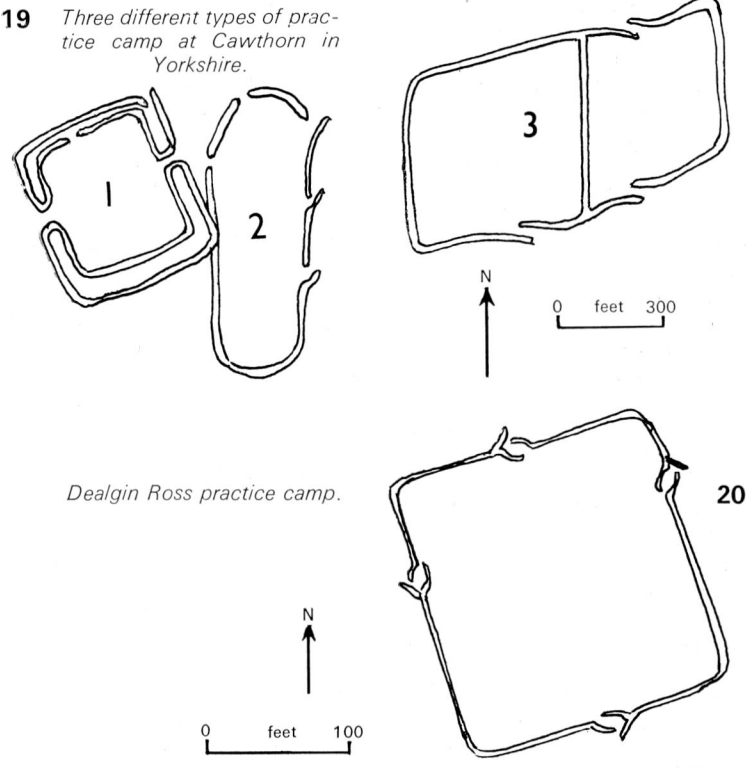

1

2

3

N

0   feet   300

Dealgin Ross practice camp.

20

N

0   feet   100

22

in Strathearn according to General Roy. (*The Military Antiquities of the Romans in North Britain,* published in 1793). The camp is no longer in existence but General Roy's drawings show us what it looked like.

AUXILIARY FORTS

Should it become necessary to camp through the winter in hostile territory, or if a newly conquered area had to be garrisoned, auxiliary forts were built at strategic points on the road system and at river crossings, each fort being normally a day's march from its neighbour. Where these forts were developed on the sites of camps, as they must often have been, they conformed to the earlier plan: forts built on new sites were usually rectangular, though not necessarily of the prescribed proportions. A few, Birdoswald and Chesters for example, obey the regulations to the letter: others such as Hardknot Castle and Portchester are square.

The forts vary in size from one to ten acres or so, an area of two to three acres being considered necessary to house a cohort. Portchester with an area of two and a half acres probably had a garrison of cohort strength, as did Hardknot Castle with just over three acres, but Birdoswald, Caersws and Castell Collen, each of about five acres, must all have held two cohorts, about 1,000 men. Piercebridge in Durham, covering almost eleven acres, held 1,000 cavalry which would have needed the extra space for stables and forage.

The defence systems employed also varied a great deal. Some forts had ditches, others had none, yet others employed sharpened stakes in pit falls. Ramparts were initially built as for camps, strengthened at front and back with stacked turves and occasionally revetted with timber. The turves were cut with a special tool and measured a precise one by one and a half Roman feet and half a foot thick. Later on this rampart was often given a stone facing up to five feet thick. A parapet of timber topped the rampart, providing cover for the legionaries: when a stone face was added the facing was continued upwards to provide a stone parapet two feet high. Merlons rose two feet higher, every ten feet along the parapet, on both stone and timber parapets. Towers were sometimes erected at intervals on the inner face of the rampart and at the corners platforms were built to take artillery in the form of ballistae. At first the towers would have been square ones of timber but these were later replaced in stone to form the solid, half round bastions usually associated with Roman fortifications.

Gateways were usually double with round headed archways, the doors of wood, metal or both. Guard-houses were built at each side of the gates in the larger forts. Birrenswark had walls three feet thick projecting beyond two of its gateways (for 30 feet on the north side, 15 feet on the west) to form a sort of barbican. Castell Collen in Radnorshire also has these projecting works, unusual in a fort of its time, the early years of the 2nd century AD.

Many of the variations can perhaps be explained by the replacement of the original timber defences by stone, and the rebuilding of such forts as were destroyed by enemy action. At Segontium for example the Romans were in occupation from AD 75–140, 210–290 and 365–380. During the long periods between these dates the site was unoccupied and the fort was probably ravaged by the local tribes. Rebuilding in different centuries must also have had an effect on the general plan. Another factor is the development of many of the forts into settlements of considerable size. At some sites, such as Gellygaer and Great Casterton, attempts were made to include these civil extensions within the defences, creating very irregular fortress lines, but as the areas became more settled so the military defences must have been allowed to decay.

Within the forts the regulation street plan was normally followed, with the Principia or HQ as the nucleus. The main road, Via Principalis, crossed the fort in front of this building and was joined by another at its centre to form a T-junction. These two roads led to the three main gates of the fort while a third road led to the rear of the fort. Two-thirds of the buildings within the walls were barracks for the garrison, the remainder were arsenals, administrative blocks and storehouses: the granaries held sufficient stocks to last a year if necessary. The largest forts also had a hospital, workshops and additional granaries.

Castle Dykes in the West Riding of Yorkshire is a good example of a minor fort which abandoned the regulations for convenience. The whole of the north side was covered by swampy ground and if a wall existed here it was so slight as to leave no trace. The three other sides enclose an area of five and a half acres within an enormous flat bottomed ditch, 15 feet deep and 50 feet wide, and a relatively low rampart, now standing at between four and ten feet.

Hardknot Castle in Cumberland is another fine example of the smaller fort. An exact square covering three acres, the fort has stone walls five feet thick and rounded at the corners but there is no ditch. An unusual feature is the square tower built against the inner face of the ramparts at each corner.

Ardoch and Birrenswark are examples of the standard rectangular fort on a larger scale but both have unusual extra ditches. Ardoch has two ramparts with a series of five 'V' shaped ditches between them. The buildings inside these defences were of timber and were never replaced by stone ones. Birrenswark is surrounded by a rampart only three to four feet high, but 40 or more feet wide. If there was a stone facing it has disappeared and the exaggerated width of the rampart may well be the result of centuries of stone-robbing. On the north and east sides there is a berm outside the rampart and beyond the berm a series of six parallel ditches, originally five feet deep and two to three feet wide at the bottom. Beyond these is a second rampart. It is not known if these complex defences were continued right round the fort for the ground has now fallen away. Such strong defences were normally only constructed in situations where the Romans expected more or less continual warfare.

THE LEGIONARY FORTRESSES

The legionary fortresses were larger, more elaborate forms of fort, covering an area of between 50 and 60 acres. Colchester, Gloucester and Lincoln must all have had legionary fortresses in the early years of the occupation but these would have been timber and earth and nothing has survived: what little there is to see at these sites belongs mostly to the civil settlements. To this era also belongs Wroxeter, although it is by no means certain that this was a legionary fortress in the true sense. First occupied by the XIV and XX Legions, by AD 81 the settlement was being extended and improved to become one of the finest Roman settlements in Britain.

The fortress at York was first built in AD 71–4, rebuilt in stone about 107–8 and destroyed by the Maeatae in 196. It was rebuilt the following year and again in 296. From being an advance base for the IX Legion from Lincoln it progressed to the position of first city of Britain, a second Rome: today it is buried beneath medieval and modern York, York Minster occupying approximately the centre of the fortress, and all that can be seen are the multangular

CAERLEON. Part of the south wall and ditch of the Roman fortress of Isca, or Caerleon (Castra Legionis) as it is now called. The ramparts were originally faced with stone. A tower stood in the break.

tower which formed the west corner and a small section of the original wall.

The fortresses at Chester and Caerleon were built between AD 74–78 on the sites of earlier, smaller forts. Chester was rebuilt in stone about 103, Caerleon about 100. Chester was again partially rebuilt about 296. Plans based on the remains of the defences, and on discoveries made during excavations, reveal what these great fortresses must have looked like when at their peak. Unfortunately it is not possible to recapture this atmosphere at the actual sites, although Caerleon is to a certain extent free of modern buildings and one can stand on the rampart and, gazing across to the distant Welsh mountains, recapture a little of what it must have been like to do guard duty on these walls.

There was one other legionary fortress, Inchtuthil, close by the River Tay, north of Perth. Built AD 83–4 by Agricola and occupied by the XX Legion, it was evacuated only six or seven years later and today there is nothing to be seen but a wide plateau and a few humps, perhaps symbolic of Rome's failure in this region.

HADRIAN'S WALL

Built about AD 121–26, Hadrian's Wall is the finest surviving Roman fortification in Britain. Stretching for $73\frac{1}{2}$ miles from Wallsend near Newcastle to Bowness on Solway, it was sited so as to take advantage of the lie of the land at all times and at its highest point reaches 1,230 feet above sea level. In the 257 years between completion and final destruction in 383 it was breached only three times.

At the eastern end, and from Newcastle for some 20 miles westwards, the wall was built of stone, nine feet thick and probably about fifteen feet high, not counting the parapet. From this point on the wall was reduced to seven feet nine inches in thickness and continued so as far as the River Irthing. West of this point the wall was originally of turf or clay (except for the turrets which were built of stone) but this section was soon rebuilt in stone, seven feet six inches in width. The defensive system was continued for another 40 miles down the Cumberland coast as far as St Bees Head with a series of small forts and turrets.

At intervals of from three to seven miles along the wall were built 23 large forts to house the garrison of the wall. Housesteads, covering five acres and capable of holding 1,000 legionaries or auxiliaries, is one of the finest examples with walls, turrets, gates, HQ building and granaries exposed by excavation. The best preserved sections of wall are also in this area. Another fine example is Chesters (Fig 21) where the gateways, HQ building and barracks have been excavated. This fort covers nearly six acres and held 500 cavalry.

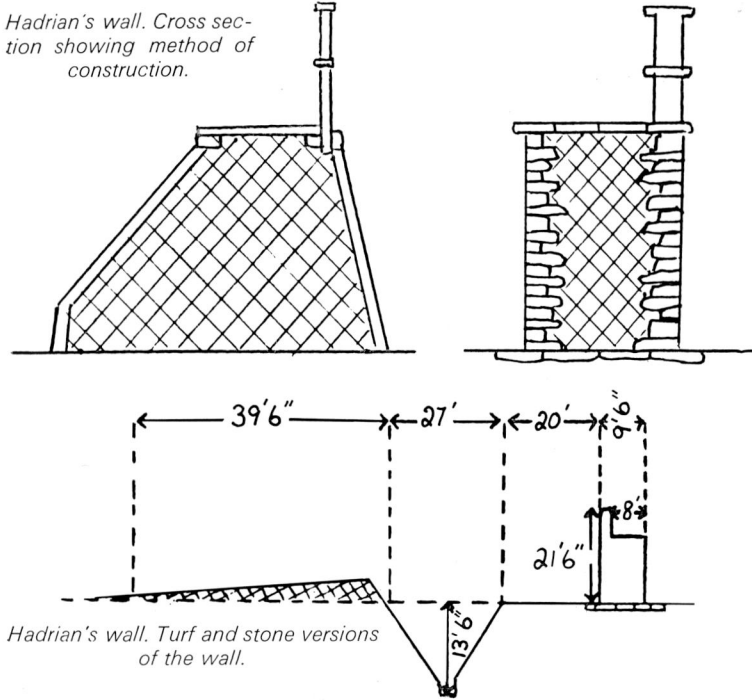

Hadrian's wall. Cross section showing method of
construction.

Hadrian's wall. Turf and stone versions
of the wall.

In addition to these main forts, smaller forts were built at every Roman mile and named mile-castles, each measuring 70 by 55 feet and capable of housing about 50 men. Between each of the mile-castles were two square turrets built of stone; these provided cover for the actual patrols.

South of the wall is an earthwork known as the *vallum*. This is thought to have been constructed to isolate the wall in the same way that a modern military zone is isolated from the public. (It is notable that only two instances of civil

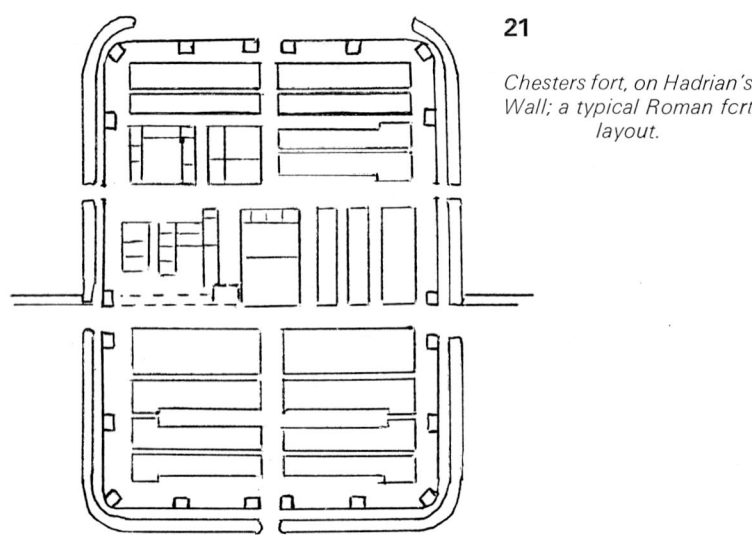

21

Chesters fort, on Hadrian's
Wall; a typical Roman fort
layout.

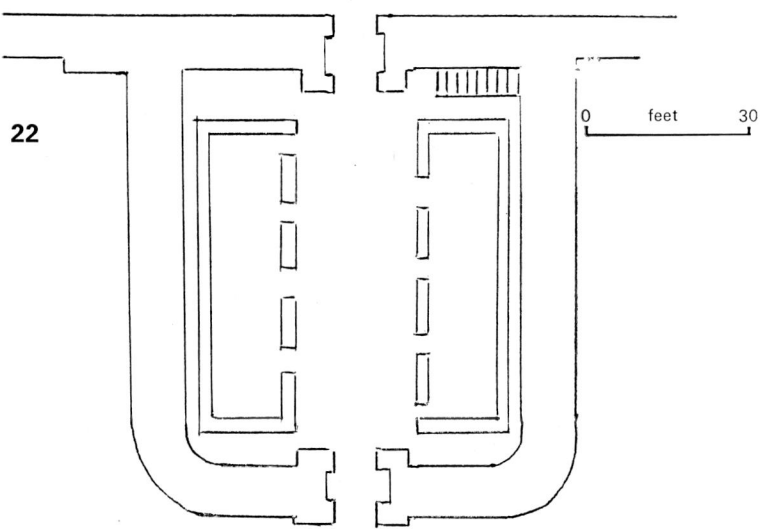

22

0   feet   30

Hadrian's wall. Plan of a typical milecastle.

occupation of the wall have been recorded: it was almost 100 per cent military). The *vallum* was seven feet deep and 30 feet wide with steeply sloping sides and a flat bottom. There were small parapets at each side. Also south of the wall, but incorporated into its defensive system, is Chesterholm, a fort covering three and a half acres. The walls, gates and HQ building of this fort have been uncovered and found to date from the early 4th century, though there are signs of work here during the 3rd and even 2nd centuries.

Until almost the end of the 4th century at least five forts were also maintained *north* of the wall: High Rochester, Risingham, Bewcastle, Birdoswald and Birrenswark. The last two of these have been described in some detail under Auxiliary Forts. The purpose of these forts was to intercept the enemy forces in front of the wall, which remained as a barrier against infiltration and provided a firm line against which the enemy could be crushed.

THE ANTONINE WALL

The most important Roman fortification in Scotland, this line between the Clyde and the Forth (a distance of approximately 37 miles) was first drawn up by Agricola in AD 80 and some of his original forts have been identified. In AD 139–42 these forts were for the most part reoccupied and a permanent line of defence was constructed to link them together. The rampart was built of turves on a stone foundation except in the eastern sector where the wall is clay. Thirteen, possibly more, forts were added to this line. The wall, believed to have been 20 feet high and 24 feet thick, was not a copy of Hadrian's Wall but rather an attempt to improve on it. There were no mile-castles or turrets, but the forts were smaller and closer together and the ditch was much larger. No *vallum* was constructed behind the wall but instead the rampart was built at a very steep angle both front and rear, making it difficult to scale from either direction and thus limiting all access except at the official points.

The wall was temporarily evacuated from AD 155–58 and after the reoccupation there are signs of reduction in the scale of the defences in order to save manpower. The wall was breached about 180–84. It may have been patched up again and held until as late as the troubles of 196 but this is not yet proven.

At Seabegs Wood, one and a quarter miles south-west of Bonnybridge in Stirlingshire is a good stretch of rampart and ditch. The most outstanding fort is Rough Castle, also near Bonnybridge. This fort was excavated in 1903 and more work has been carried out at the site recently. It covers an area of about an acre, on the brink of a ravine, and is protected by a double ditch with an annex added to the eastern side. The fort is famous for its *Lilia* (lilies), a rather ironic name for a series of pits, at the bottom of which awaited sharpened stakes. These protected the left front of the fort and are the only known examples of this type of fortification in the British Isles.

CIVIL SETTLEMENTS

At first glance these may seem by their very name to be outside the scope of a book on fortifications but it should be remembered that the early settlements had a precarious life in a largely unconquered country, while in the subsequent centuries raiders from the seas and the north perpetuated the need for defensive works.

The line taken by the walls of these civil settlements may still be traced today in modern cities. At Chichester for example the four main streets follow exactly the line taken by the Roman ones. The same may be said of Gloucester and even in London, where rebuilding after the damage of the Great Fire and the World War 2 bombing have not obliterated them, many Roman roads still exist: Old Kent Road, Edgware Road, and Oxford Street to name the prime examples.

There was no regulation plan as for military establishments and since most Roman settlements were built on the sites of earlier towns they often adopted the outline of these towns. Thus Bath is pentagonal, Wroxeter oval and Silchester an irregular octagonal shape. In some cases the new Roman town occupied only a fraction of the earlier town, as at Colchester, St Albans and Lincoln.

London, Colchester and St Albans were all burnt and sacked by Boudicca in AD 61 but rose again, encompassed this time by stout stone walls. Roman London is buried under the modern city and little remains of what was once an important port and town. At Colchester much of the one and three-quarter

CAERWENT. The rubble core of the walls of the town.

CAERWENT The south wall and bastion. This is one of the finest stretches of Roman walling in Britain.

mile circuit of the eight feet thick wall still stands, mostly minus its parapet, but in places even this remains. The wall was probably fifteen feet high originally. Internal towers, bastions and sections of the outer ditch can also be seen and the town can also boast of Balkerne Gate, the largest Roman gateway in Britain and the original west gate of the Roman city. St Albans has survived the centuries well also, mainly because the modern city was built a mile from the old site. Much of the two mile circuit of the stone walls remains, together with its outer defences.

Probably the finest example of a civil settlement in Britain is Caerwent. Some eight miles east of the fortress of Isca at Caerleon, Caerwent was first occupied about AD 75–80 when the region was still unsettled. Consequently it is military in appearance and built on the traditional rectangular plan, enclosing the standard 50 acres, factors which once led archaeologists to believe it had started life as a legionary fortress. This belief has now been abandoned for it is realized that Caerwent was merely a pioneer town on the edge of Rome's frontiers, built not so long after the sacking of London, Colchester and St Albans, and this alone explains its military aspect.

Originally Caerwent was surrounded by a clay rampart and two ditches but these were supplemented in the early third century by a stone wall 30 feet high and about five feet thick, built on the face of the rampart and with shallow internal projections, perhaps designed to take ballistae. About AD 350 six polygonal bastions were added to the south wall and recently more bastions have been discovered on the east wall. There are none on the west or north walls and this seems to indicate that the extra defences were because of Irish raids up the mouth of the Severn. The east and west gates have been destroyed by the Newport-Chepstow road, which thus traces the original main west-east road of the town. The north and south gates were single arch openings, blocked during the 5th century, either because of the decline of the town's trade or because of increasing trouble from the raiders. The town was not sacked and destroyed but seems rather to have gradually lapsed into decay, perhaps surviving until as late as the middle of the 5th century, when all hope of help from Rome had long gone.

THE SAXON SHORE FORTS

The forts of the Saxon shore were a series of large forts built along the east and south coasts of England from The Wash to Portsmouth between the end of the 3rd century and the beginning of the 4th. Originally ten, possibly eleven, in number, there are nine surviving examples; from the top of the east coast: Brancaster and Burgh Castle in Norfolk, Walton Castle in Suffolk, Bradwell in Essex, Reculver, Dover and Lympne in Kent, Pevensey in Sussex and Portchester in Hampshire, overlooking Portsmouth Harbour. All were built in strategic positions to guard river mouths or Roman harbours and all could hold a large garrison.

At Dover and Brancaster nothing remains: Walton and Reculver have disappeared into the sea, while Lympne and Bradwell have little to offer but a few fragments of walls, but at the other four sites the forts remain as impressive fortifications.

Burgh Castle retains its east wall and portions of the north and south walls, together with six solid bastions, one of which still has the socket designed to take a ballista. Richborough (Fig 17), rescued from the dull life of a depot, still has most of three of the walls and the double ditches constructed about AD 290 when the clutter of a less military way of life was swept away. There is a causeway over the outer ditch to the west gate but the inner ditch was spanned by a bridge. Both ditches at the postern in the north wall were probably crossed by a removable bridge. Richborough has shown signs of being densely occupied towards the end of the Roman period, which suggests that this original invasion port was used for the withdrawal of the last legionaries from Britain.

At Portchester there remain the four walls with their hollow, semi-circular bastions, and outside the north wall there is a defensive ditch, but the east and west gates have been replaced by medieval works, part of the castle complex in the north-west corner. Pevensey is perhaps the finest of all the Saxon shore forts, with its tweve-foot thick walls, solid semi-circular bastions and the original east and west gateways. Here also there is a medieval castle in one corner; William the Conqueror made his first camp within these strong walls, while even as late as World War 2 the old fortifications were still being pressed into service. (See Section 11).

This chain of forts has always been thought to have been constructed to defend the coasts against the Saxon raiders but recently a theory has been put forward which challenges this belief. In AD 287 Carausius, the commander of the British fleet and a Celt by birth, usurped the title of Emperor of Britain. Not until 296 did a Roman force cross the channel to reclaim Britain for the Emperor of Rome and the new theory suggests that the Saxon shore forts were in fact built by Carausius to repel the Romans, not the Saxons, who at this time were making only raids which did not warrant such massive fortifications. Whatever the truth of the matter, the chain of forts was used to hold off the Saxons during the subsequent centuries and succeeded in this role until Constantine III stripped Britain of troops for his conquest of Spain and Gaul.

FORTS OF THE WELSH COAST

About AD 270 an Irish tribe called the Deisi settled in Pembrokeshire and from that time on pressure from sea raiders began to increase along the Welsh coast. An attempt to occupy the fertile land of Glamorgan and Monmouthshire was thwarted by the building of a large fort at Cardiff, Caerleon not being very well placed for defence of the coast. The Cardiff fort, with walls ten feet thick,

PEVENSEY. The great bastions of the Roman west gate which have outlasted the Norman gatehouse and a World War 2 anti-tank blockhouse set up in this same spot.

twenty feet high and projecting bastions, covered eight and a half acres and was built on the site of an earlier fort. The walls and gates survive in the present castle.

The raids were diverted but not stopped and in the 4th century Irish sea rovers began attempting to gain a foothold on the more northerly, unguarded shores. Segontium (Caernarvon), Carmarthen, Gaer Gybi and Caerhun (Conway) were all rebuilt about 360 and, with Chester in the extreme north, these provided a chain of protected harbours from which Roman fleets could operate.

The system was far less extensive than that on the south and east coasts of England and it is not known if it was successful. In 383 Britain was drained of troops by Maximus and Segontium was probably abandoned for the last time in this year, as were the other forts. By 400 Wales was devoid of Roman troops and the Cymry were left to fight it out with the original occupants.

SIGNAL STATIONS

The Roman Army had developed a signalling system by the end of the 1st century and the discovery of numerous signal towers in northern Britain suggests that forward camps maintained contact with their bases. It is known that a network of such signal stations connected Hadrian's Wall with the legionary fortress at York. The details of the system used are not known, but one station excavated on Dere Street in Redesdale had six platforms, suggesting a combination of fires or smoke columns.

Around AD 370 the threat of sea raiders along the coast of Yorkshire provoked the building of a system of signal stations between the Tees and Flamborough Head to provide an early warning system for the garrison further inland. A good example has survived on Castle Hill in Scarborough, on the eastern-most part of the headland and within the castle walls, where the layout can still be seen. It consisted of a very high square tower within a square walled enclosure, the whole enclosed on three sides by a wide deep ditch and on the fourth side by the cliff. There was only one gate, on the west side.

It is interesting to compare this with examples of signal stations elsewhere. Within the 3rd-century fort at Richborough (Fig 17) was constructed a signal station, three sides protected by an earthwork, the fourth having been lost owing to soil subsidence. Along Hadrian's Wall are three more very good specimens : Pike Hill, Mains Rigg and Robin Hood's Butt. The first was 20 feet square with exceptionally deep foundations, indicating construction to an unusual height. Mains Rigg is 21 feet square, surrounded by a ditch which is bridged by a causeway. There is no door at ground level and access must have been at first-floor level via a ladder, exactly like the Martello towers of the 19th century ! This reveals an interesting point. Bearing in mind the lack of escape routes for the small garrisons, it would appear that the signal stations were in fact isolated strongpoints, to be held during any raids for obviously any station abandoned to the raiders would be destroyed.

Robin Hood's Butt is similar to Mains Rigg. Signals sent from this station could be seen at Birdoswald fort and on the wall, but not by an enemy approaching from the north. It is rather a nice thought that by means of such towers the Romans could, owing to the rugged terrain of the area, arrange an ambush for the raiders by long-distance signalling.

The Yorkshire coast system was abandoned at the beginning of the 5th century when the Roman troops were withdrawn from Britain.

(opposite page)   **Plate 1**

A Roman Legion storms a hill fort constructed with a double rampart and ditch. This type of fort was usually held by an entire tribe with women, children, cattle and warriors all crammed in together. It is therefore not surprising that the Romans met fierce resistance when they attacked one of these strongholds as they were threatening the very existence of the tribes concerned.

When actually storming the fort the Legion would attack in cohort strength (about 600 men) at the main fortified points such as the gates and the narrowest part of the ditch. There would also be several Centuries (90–100 men) detailed off to cause a diversion and switch the defenders' attention from the main assault. The entire attack would be covered by the Legion's artillery pouring boulders and assorted hardware into the defenders manning the walls and assembling in various parts of the defences to meet the anticipated assault.

The main attack would be carried out in 'testudo' or tortoise formation, as shown below, when the opposition was particularly heavy or their was no artillery available. Otherwise the Roman troops charged straight in as depicted in the colour illustration. This charge carried out with speed and discipline usually cleared the ramparts and spilled over into the main parts of the fort itself where the fighting degenerated into small individual engagements. Once this attack was over the ramparts the fort usually fell very quickly as in many cases the only defences were in the outer ring and there was no provision for a series of 'strongpoints' within the walls. This meant an attacker could roam the length and breadth of the defences from the inside without meeting a check of any sort apart from the disorganized defenders' families and livestock.

3: The Dark Ages

THE BRITONS

THERE is a brief gap in British history after the Romans left the country but fortunately the Anglo-Saxon Chronicle takes up the story again from AD 443 when the Britons invited the Saxons to help them fight the Picts. The Picts defeated, the Saxons soon began to push the Britons back too, calling in the Jutes and Angles to help them, and the Chronicle records defeat after defeat for the Britons, who were pushed westwards until they were finally forced to take refuge in Cornwall and Wales. No mention is made of any sieges at first and the struggle appears to have taken the form of a pitched battle whenever the Saxons needed more land. Later, from 491 on, we begin to get a different picture: '... besieged Pevensey and slew all its inhabitants' (in 491) : '... fought the Britons at Old Sarum and put them to flight' (in 552) : '... fought against the Britons at Barbury Castle' (in Wiltshire, 556) : '... fought against the Britons at a place which is called Dyrham; and captured three cities, Gloucester, Cirencester and Bath'.

From these entries it seems that to begin with the Britons made no attempt to form a line of defence against the invaders. This was probably because the Saxons arrived in dribs and drabs, slowly encroaching on the land: there was no military invasion as such and consequently no organized defence to oppose it. Later, with the Bristol Channel and the barrier of the Severn at his back, the Briton appears to have at last realized the danger. To my mind the appearance of Pevensey, Old Sarum and Barbury Castle in the records signals the beginning of an attempt by the Britons to form a defence system which would protect Cornwall, Devon, Somerset, Dorset and parts of Wiltshire and Hampshire.

To defend this area the Britons began reoccupying the Roman and Iron Age forts and about the same time, the end of the 5th and beginning of the 6th centuries, constructed Wansdyke and Bokerley Dyke, which were not dykes in fact but walls. Wansdyke is the most extensive of its kind in the country with a total length of 80 miles, stretching from near Hungerford in Berkshire, across Wiltshire and Somerset to Portishead, where the mouth of the Severn meets the Bristol Channel. As much as possible the 'dyke' takes a straight line, but never abandons the strategic ground, and may be called a British, and inferior, copy of Hadrian's Wall. There is a single rampart, at the best preserved parts still some nine feet high and eighteen feet above the floor of the outer ditch, which is on the north side. Rampart and ditch together make an enormous obstacle about 80 feet wide. There is a definite parapet along the northern edge of the top of the rampart. The wall links up with several important camps, either British or earlier, at Bathampton Down, Stantonbury, Maesknoll and Portishead Camp. Some 20 or so other camps lie to the rear or front of the wall.

Bokerley Dyke is a much smaller affair, only four miles long, with a single rampart and ditch, the latter on the north and east sides. The wall runs generally south-east to north-west, marking the modern boundary between Wiltshire and Dorset, and barring the approach to the Dorset centre of Badbury

CANTERBURY. Known as the Dane John, possibly from donjon, this would appear to be the site of a Norman castle, perhaps an earlier structure than the nearby Norman keep. However, it has been proved that the mound existed as early as the 3rd century, even prior to the Saxon settlement in the town, and this indicates it has its origins in the Iron Age.

Rings in the same way that the Wansdyke bars the way to Bath from the north.

Between the eastern end of the Wansdyke and the northern end of Bokerley Dyke there is a gap of over 30 miles, facing the very direction from which a Saxon attack might have been expected to come. At that date the gap was bridged by a dense forest which stretched from the New Forest right up into Berkshire, but it is unlikely the Britons would have relied solely on such a barrier. A glance at a map of the area shows another reason for the absence of a wall on the east flank: scattered between the dykes are Old Sarum, Yarnbury Castle,

(Page 36) **Plate 2**

A Roman patrol point on Hadrian's wall. As the name suggests these small square turrets were for the protection of the Legionaries patrolling the Wall and were established mid-way between the mile-castles which housed the men responsible for guarding that stretch of the Wall. Although really for protection against the weather they could be used as strong points to fend off a sudden attack until help came, either from the nearest mile-castle or from one of the twenty-three main forts along the entire length of the Wall. If even this was not enough more force could be gathered from the various Legionary fort-resses established throughout the country to guard against just this sort of possibility.

(Page 37) **Plate 3**

William the Conqueror's pre-fabricated castle being assembled above the beach at Hastings. This is the first recorded instance of a pre-fabricated fortification. The individual pieces were cut from forests in Normandy and fashioned into a fort. The whole assembly was then taken apart and fitted into the ships taking the rest of the Conqueror's invasion force to England.

Once the main force had landed and marched inland, the fort was set up and garrisoned so that it could form an effective defence against King Harold's Britons should they, for any reason either break through, outflank or otherwise elude the main army. This would then safeguard the army's lines of communication and hold open the beach-head should the army have to withdraw. In the event this did not happen and after Harold's defeat at the Battle of Hastings the wooden fort was dismantled and replaced by a more permanent structure made of stone (see also page 48).

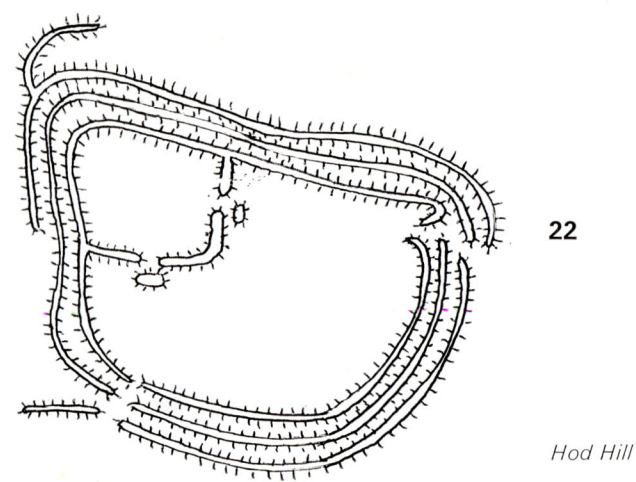

22

Hod Hill

Scratchbury, Battlesbury, Bratton Castle, White Sheet Hill; hill forts and other earthworks by the dozen. Reoccupation of these would have provided defence in depth in an area already difficult for a large force to manœuvre in because of the thick forest.

Hod and Hambledon Hills, north and west of Badbury Rings, show best how these old forts were adapted by the Britons in their hour of need. Hod Hill (Fig 22) is a strong fort with twin ramparts, reinforced in places by a third, covering 50 acres on the flat summit of a hill 470 feet high. It appears to be a normal Iron Age hill fort but in the north-west corner another fort has been built, covering only seven acres. This is known as Lydsbury Rings and looks Roman in design. However, there are no indications that it was built by the Romans and there is no precedent in Britain for them building their fortifications within those of an earlier age. The south-west and north-east gates on the other hand are characteristically British.

Hambledon Hill has also been altered at a later date by the addition of a ditch and rampart cutting across the three-quarters of a mile long camp. The two hill forts are only one and a half miles apart and both overlook the valley of the Stour. They would have provided ideal outposts for Badbury Rings, or for the interior of the line of defences should Badbury Rings have fallen.

The sites of the battles of Mons Badonicus in 516, after which the West Saxons gained their kingdom of Wessex, and of Dyrham or Deorham in 577, which resulted in the destruction of Bath have never been traced. Some experts believe that Mons Badonicus was Badbury, which would have spelt the end of the eastern defences and the Bokerley Dyke. Similarly, once Bath fell, the Wansdyke would also have become obsolete. By 577 therefore these defensive works were useless: the Britons had lost and the Welsh of Cornwall were isolated from those in Wales.

In Wales the Britons apparently took steps to see that they were not driven into the Irish Sea and there are innumerable small forts in the hills which are either post-Roman or were reoccupied after the Roman evacuation. Dinas Emrys, near Beddgelert in North Wales, is one of the best examples of these later hill forts, dating from about 550. Situated on an isolated hill, the naturally strong defensive position has been strengthened by the judicious use of short lengths of walling between rock outcrops.

In Cornwall the situation is reflected by a similar crop of small hill forts of uncertain date, while the same picture emerges in Scotland, where some of the forts were occupied up to the 9th and even 10th centuries.

THE SAXONS

The Saxons do not appear to have had any knowledge of military fortifications and, being on the offensive for many years, had no need of them. The first known example occurs at Bamburgh in 547 when the first Angle king 'built Bamburgh, which was first enclosed by a stockade and thereafter by a rampart'. (Probably a ditch too.) Bede calls Bamburgh a city, which only emphasizes the lack of fortification of an important site at such a time in a troubled area.

The Saxons remind one of the American pioneers, pushing inexorably westward, driving the native population before them, settling in the valleys and lowlands, clearing the forests and breaking the waste lands with their heavy iron ploughs, while all the time the Britons lurked in the hills. At the most they may have erected timber stockades, but all traces of these have long since disappeared.

From the arrival of St Augustine in 597, and the subsequent development of the churches, the art of building in stone was slowly revived, but even so the Saxons avoided the confines of towns, which they hated, and their only real centres were the royal manors such as Wilton, Chippenham, Old Sarum, Winchester and Canterbury. Only when forced on the defensive by the Britons of Cornwall (the fortification of Taunton against the Britons in 720), or by the raids of the Danes and Vikings, from 789 onwards, did the Saxons begin to erect defences, and then only in the form of *burhs*.

THE SAXON BURH

A *burh* was merely a fortified settlement covering perhaps twenty or more acres and containing the huts of the people, a church, a mill and an inner stronghold for the local lord. The fortifications were a ditch, an earthen rampart and a timber palisade, repeated on a smaller scale for the inner stronghold of the lord. One innovation was the wet ditch or moat, probably the result of Saxon settlements invariably being on low land, close to rivers.

Mostly the fortified *burhs* date from the 10th century, after the granting of lands to the Danes by Alfred the Great in 878. Chester was fortified in 907, Stamford and Tamworth in 913, Witham and Maldon in 914, Warwick and

(Page 40)   **Plate 4**
This impression shows Harlech Castle as it might have appeared in the 13th century, based on descriptions of the period. A notable feature was the roofing in of the tops of the towers with local timber to provide added protection and shelter for the men manning the walls.

(Page 41)   **Plate 5**
Siege warfare in the 13th century, as it looked to the attackers. The siege towers were usually mobile — with rollers or crude wheels — sufficient enough to be pushed into position for an attack. The wood towers were built higher than the castle walls if possible so that the men on top of the tower had some tactical advantage over the defenders in the castle.

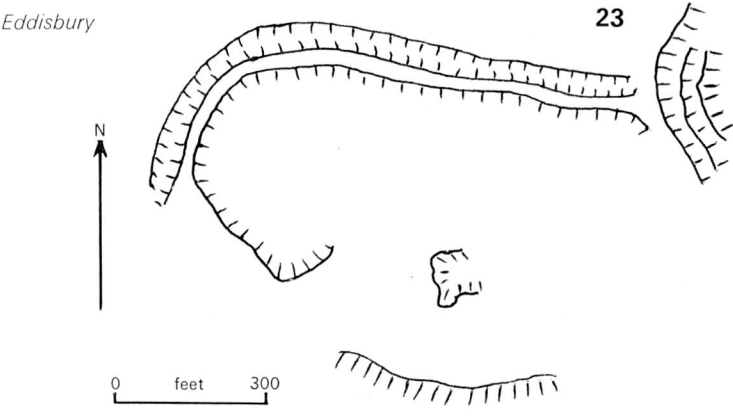

N

| 0 | feet | 300 |

Eddisbury in 915, Towcester and Thewall in 920, to list but a few. Modern building or cultivation has destroyed most traces of these comparatively slight fortifications, but a few have survived. At Hoggeston in Buckinghamshire the village is still surrounded by an oblong rampart with rounded corners, the ditch also discernible occasionally. At nearby Cubblington there are remains of another rampart and ditch, still in good condition on the north-west side. This is not the modern Cubblington, but the old one close by. (The old village and its defences were abandoned at the end of the 14th century, probably because of the Black Death.) Avebury is an example of the Saxons utilizing an existing earthwork to defend a settlement.

Eddisbury (Fig 23) near Delamere, ten miles east of Chester, is perhaps the best surviving example of genuine Saxon work. Built to command the roads from the east to Chester and Wales, the defences were a double rampart with a central ditch, half surrounding an area of over 12 acres, the remaining sides being protected by naturally steep cliffs. The ramparts still stand up to 14 feet high and the ditch was originally 35 feet wide. Although now just grassy mounds the ramparts were probably built in stone originally, an interesting exception to usual Saxon practice, repeated at Towcester where in 920 Edward the Elder reinforced the fortress with stone walls.

THE SAXON DYKES

There are three main systems of Saxon dykes in Britain, all built in very much the same manner: a single rampart and ditch with heights nowadays of from 2 to 40 feet. Grim's Dyke runs almost the entire length of the Chilterns and divided the villages of the Icknield Way from the kingdom of the East Saxons. Offa's Dyke runs from the Flintshire coast to the mouth of the Wye, sometimes in England, sometimes in Wales. It was constructed between 757 and 796 and is probably on a line mutually agreed between the Welsh and the Saxons. The Cambridgeshire Dykes, which cross the Icknield Way where it fords the Cam, probably separated East Anglia from Mercia. Here there are three parallel lines of dykes, known as the Roman Way, the Fleam Dyke and the Devil's Dyke.

Another interesting dyke is that on Flamborough Head known as Dane's Dyke and consisting of a series of entrenchments cutting off five square miles of the headland from the mainland, an area still known locally as Little Denmark.

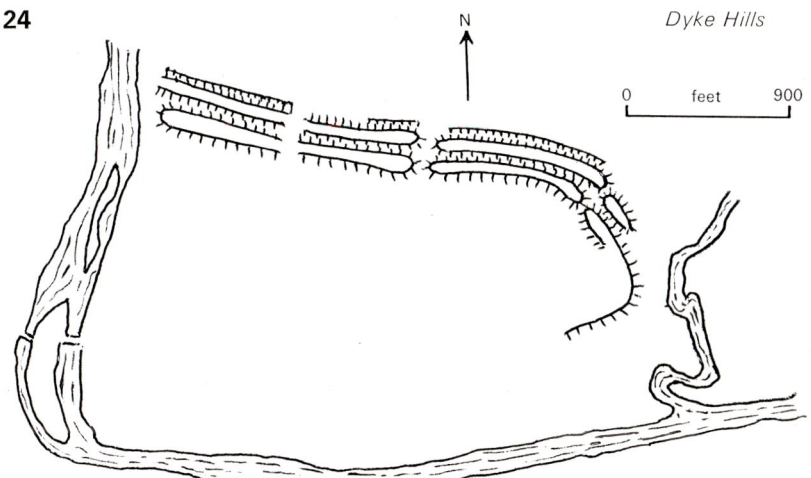

N

0   feet   900

Experts are divided in their opinions as to whether it was constructed by the Saxons to keep the Danes out, or by the Danes to maintain a foothold on the coast.

Except for Dane's Dyke none of these dykes can be genuinely termed fortifications, since they do not appear to have been manned and may only have acted as boundaries between the kingdoms of the time. If this is true, and the Saxons are certainly not renowned for building fortifications, then Little Denmark may indeed have been just that, and Dane's Dyke may really have been built by the Danes!

THE DANES

The Danes rarely strayed far from their ships and water, and since they were on the offensive, fighting a war of a cut and dash nature, they had little need for fortifications. In 871 they built a rampart near Reading between the Thames and the Kennet, but this was merely a winter camp. Dyke Hills (Fig 24) near the Dorchester in Oxfordshire, was a similar type of temporary camp and enclosed 114 acres. The Danes used the Thames and Thame here to protect three sides of the site and the only defences to be constructed were on the north side. Here were two ramparts 1,000 yards long and about 16 feet above the floor of a central ditch which was 55 feet wide. There was also a smaller outer ditch. Despite centuries of cultivation the defences may still be traced and one section of about 200 yards has survived, minus its outer ditch. The camp stood on ground higher than the surrounding fields and the ditches must have been flooded to form moats.

The Ouse in Bedfordshire was the scene of much fighting during the early 10th century and two examples of Danish fortifications have survived on the river banks. Willington (Fig 25), on the south bank, must have been a formidable task although now much obliterated by road and rail construction. Built in 921 it had two ramparts and ditches on the south and east sides and an inner citadel with a 40 foot wide ditch. All three ditches were filled by the river. The ramparts have more or less disappeared now. The Danes also excavated 'docks' for their precious ships, the largest being 105×176 feet, a smaller one off this measuring 110×60 feet, and a third of 72×35 feet which provided a separate dock for a single vessel.

Unfortunately for the Danes these fortifications did them little good and

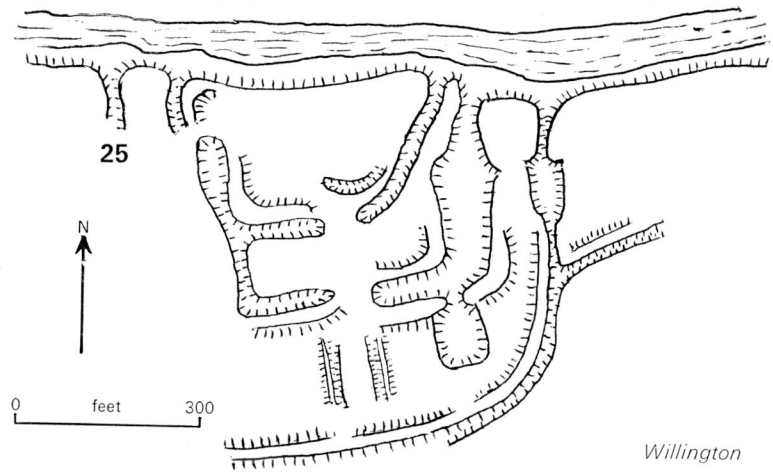

25

N

0 feet 300

Willington

they lost many men and most of their fleet here. The same year some 3,000 Danes made their way back to Tempsford and built a second fortress. Only the central citadel survives, measuring 180×84 feet, enclosed by a 20-foot wide wet ditch and a rampart about ten feet high. In the north-east corner is a low mound about twelve feet high and the entrances were to each side of this. In that same year Edward the Elder besieged the fortress, killed the leaders, captured the rest and 'seized everything inside the fortress'.

IRISH ROUND TOWERS

Although classed as ecclesiastical buildings these do in fact represent fortification against the Scandinavian raiders of the 9th to 12th centuries. Tall, slender towers of dressed stone and mortar, they are invariably found close by churches and monasteries and served the dual role of watch towers and depositories for religious treasures in times of strife, occasionally being used as belfries also. Unlike the Scottish brochs these round towers with their conical stone roofs do have exterior windows, albeit high up, and their doors are on the first floor, in one case 27 feet above ground level, although the average is more like eight to fifteen feet. Access was by ladder and the doorways were usually kept very small, often as narrow as 19 inches or as low as four feet three inches. Height varies from 50 to 100 feet or more, those at Kildare, Kilkenny and Ardmore being 103, 100 and 97 feet respectively.

Over a hundred examples survive in Ireland: the only other known examples are three in Scotland, that at Brechin in Forfarshire being 86 feet high, and one in the Isle of Man. Antrim possesses one of the finest examples, the tower being 93 feet high with a diameter of 17 feet. The walls are four feet thick at ground level, but only 20 inches at the top, being stepped at each floor level.

Plate 6

OPPOSITE: The Martello Tower, many of which remain around Britain's east and south coasts, dates from the Napoleonic era when Britain seemed faced with the threat of invasion in the 1804–1812 period. The chain of towers, armed with guns, was quickly erected, each sited to give a good field of fire at any enemy ships which might approach. These simple stone structures varied in precise shape and dimensions – some were taller and narrower. In the foreground stand men of the local militia and fencibles who, together with artillery men, were responsible for the defences (see page 107).

4: Norman Castles (1048 – 1250)

DURING most of the Dark Ages the art of fortification had come to an almost complete standstill in Western Europe but by the end of the 10th century the form of fortification known as the castle was becoming widespread, except in the British Isles. This was because in France the raids of the Norsemen had brought about the downfall of the central government and the country had split into small kingdoms with each 'king' having his own stronghold or castle, but in England the Norse raids had been resisted at an organized national level and the only strongholds were the *burhs*, designed, in the words of the Anglo-Saxon Chronicle 'to shelter all the folk'. It was this lack of castles, or an organized system of fortifications, which enabled the Normans to complete their conquest of England so swiftly and easily.

Before going further it is perhaps wise to define precisely what is meant by the term castle. We almost invariably associate the word with a strongly built stone fortress but this is to a large extent a false picture of the early Norman castles. We shall see shortly that until as late as 1150 the bulk of all Norman castles in the British Isles were in fact strongholds of earth and timber, materials which had been used in British fortifications for 1,500 years or more.

A fortress or fortification is built for a purely military purpose, housing only a garrison, but the Norman castle was also the private home of the lord, be he baron or king. This dual role distinguishes the castle from all the fortifications which have been described up till now. The hill forts of the Britons and the burhs of the Saxons and Danes were built to protect communities; the Scottish brochs and Irish crannogs were primarily dwelling places or the fortified home of a small community; even the Roman fortresses had their civil settlements and so lived a form of community life. The castle always remained the private home of an individual, and his private fortress.

THE ROLE OF THE CASTLE

The primary role of the castle was not a place of refuge but a centre of military power from which the surrounding countryside could be dominated. A large proportion of a castle's garrison therefore consisted of mounted men and they were used to constantly patrol an area with a radius of about 30 miles from the castle, thus providing some protection for the peasants who worked the land for the lord of the castle. In times of siege these mounted men usually made frequent sorties from postern gates, for even when under siege the castle still maintained its ability to take aggressive action.

The castle was also a storehouse for munitions of war, an advance HQ and observation post in troubled areas, as well as being the home of the lord, a place where he could be secure from attacks by his neighbours and/or enemies. The king's castles could in times of emergency also act as havens for his field army or supply the men to raise a new army. In the event of an invasion castles served to draw off large numbers of men from the invading force who had to capture or at least contain the castles being left to the rear and flanks of the main army in order to prevent the garrisons sallying out to take the offensive.

PRE-CONQUEST CASTLES

The castle was introduced into Britain by the Normans, but not after the 1066 invasion as is popularly imagined. Edward the Confessor spent a great deal of time in Normandy and admired the Normans and their castles. During his reign many Normans came to England as members of his court and, seeing a chance to secure the troublesome Welsh border, Edward gave a number of these Norman knights permission to erect castles along this border. The Anglo-Saxon Chronicle mentions these castles several times, the earliest mention being in 1048, and very definitely distinguishes them from the *burhs*, referring to them as the foreigner's castle and novelties.

To this pre-Conquest period belong Clavering in Essex, and Hereford, Ewyas Harold (built by Osbern Pentecost) and Richard's Castle (built by Richard FitzScrob) in Herefordshire. Although the garrisons of these frontier castles helped to keep back the Welsh they also oppressed the local population and in 1052 the people rose under Harold, Earl Godwyn, and drove the Norman owners from the country.

Richard's Castle is the best example of these first Norman castles in England. Placed in a position of great natural strength on the Herefordshire bank of the River Teme overlooking Ludlow, the castle consists of a massive 60 foot high mound with a flat summit 30 feet in diameter surrounded by a very broad and deep ditch. The few surviving pieces of masonry on the site date from a much later period.

THE MOTTE AND BAILEY CASTLE

Richard's Castle was, of course, what is known as a motte and bailey castle, as were almost all the castles built in England during the 11th century by the Normans. The term is derived from the Norman words for the two main parts of these castles; motte being the mound and bailey the enclosure at the foot of that mound.

The method of construction was to excavate a deep ditch, throwing the earth from this inwards to contribute to the mound. Some of the earth was also used round the outer circumference of the ditch to form a counterscarp or earthen rampart, which was often topped by a palisade of sharpened stakes or a close set thorny hedge. The ditch itself was usually dry by design, although on occasions a wet ditch was utilized, for example where a castle was on a lowlying site or close by a river. Rarely was the site of a Norman castle chosen with a view to obtaining a wet ditch.

Where possible the motte was wholly or partially formed by a natural hillock or rock outcrop in order to save time and labour and to provide a more secure base on which to build. As can be seen from Fig 26, which is based on the Hastings castle as shown on the Bayeux Tapestry, where a motte was entirely artificial it was not constructed of earth alone but of a mixture of earth, gravel and stone, stacked in layers which bonded together more firmly and so eliminated some of the inevitable sinking. This 'sandwich' method was also discovered at Silbury Hill during the BBC's excavations in 1968.

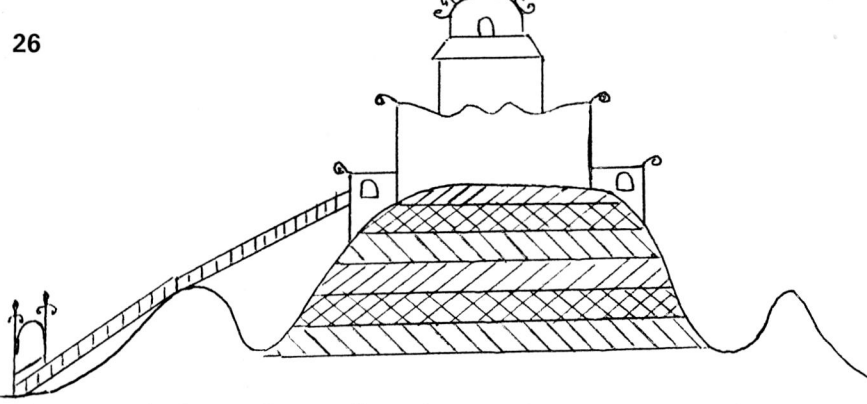

Hastings castle, Bayeux Tapestry illustration portraying a Norman bretasche *and motte.*

The mottes were normally circular in plan, although examples do occur of oval and occasionally almost rectangular mottes. The sides were made as steep as possible and the height ranged from a common 20 to 30 feet to over 100 feet in exceptional cases, with a circumference of from 300 to more than 1,000 feet. The top of the motte was levelled off to provide a building platform and could be anything from 30 to 300 feet in diameter. Round the outer edge of this summit was constructed an earthen rampart, again varying considerably in size at different castles. At Croft Castle in Devon this rampart has survived extremely well and would appear to have been six feet wide and twelve feet high. The rampart was then topped by the stout timber palisade of sharpened stakes always associated with earthworks of this nature, or by a less effective wattle fence. On this well guarded summit was erected the lord's residence and stronghold, referred to as the tower or *bretasche*. Where subsidence in the newly constructed motte was to be expected these towers were often built on stilts in the form of four great baulks of timber, one at each corner. This practice was still in use up to the second quarter of the 12th century.

Of the hundred or more motte and bailey castles built before the end of the 11th century not more than twelve had any stone work and even such future giants as Windsor and Warwick Castles began life as a simple wooden tower on a motte. We know that William the Conqueror erected one of these wooden towers at 'Hastings' when he landed in England, even before engaging the English army, and that he brought with him the already shaped and jointed timber for the tower, in prefabricated form as it were. When his men landed they unloaded these parts and within hours had erected the tower, inside the stone walls of the old Roman fort at Pevensey, to provide a protective base for the beach-head. One is reminded of the Normandy Landings, in reverse. At York the Normans erected William's own castle of wood in eight days, presumably in this instance having to start from scratch.

The entrance to these wooden towers was on the first floor, protected by the quarters of the garrison. The first floor also contained the larders, kitchen if any, and the rooms of the other common residents of the lord's household. Steps led down from this floor to cellars and granaries in the ground floor, and up to the lord's rooms on the second floor. The top storey, which had a parapet surrounding the roof of the tower, was used as a high vantage point by the guards to keep a watch on the surrounding countryside, and in times of attack provided the only position from which the garrison could take offensive action.

The whole design of motte and tower is best summed up by the biographer of the Bishop of Terouenné, writing about 1130: 'The nobles . . . make a hill of earth as high as they can, and encircle it with a ditch as broad and deep as possible. They surround the upper edge of this hill with a very strong wall of hewn logs, placing small towers on the circuit, according to their means. Inside this wall they plant their house or stronghold, which *looks down on all the neighbourhood.*' (Author's italics.) The use of small towers on the encircling wall has not been mentioned before because information about these is almost non-existent. The castles on the Bayeux Tapestry often have what look like towers, but these were probably merely raised parts of the tower parapet rather than projecting or flanking towers as we know them.

The bailey which nestled at the foot of this stronghold, separated from it by the ditch, contained the timber buildings necessary for the support of the castle : stables, barns, smithy, chapel, workshops etc, and had its own defences within which the population of the surrounding area might also shelter in times of danger if the lord so permitted. (Of course, the lord was usually only interested in men capable of bearing arms in the defence of the castle.)

Like the motte the bailey was surrounded by a counterscarped ditch and an earthen rampart topped by a wooden palisade. The palisade was continued up the sides of the motte and linked up with that of the tower, while the ditch of the bailey linked up with that of the motte, usually resulting in a figure of eight plan. The bailey was rarely of large proportions, the whole area of these castles perhaps not occupying more than one and a half to three acres. The actual shape of the bailey varied considerably and probably the lay of the land was the major influence.

The plan of the motte and bailey castle also varied occasionally. In some cases the motte was placed in the centre of the bailey, as at Bramber Castle in Sussex and Pickering Castle in Yorkshire, but this is unusual, the idea of having the motte to one side of the bailey being that as a last resort the garrison could escape from the tower, no longer possible when the bailey, which must fall first, surrounds the motte. There are also occasional instances of mottes with two baileys, Windsor Castle and Castle Acre in Norfolk are two examples. In these cases the second bailey was very small and was probably in reality only an outwork designed to protect the approach to the castle. One other interesting variant is Lewes Castle, the only castle in Britain to have two mottes. (Lincoln has what appears to be a second motte, but it is not so pronounced as at Lewes.) Brack Mount, to the north-east of the latter castle, was probably raised for the first motte and bailey castle, immediately after the Conquest. The second motte, on which was built the shell keep, was closer to the existing town. Both mottes were built with large roughly squared blocks of chalk, which indicates that stone buildings were expected to be constructed on them soon after. It is also interesting that the Norman de Warenne built both Castle Acre and Lewes Castle.

Entrance to a bailey was via a drawbridge over the bailey ditch and a gateway in the palisade. Sometimes this gateway was strengthened by wooden towers. The only means of access to the motte from the bailey was a long, narrow, sloping bridge supported on wooden piles and leading from the bailey to the top of the motte. Often wooden towers protected the ends of this bridge where they met the counterscarp of the mound ditch and the palisade at the top of the motte, and there must have been some form of drawbridge so that the bridge could be 'broken' if the bailey was captured.

The one great weakness of the motte and bailey castle lay in the basic plan,

SHREWSBURY CASTLE. Postern gate and tower in the east curtain wall. The wall leading up to the motte is to the right of the picture. Notice how this tower is set back and does not project its full depth in front of the curtain wall.

for the defences formed one barrier after another and were not related to each other throughout. They could not therefore be used as a co-ordinated defence system. However, this fault in castle building was not corrected until the 14th century and this one inherent weakness does not seem to have affected the strength of the castles in the period covered by this chapter.

On the other hand the vital factor in favour of the motte and bailey castle was, of course, that it could be quickly and easily constructed. (When Henry II set out to conquer Ireland a hundred years later he used precisely this style of fortification.) That the castles were strong enough to combat the siege methods of the day is borne out by the fact that, despite all the advances in military fortifications and the new techniques of siege warfare introduced, the motte and bailey castles continued to be inhabited throughout the Middle Ages.

ADULTERINE CASTLES

During the disturbed reign of King Stephen (1135–54) a large number of castles were constructed without the authority of the king, thereby earning the name of adulterine castles. These castles sprang up in every part of the country and there were more castles in England during this period than at any other time. Henry II is stated to have been kept busy during his long reign (1154–89) destroying 375 (another account claims it was 1,115) of these unlicensed castles. Had they been of stone the destruction of so many would have been impossible and this, together with numerous mentions in the records of the accidental or deliberate burning down of castles, confirms the conclusion that certainly until as late as about 1160 the term castle meant a construction of earth and timber.

As the king grew stronger the licensing of castles was more and more restricted while the barons, gradually abandoning their private wars, began to seek surroundings designed more for comfort than security. These factors played an important part in the subsequent development of the castle.

11th CENTURY STONE CASTLES

During the reigns of William the Conqueror and his son William Rufus (1066–1100) very few castles were erected in stone and none at all prior to about 1075. There were two main reasons for this: William was too busy conquering the country and at this stage made do with the quick but effective earth and timber castle, and at this stage there were few Norman masons in the country and insufficient organized labour for the task. As soon as the Conquest was reasonably established William set about constructing stone castles at the strategic points in his new kingdom and from this period date the great tower keeps of London and Colchester, the keeps of Canterbury and Chepstow, and parts of the castle at Richmond in Yorkshire. With these, though slightly later, may be grouped the keep at Pevensey Castle and parts of Peveril, Durham, Ludlow, Tamworth and Shrewsbury castles.

It is interesting to note from these rare examples that the design followed very closely that of the motte and bailey castle, ie, raising a fortress which relied on passive defence in the form of height and thick walls. The White Tower (Fig 27) at the Tower of London, dating from 1078, has survived beautifully and enables us to see precisely what these first English stone castles looked like. Distinctive points are the towers at each corner and the pilasters or flat buttresses which reinforce the walls. The White Tower measures 107 feet from north to south and 118 feet from east to west. The walls are 15 feet thick at ground floor level.

Colchester Keep (Fig 28) follows an almost identical pattern but is even larger, measuring $151\frac{1}{2}$ feet from north to south and 110 feet from east to west, with walls $12\frac{1}{2}$ feet thick at the base. Construction commenced about 1085 though it may have been earlier, but was abandoned at first floor level and the existing work then hastily prepared for defence. However, work was resumed soon after and the tower eventually had four storeys and stood 90 feet high with the corner towers rising about another ten feet. The battlements built at first floor level may still be seen in the outer wall, being especially clear on the eastern side.

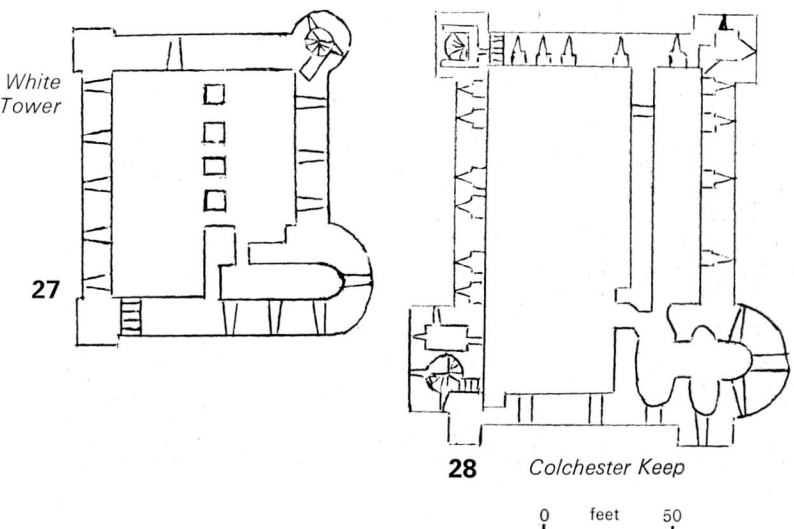

White Tower

27

28   Colchester Keep

0   feet   50

The Tower of London was obviously built to overawe the city, and Colchester was ideally placed for guarding against a seaborne invasion on the coast between the Thames and the Stour. Bramber Castle on the River Adur in Sussex was probably erected for the same purpose (see also World War 2 pill boxes). The keep of Bramber Castle was built about 1087, though the earthwork is probably pre-Conquest, the site being mentioned as belonging to an English earl during Edward the Confessor's reign. Ludlow, commenced 1085, was also built on the site of an earlier fortification and its position on the Welsh border speaks for itself.

Pevensey keep, built at the very end of the century by William de Mortain for his rebellion in 1101, is of highly irregular form. Measuring 55×30 feet it incorporates a length of Roman wall and a Roman bastion. The other five round-fronted towers are probably based on the Roman style. Nothing now remains above ground floor level but the keep may have stood 80 feet high with the entrance on the first floor.

Richmond Castle, 1075, and Peveril's Peak, end of the 11th century, were undoubtedly built in stone because of their rocky sites, which made it impossible to construct the standard ditch and motte. At Peveril two sides are made almost impregnable by steep cliffs and the stone curtain wall was erected on the other two sides to complete a perimeter defence. Richmond also has a curtain wall of stone, and also the remains of an 11th century stone hall, but it is significant that neither of these castles had a stone tower keep : stone was only used in this period where earth and timber construction was not possible.

THE TRANSITION TO STONE

The change over to stone for castle building was brought about by a combination of factors. As we have seen, in the 11th century a few stone castles were built to secure strategic points in the conquered land. These were followed in the first half of the 12th century by more stone castles

PEVENSEY CASTLE, north curtain wall and angle towers which replaced the old wooden palisade c.1250. The great towers reveal their later date.

GROSMONT CASTLE. The four storey west tower, seen from the interior of the castle.

designed for the same purpose. Carlisle, Norwich, Rochester and Castle Hedingham were some of the more important ones of this period.

The existence of these stone castles led to improvements in the art of siege warfare and these improvements in turn forced more and more castles to change over to stone. However, this transition was not achieved overnight but continued for over a century, the main period being approximately 1150 to 1250. Similarly the transition to stone at individual sites did not take place instantaneously and there were no doubt many instances where a stone keep still had an earthen and timber bailey, or a brand new curtain wall of stone encircled an old timber keep. The old timber keep at York, for example, stood

BERKELEY CASTLE shell keep, c.1153, seen from the west. The breach in the wall was made during the Civil War and conveniently shows the thickness of the wall where it abutts on a square tower.

for nearly 200 years before it was replaced by the stone-built Clifford's Tower during the reign of Henry II.

The majority of the stone castles were naturally built on the sites of the old motte and bailey castles, although not all the motte and bailey castles in existence were necessarily converted; some never graduated to stone at all, mainly because of lack of funds, the restrictions on licensing castles imposed by Henry II, and the gradual cessation of private wars between the barons. New castles were built, but not as profusely as during the previous hundred years, and even up to as late as the beginning of the 13th century some new castles were constructed of earth and timber in the old fashion, mainly in cases of emergency when speed was the main concern.

Because the vast majority of the stone castles of this period were built on earlier sites the basic plan of the castle did not change drastically and most retained their original form of motte and bailey, with a stone keep added either to the motte or in the bailey. The simplest form of keep merely replaced the palisade round the edge of the motte summit and was known as the shell keep. The bailey wall was continued up the motte and linked to this keep,

BERKELEY CASTLE, the north face of the keep. The towers on this face are square, but round on the other sides. The roof in the foreground belongs to a modern addition.

just as the timber wall had done previously. The other, and most popular, form was the tower keep following on a smaller scale the style of the great keeps of London, Colchester and Rochester. This word keep needs some explanation before proceeding.

Until now I have deliberately tried to avoid using the word keep for although it is now the accepted term for the main tower or stronghold of the 11th–13th century castle, in the period I am writing about the word was unknown. The shell keep was known simply as the motte, having changed only in material and not form, while the tower keep was referred to as the tower, a practice which has continued through the centuries in the case of the Tower of London. The term donjon was later applied to the tower keep, being low Latin for dominant point and neither motte nor donjon should be confused with moat and dungeon, words which erroneously developed from these original terms and eventually evolved meanings of their own.

SHELL KEEPS

This form of keep was easy and cheap to construct but, lacking the great strength of the tower keep, it did not become widespread. Its main advantage was that it could be added quickly to the existing fortifications, the timber *bretasche* being replaced at a later, more convenient date. The buildings which replaced the *bretasche* might be in stone or wood, but in either case they were built against the keep wall, thus leaving an open courtyard in the centre. Windsor Castle, although much added to over the centuries, is the classic example of the shell keep, still standing on its dominating motte. Restormel in Cornwall is another fine example, with a near perfect crenellated wall, and other shell keeps may be seen at Carisbrooke, Cardiff, Arundel and Lewes.

In most cases the shell keep was built where the motte was artificial and there was a danger of it slipping under the massive weight of a tower keep. There are also occasional instances where the shell keep was built round the base of the motte, as at Berkeley Castle situated in Gloucestershire. Here the shell keep provides a revetment for the motte and is then continued upwards, forming a keep of which the base is made all the more impregnable by the solid earth behind the stonework.

TOWER KEEPS

The square or rectangular keep of fine ashlar stone was the most outstanding feature of this period of castle building. Although crude, in that it relied on the brute strength of its walls to defeat attacks, it was extremely effective and this form of keep continued to be used for as long as castles had a military role to fulfil. However, the majority were raised in the reign of Henry II and many of the finest surviving tower keeps, Scarborough, Peveril, Bamburgh and Dover to name just a few, were built for that king.

Where a motte was wholly or for the most part natural the towers were built on their tops, as at Castle Hedingham and Norwich, but most frequently the mottes were incapable of supporting the weight of a tower keep, the rectangular shape of the tower was also unsuitable in many cases, and more often the motte was abandoned in favour of the bailey. Where there were two baileys the keep was normally built on the cross wall which divided them, as at Scarborough and Bamburgh. Most newly raised castles, therefore, did not have a motte. At Kenilworth the keep was built round the motte so that the basement was backed by solid earth, exactly the same method used at Berkeley Castle for the shell keep.

The walls of the tower keeps, being their main defence, were enormously thick and rose to great heights, supported by pilasters and angle turrets in the same manner as their predecessors in London and Colchester. The walls of the keep at Dover are from 21 to 24 feet thick, the tower rose to a height of 80 feet and the ground plan covers an area of 98 × 96 feet. However, this is the finest of the 12th-century keeps: a more average keep of the period was likely to have walls 14 feet thick, a ground plan covering say 60 × 50 feet, and stand some 50 feet high. Except in some of the earliest examples the base of the walls was splayed out to form a plinth which would resist the action of such siege weapons as the ram, bore and pick.

At the lowest levels there were slits for ventilation and light: they were not designed as arrow slits at this date. From the second floor up 'windows' were used, but often this meant apertures only a foot or eighteen inches wide and four feet long. By the end of the 12th century these openings reached five feet

CHEPSTOW CASTLE, the great hall of 1067–72. This was one of the early stone 'keeps', utilizing the usual tower keep principles of entrance at 1st floor, pilasters, small apertures etc, but was altered to become the Great Hall when the bailey walls were added between 1190 and 1245.

CHEPSTOW CASTLE. The east curtain wall and tower, added c.1190. The gatehouse beyond belongs to the 13th century.

in length and were close to two feet wide but they were still few in number and were heavily barred and shuttered in times of unrest. Even the larger windows which developed after this date were not so vulnerable as they would at first appear, being protected by strong iron grilles.

The entrance to the keeps was usually at first floor level, occasionally at second floor level. Steps to the doorway were built at right angles to this entrance, either against the keep wall or separated from it, when the resulting gap was bridged by a drawbridge. The doorway and drawbridge were often protected by a small forebuilding.

The interior of these keeps followed a more or less general pattern and this is shown in Fig 29. In the largest keeps, such as London, Colchester, Rochester, Dover and Castle Hedingham, the interior was divided by a strong cross wall so that, should the entrance to the keep be forced, the defenders could retire behind yet another line of defence. This happened at Rochester in 1215 when one corner of the keep was undermined. The cross wall was solid at ground floor level, except for a small doorway, but in the residential floors it was usually

CHEPSTOW CASTLE. The nearest tower marks the end of the east curtain. The other tower and connecting curtain, on the south side and joining up with the keep, date from 1225–45.

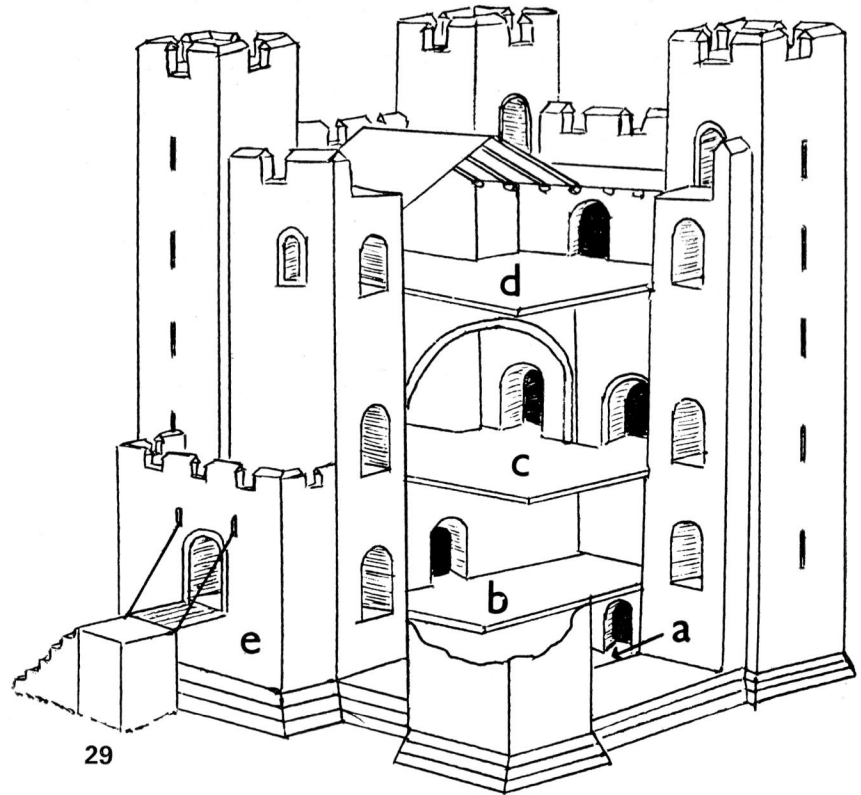

29

Cut away diagram of a typical Norman keep, showing the internal arrangements: A: storage cellars; B: garrison quarters with dividing cross wall; C: great hall; D: lord's quarters; E: forebuilding.

pierced by large arches to admit more light and give more space.

Spiral staircases were built in one or more of the corners of the keep to connect the various floors and were continued up to the corner turrets. The spiral was normally right handed so that defenders retreating up into the towers would have plenty of room to swing their swords while the central pillar of the stairs protected their left side. Conversely the enemy had no room to swing his sword and his shield also became practically useless in the circumstances.

Two other vital parts of the keep were a small chapel, for the good of their souls, and the well. The latter was frequently continued up to the residential floors, not only for convenience but also for safety.

THE CYLINDRICAL KEEP

This type of keep began to appear towards the end of the 12th century when it had become obvious that the major weakness of the tower keep lay in its corners. Not only was it comparatively easy for a pick or bore to break away the corner stones, which had only two sides secured against other stones, but the corners were also blind spots except for a man stationed directly overhead and if he bent over the rampart to bombard the attackers he would almost certainly be picked off by enemy marksmen. No other fire could be

CHEPSTOW CASTLE from across the Wye, showing the strong natural position chosen by the builders. The 13th-century gatehouse lies at the bottom of a steep slope.

brought to bear on the corners by the defenders.

The obvious answer was the round or cylindrical keep, but this was not immediately forthcoming and there was a transitional stage of polygonal keeps. Orford Castle (Fig 30), built between 1165–73 for Henry II, was one of the first of these transitional keeps. Although perfectly cylindrical inside, the outer face was broken by the three great buttresses which supported the keep, and these were again a weak point, though they could be defended more adequately than the corners of the tower keeps. Chilham Castle, again built for Henry II, and dating from the 1170s, was octagonal in plan, as was Odiham Castle, built for King John in the 1200s. Conisbrough Castle (Fig 31) is another attempt, once again spoilt by the use of buttresses. Built about 1185–90 it survives practically intact except for the roof and floors, which were of timber.

The first truly cylindrical keeps do not appear until the 13th century. Pembroke Castle is one of the earliest of these round keeps, and other examples

Orford keep　　　　　　　　　　　　　*Conisbrough keep*

Scale: ¾ inch to 20 ft

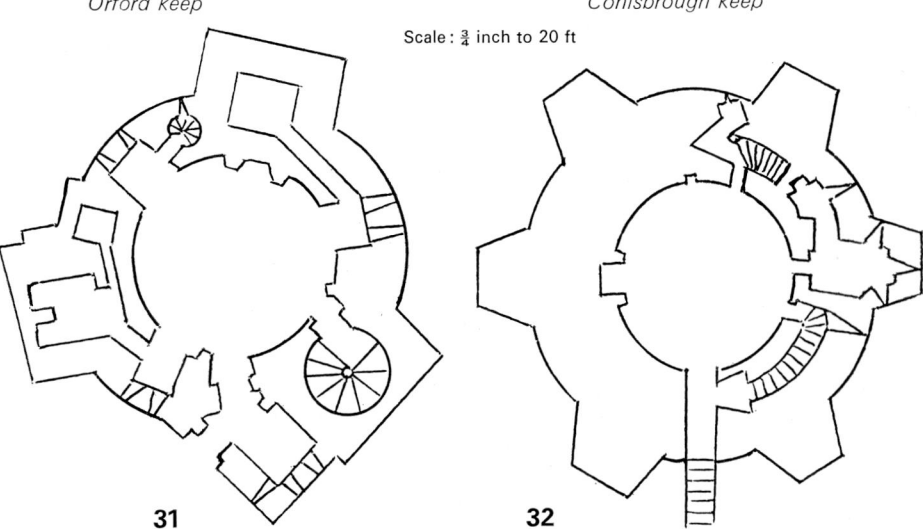

31　　　　　　　　　　　　　　　　　　**32**

RICHMOND CASTLE. The great keep, built over the 11th-century gatehouse. Chapel and great hall were all built in stone in the 11th century.

survive at Caldicott, Bronllys, Skenfrith and Launceston, all except the latter being in Wales. Launceston and Skenfrith are also of interest in that they are built on a motte.

Despite its obvious advantages over the tower keep, the cylindrical keep never became common. There were two main reasons for this. Firstly, the tower keeps could stand up to almost any assault likely to occur unless in actual rebellion against the king, as at Rochester, and it is significant that cylindrical keeps are mostly confined to areas of great unrest. Secondly, just as the cylindrical keep was nearing perfection, the hitherto unchallenged belief that the keep was the ultimate stronghold of a castle was made obsolete by other developments in castle architecture dealt with in the next section.

SKENFRITH. The round keep.

5: The Golden Age of Castles (1250-1350)

IN the previous section we have seen how the castle was designed in two parts, a bailey and a keep, the basic theory behind the design being to present the attacker with one line of defence after another. This system was based on the fact that the keep, the ultimate stronghold of the castle, was the lord's residence and as such was to be defended to the last. Whilst this system had some advantages its inherent weakness lay in the fact that the lines of defence could not be co-ordinated to present a mutually supporting system of defences capable of withstanding an attack from any direction, while advances in methods of siege warfare had made it possible for the attackers to breach the thin bailey walls with comparative ease and even in some cases cause the downfall of the mighty tower keeps.

Chateau Gaillard, Richard I's castle in France, one of the finest in Western Europe and considered impregnable, fell in 1202, only five years after its completion. Rochester keep was undermined in 1215, Bedford in 1224. In each of these cases the castles were reduced systematically, the attackers able to concentrate their assault on one line of defence at a time. Castles could no longer be relied on as a secure base and men began to seek improvements.

During the 13th century new ideas on fortification were brought back to England by the Crusaders and many new features began to be added to existing castles or incorporated into new ones. The emphasis of defence began to shift from the keep and the aim became to prevent an enemy overrunning the entire castle should he once gain entry at any one point or, better still, keep the enemy out altogether, for no castle owner could now be certain his keep would survive a siege, nor would he wish to see the outer bailey overrun and sacked. Obviously therefore the best defences were those which could keep the enemy outside the castle altogether and this meant moving the emphasis to the bailey walls.

BAILEY DEFENCES

From an early date the bailey curtain wall had had crenellations to provide cover and a wall walk to allow movement along the top of the wall behind the parapet, and these measures allowed assailants to be held back or, failing this, to be repulsed from the top of the wall. However, should the enemy gain the *base* of the wall and bring rams or bores to bear there was no defence except by leaning over the parapet, when the defenders were exposed to the waiting marksmen. The base of the wall was splayed or battered for extra strength but this was no permanent solution to the problem.

Another answer was to keep the enemy away from the base of the walls and this could be achieved by firepower. The merlons were narrowed to permit a greater number of embrasures and early in the 13th century the merlons themselves were pierced. This increased firepower and also provided more cover for the bowmen. Further refinements were angled coping stones on top of the battlements to deflect arrows upwards and away from the defenders, and shutters over the embrasures which gave the archers more time to select a target, aim and fire.

The arrow slits in the merlons were at first designed for the long bow which was fired vertically and they were therefore long and narrow with reveals on the inside to allow for the handling of the weapon and give a wider field of fire. With the advent of the crossbow, which was fired horizontally, a cruciform arrow slit was adopted, suited to both types of bow. When flanking towers and gatehouses were introduced these arrow slits were applied to them also. At a later date, such as at Caernarvon (12831–323), firepower was further increased by building firing galleries into the walls below the rampart. This also had the advantage of allowing archers to fire *beneath* the protective roofs of siege engines.

However, except for the example quoted at Caernarvon, which was a very late development and came about after the problem had been solved by other means, these improvements still did not protect the base of the wall. The first attempt to solve the problem was the use of hoardings or brattices, wooden platforms built out from the front of the battlements and having their own embrasures and roof. Arrows and stones could thus be discharged through slots in the floor at the attackers at the base of the wall while the embrasures provided the normal opportunity to fire as the attackers approached. The Tower of London had a hoarding fitted in 1240 'made of good strong timber and well leaded over, so that men may see as far as the foot of the tower'. These hoardings were often of a temporary nature, being taken to pieces and stored in times of peace.

Of course, a good hit with a hundredweight stone thrown by a siege engine could have a detrimental effect on these wooden structures, though wood could be far more resilient than stone in these instances, and on the Continent hoardings were replaced by stone machicolation from the end of the 12th century onwards. Machicolation did not become common in England until the end of the 14th century and even then was mainly restricted to gatehouses, the bailey walls having by that time ceased to be the prime target owing to improved methods of defence.

THE FLANKING TOWER

Until the second half of the 12th century the great length of a bailey curtain wall had ruled out the possibility of it being constructed to the same massive proportions as the keep while, as we have seen above, there was little chance of defending the base of the wall against siege engines. These factors had made the bailey wall the main target of an attacker, until the Crusaders brought home the idea of the flanking tower, the most important development in the art of castle-building in the 13th century.

Based on the Roman bastion, perpetuated in the Byzantine fortifications, these towers were built at intervals along the bailey wall, projecting outwards so that defenders could fire from their tops or from arrow slits in their sides along the outer face of the curtain wall. Entrance was at ground level in the bailey with doors on the first floor to give access to the ramparts. The towers were then continued up to a second storey so as to be higher than the walls. These factors enabled the towers to act as individual strongpoints along the

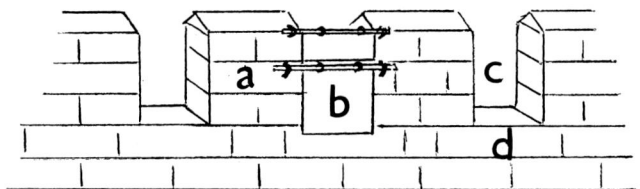

Section of parapet showing A: merlon, B: shutters, C: embrasure, D: sill wall. Embrasures in later battlements were two to three feet wide with a sill wall up to three feet high. The merlons were five to six feet wide and between seven and ten feet high overall.

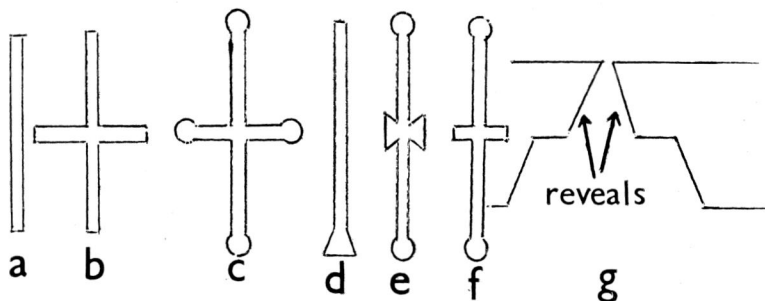

Various types of arrow slits: A: the plain vertical slit for long bow; B: crosslet for long and cross bow; C: crosslet with oilets, c.1150 on; D: variant of C; E: variant at Caerphilly Castle, late 13th century; F: variant at Rockingham Castle, c.1275; G: slit seen from above.

wall, to divide the rampart into sections so that a captured section could be isolated and dominated by the towers, and if sited correctly the towers could also provide covering fire for each other. The towers were capped by steep conical roofs which made them look completely different from the open topped towers we are accustomed to seeing nowadays. (Roofed towers may be seen quite often on the Continent.) Sometimes accommodation and store rooms were housed in the towers.

Ludlow Castle had flanking towers as early as the beginning of the 12th century but this is an isolated example and the towers were sited rather haphazardly. The bailey wall built round the keep at Dover in the last quarter of the 12th century (now the inner bailey) has some of the earliest flanking towers, while those in the inner bailey wall at Framlingham Castle were built in the 1200s. In these examples the towers were square, their inner faces flush with the bailey wall and in most cases the backs of the towers were left open, an advantage if they were captured since there was then no shelter for the attackers, but a disadvantage in that the tower was not an individual strongpoint. Later towers did not have this open back.

Conisbrough Castle, built 1180–1200, is an interesting example of the application of round towers at the same time as the round keep was replacing the square or tower keep. Here the towers are half round and solid, but not all are mutually supporting. Pembroke and Llanstephan castles both have rounded or transitional polygonal towers. From about 1250 the massive drum tower became a characteristic feature of English castles and reached its peak at the end of the century in such great castles as Conway, Harlech and Beaumaris.

GATEHOUSES

By its very nature the gateway into a castle had always been vulnerable and extra precautions had been taken for its defence. The earliest examples of gatehouses occur at Richmond Castle in Yorkshire, Exeter Castle and Ludlow Castle, all built in the late 11th century. In these examples the gateway was formed by two square towers with the gate between them. Most of these square gatehouses were later converted into keeps by blocking up the gates and adding more storeys.

Towards the end of the 12th century, at Dover, two towers were placed at either side of the gate. Rockingham, mid 13th century, has the same plan, but now using rounded towers. These developments, together with the custom of hiring mercenaries (a side effect of the Hundred Years War) gave rise to the great gatehouses of the late 13th, early 14th centuries, the towers being joined together above the gateway to form a long narrow passage, blocked at each end by a portcullis and gates. The passage was further defended by the use of pits, arrow slits in the side walls, and 'murder holes' in the floor above. The common method of gaining access through a gatehouse of this nature was to set fire to the gates by filling the passage with combustible materials. This method had the advantage of roasting the defenders on the floor above at the same time. The 'murder holes' were used to pour water on these fires, or to pour other materials and fire arrows at the attackers as they prepared the fire. In the Bloody Tower in London an original portcullis and its machinery can still be seen and many other castles have examples of the fighting rooms over the gate, sandwiched between the residential apartments in the two towers.

The use of mercenaries had led the castle owner to revise his position within the castle. Hired professional soldiers were far different from the earlier feudal serfs and henchmen and might easily mutiny. There was therefore no point being safe within a keep if at the same time you could not control the gateway into the castle. This factor, and the ever increasing strength and importance of the gatehouse at the end of the 13th century, led to the development of the keep-gatehouse. Beaumaris, Alnwick, Harlech and Kidwelly, to mention a few, all had gatehouses which were strong enough to supersede the keep, and this permitted the lord to house his family in the gatehouse where he could also keep control of the entrance to the castle.

Harlech, with two gates and three portcullis, had no access to the upper floors from ground level so should the gates fall the remainder of the gatehouse continued to operate in the manner of a keep. However, the gatehouse was in the forefront of the fighting, unlike the keep which was normally used only as a last resort, and this is reflected in the construction of the gatehouse. With its portcullis, gates, pits, drawbridges, arrow slits and murder holes the gatehouse of this period was very much on the offensive, whereas the keep had relied solely on passive defence.

Because the gatehouse had become so strong, from the late 13th century onwards many castles had two main gates and two or three posterns or lesser gates. This greater freedom of movement enabled the defenders to sally out to take the offensive more easily. Thus it can be seen that gatehouses played an important part in the defence of the castle, supporting the other defences by forcing an enemy to invest the whole perimeter of the castle and so preventing him from concentrating his forces at any one point.

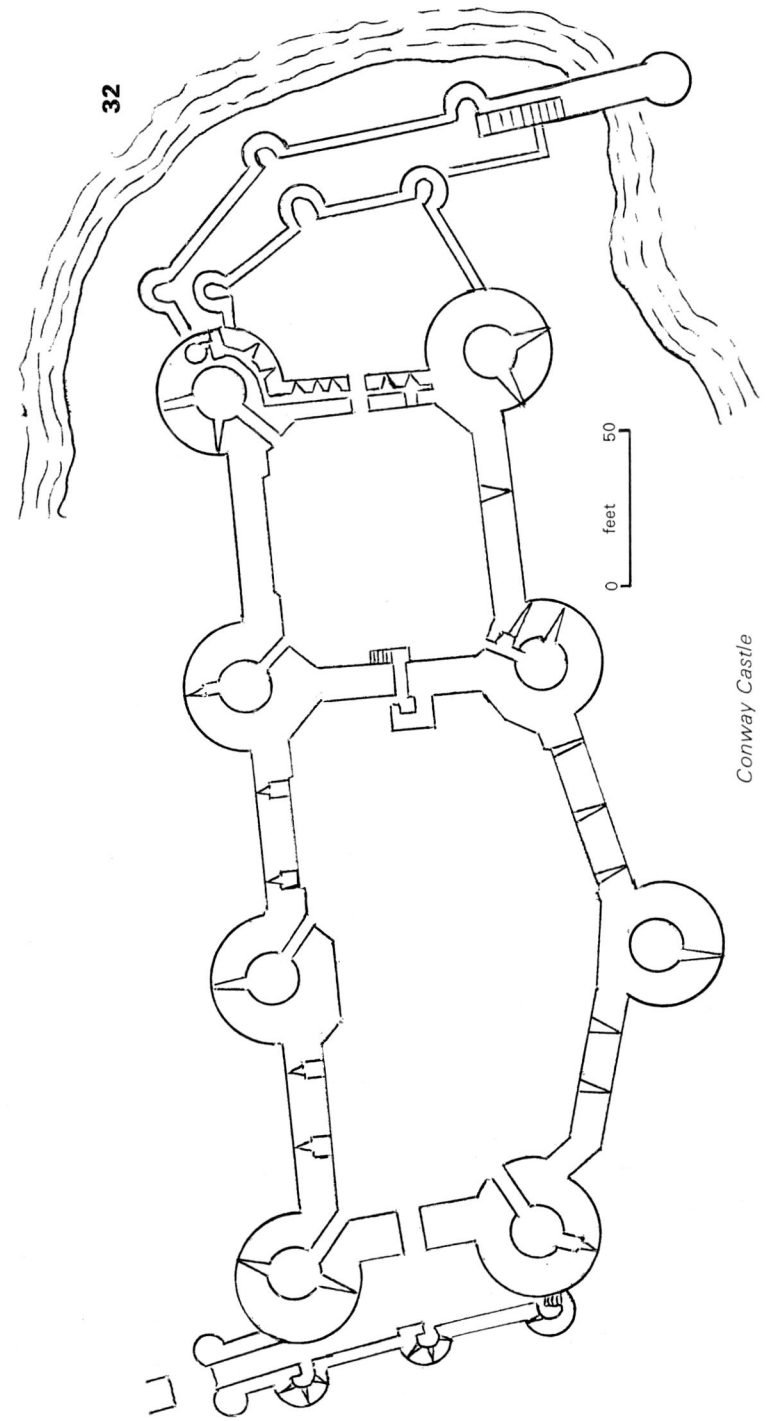

32

Conway Castle

0   feet   50

BARBICANS

These were additional defences or outworks of the gatehouses often, as at Conway (Fig 32), acting like smaller outer baileys to the gatehouses. Here they have their own flanking towers. In its simplest form a barbican consisted of two parallel walls built out at right angles to the gatehouse, thereby forcing an attacker to approach the gates by a narrow defended passage. At Beaumaris (Fig 33) the walls of the south barbican are constructed so that the attacker is made to approach at an angle, thus exposing his flank to fire from the gatehouse. Sometimes the outer end of the barbican might be covered by yet another work, as for example at Goodrich in Herefordshire where there is a large semi-

35

Beaumaris Castle

Scale 1 inch = 200 feet

N

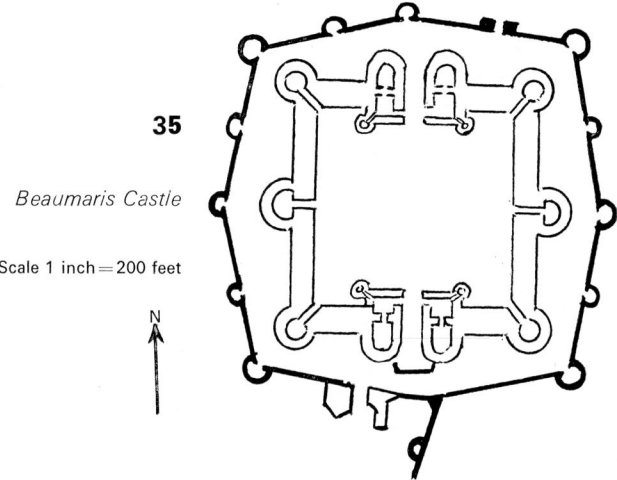

circular covering wall, or by another system of moat, drawbridge, portcullis and gate, as at Warwick Castle.

The gatehouse and barbican at Warwick is in fact outside the period covered by this section, being built about 1370, but it does serve to illustrate the complexity of these defences, the entrance to the castle being transformed into an ambush area or killing ground. First there is the barbican moat, then a raised drawbridge to be burnt or hacked away. Behind this is a gate, and behind the gate a portcullis. Beyond the portcullis is a long narrow passage to the main gatehouse. Here the attacker must start again, moat, drawbridge, gates and portcullis. Once through this second set of obstacles there remains another long narrow passage, commanded by the defenders from both sides and above, and at the end — another portcullis!

THE EDWARDIAN CASTLES

During the reign of Edward I (1272–1307) castles reached their peak and some of the finest examples of military architecture in Britain are to be found among the royal castles built by Edward I to consolidate his conquest of Wales. These are Aberystwyth, Beaumaris, Builth, Caernarvon, Conway, Flint, Harlech and Rhuddlan. In these eight castles Edward I was able to incorporate all the refinements which have been covered above.

Of Aberystwyth and Builth, built in 1277, no masonry now remains but we are fortunate in having the other six survive in very good condition.

ST BRIAVELS CASTLE. Half round tower built c.1290. The roof is a restoration but does give a good idea of what the towers looked like at the time. Note the flat rear of the tower especially.

Conway (1282–87) and Caernarvon are two of the finest examples of the castle whose main strength lay in a single circuit of walls. Both were originally divided in two by cross walls. The keep is abandoned totally in these castles but the walls are as high and as thick as those of many earlier keeps and the flanking towers are massive strongholds in their own right. The towers are also placed so that any attacker is exposed to a withering crossfire, no matter from which angle he approaches the castle. Both castles have two main gates, Conway also having two posterns while Caernarvon has three. There is an interesting development in the spiral staircases too. At Conway one tower has a left hand spiral, at Caernarvon four towers have this feature. This reversal of the standard right hand spiral was to allow for the possibility of the enemy gaining the walls or towers and forcing the defenders *downwards*. The planners appear to have thought of every eventuality.

Another interesting castle of this period, built by the Earl of Lincoln, is Denbigh (Fig 34). The north-west and south-west sides date from 1282 and are portions of the original town walls: the other two sides were built later within the town defences to form the castle. Subsequently the earlier walls were strengthened. The most impressive feature is the great triangular gatehouse and the south barbican and gate complex.

34

Denbigh Castle
South Barbican

N

0   feet   60

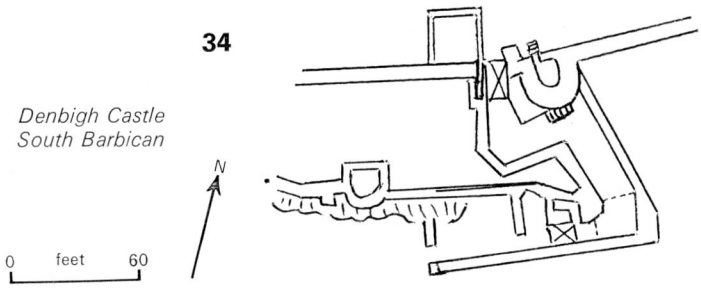

CHEPSTOW CASTLE. The massive Marten's Tower, built c.1270–1300 and commanding the approaches to the main gate. The curtain wall to the left was breached in the Civil War and rebuilt later.

It should not be thought that all the castles built in Wales by Edward I were of totally new concept. Flint Castle (Fig 35) is a notable exception, being basically the old traditional great keep and bailey updated by the use of a cylindrical keep and round towers to provide the vital flanking fire along the walls.

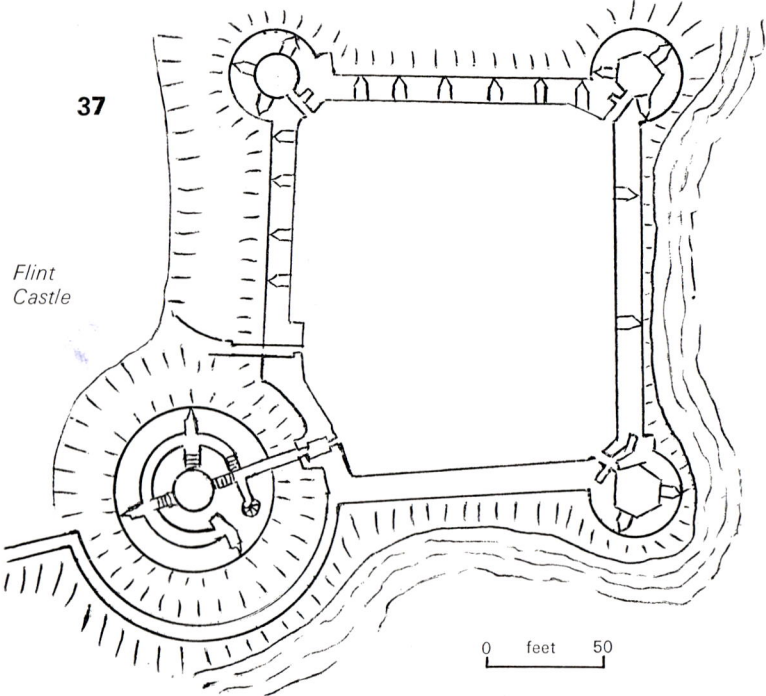

37

Flint
Castle

0   feet   50

CHEPSTOW CASTLE'S great gatehouse, built 1225–45.

CONCENTRIC CASTLES

The other Edwardian castles in Wales are concentric castles, a term aptly described by the illustrations of these castles in this section. They were very similar to those developed in Syria by the Crusaders, and on the Continent, and consisted of a circuit of walls and towers, usually quadrangular in plan, surrounded by another lower wall with its own flanking towers. The area between these two walls, usually very narrow and known as the lists, was divided by cross walls so that any force penetrating the outer wall could be confined to one sector which would then act as a killing ground. The higher inner wall provided covering fire for the outer wall.

Rhuddlan Castle (Fig 36) built 1277–81 and the earliest of the three concentric castles built by Edward I is very simple in plan. No towers were considered necessary for the outer wall because three sides were protected by a wide moat, the fourth side by rocky cliffs. Note how the gates in the inner wall are set obliquely to the outer gates so that an attacker must expose his flank to the concentrated fire from the gatehouses in order to reach them.

Harlech Castle (Fig 37) built 1283–89, has only one gatehouse, aggressively facing the side most easily scaled by an enemy. Again no flanking towers were included in the outer wall, the castle being adequately protected by its lofty position and the moat on two sides. Beaumaris Castle (Fig 33) built 1295–1323, is the culmination of Edward's castle building, perfectly symmetrical in plan, surrounded by a sea water moat and with two gatehouses which epitomise the peak of military architecture in Britain. Note how the gates are again set obliquely in the two circuits of walls.

Perhaps the finest concentric castle, certainly the most developed and largest, with an area of 30 acres, is Caerphilly Castle (Fig 38) built by one of Edward's earls. Added to the basic strength of the quadrangular concentric castle is an extensive system of water defences, barbican and outworks. The magnitude and strength of these defences is best shown by the plan and photographs of the castle in this section.

However, it should be borne in mind that these 'Welsh' castles are exceptional examples, all being new castles, built without consideration of the cost and raised within a very short space of time, all in an area where warfare was still

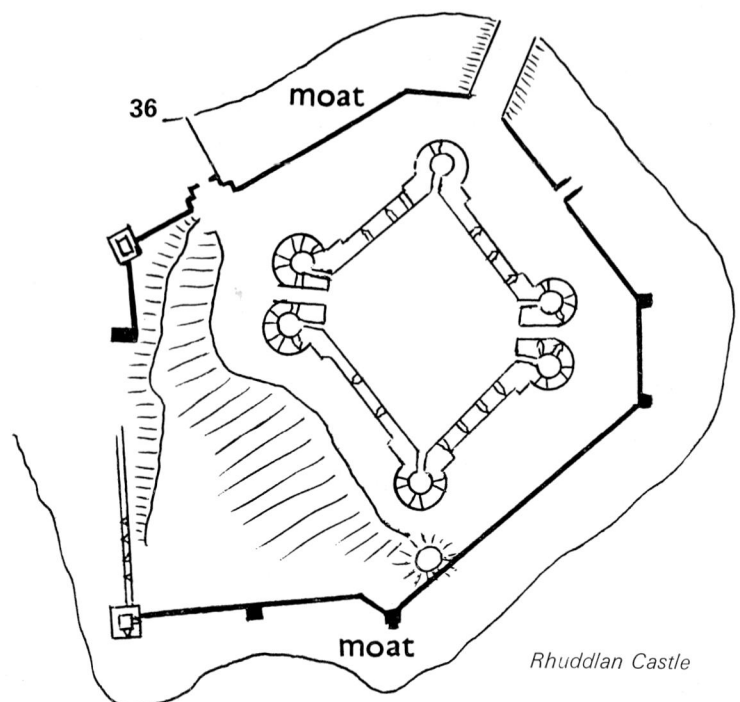

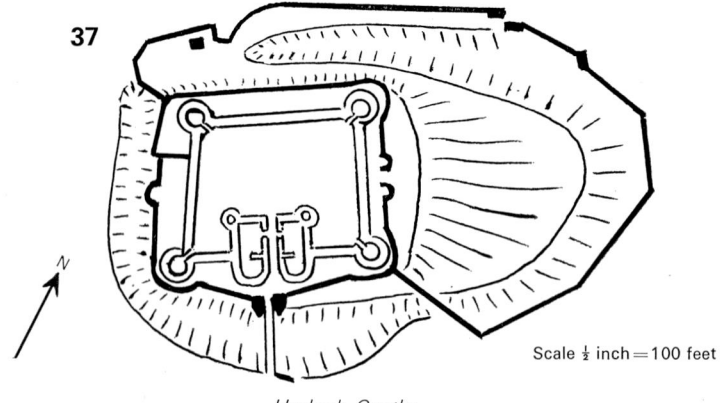

36 moat

moat

Rhuddlan Castle

rampant. Not all new castles of this period, not even all the new castles in Wales as we have seen, were of such excellent design. By far the greater bulk of castle building during this period was in the form of adaptation and strengthening of existing defences, though this work should not necessarily be considered inferior to the new castles. The Tower of London (Fig 40) was extensively 'modernized' in the 13th century and developed into one of the largest concentric castles in Britain, making the White Tower obsolete. Dover Castle was also improved in this century to become a concentric castle of great strength.

Where conversion to the concentric plan was not possible because of the

37

N

Scale ½ inch = 100 feet

Harlech Castle

70

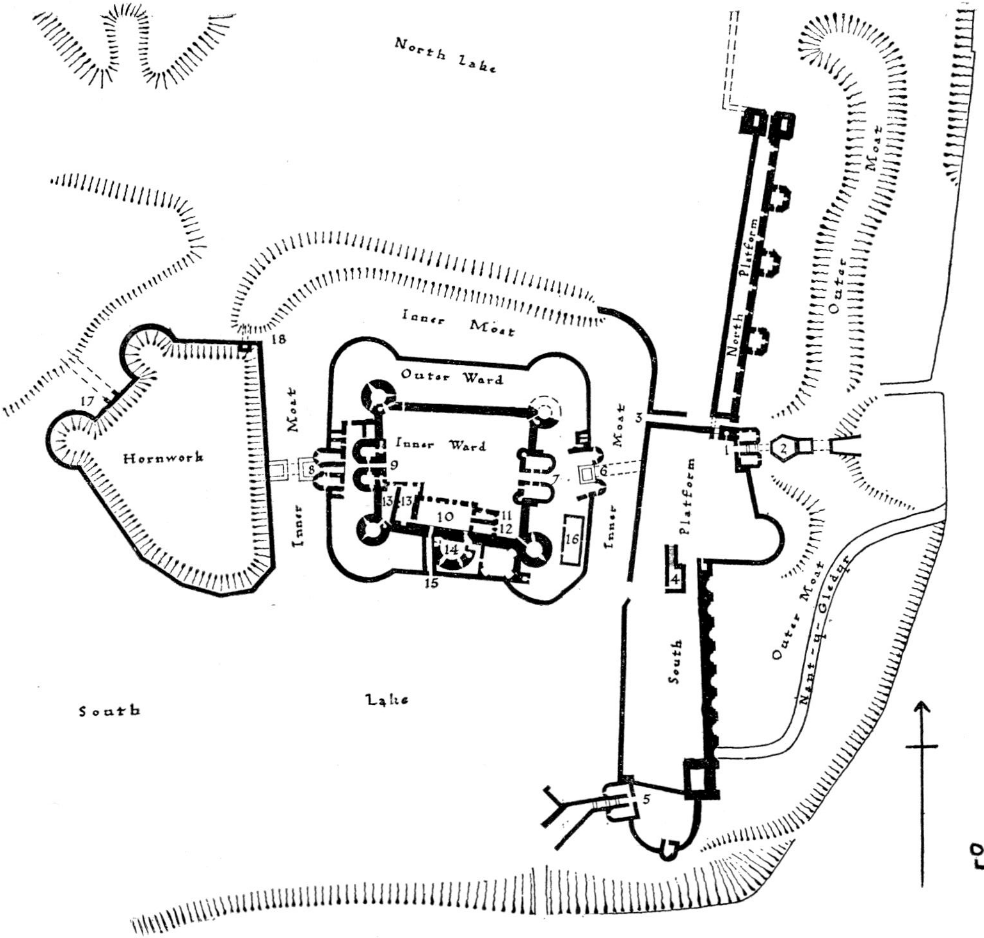

Caerphilly Castle

KEY 38

Eastern Front, comprising North and South Platforms

1 Main Gateway
2 Barbican and double drawbridge
3 Channel from Inner to Outer Moat
4 Watermill
5 South Gateway

Inner and Outer Wards

6 East Gate to Outer Ward
7 East Gate to Inner Ward
8 West Gate to Outer Ward
9 West Gate to Inner Ward
10 Great Hall
11 Buttery, etc.
12 Chapel
13 State Rooms
14 Kitchen Tower
15 Water Gate and covered passage
16 Storehouse

Hornwork

17 Gateway and site of drawbridge
18 Gateway and site of drawbridge

0   100'

North Lake

Moat
Outer
North Platform

Outer Moat
Nant-y-Gledyr

South Platform

Inner Moat

Outer Ward
Inner Ward
Inner Moat

South Lake

Inner Moat

Hornwork

South

CAERPHILLY CASTLE'S forbidding main gate, late 13th century. There is a drawbridge between gate and barbican and another bridge from the barbican to the far side of the moat, not seen here.

lay of the land the new ideas were still utilized. At Corfe Castle for example the middle and outer baileys were added during the 13th century while at Chepstow Castle a new bailey was added to each end of the original castle, both defended by drum towers and massive gatehouse complexes. Kidwelly was adapted about 1275 by building a rectangular 'bailey' with four

The triangular gatehouse

39

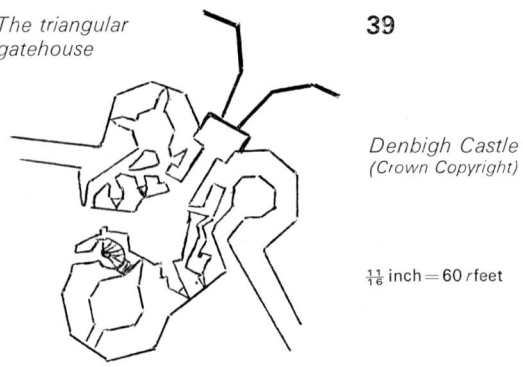

Denbigh Castle
(Crown Copyright)

$\frac{11}{16}$ inch = 60 *r*feet

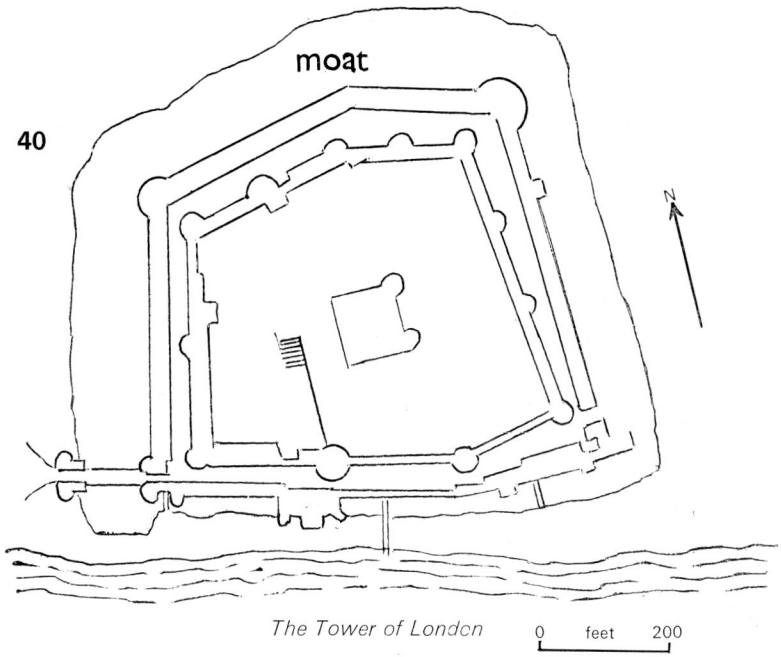

moat

40

N

The Tower of London

0   feet   200

CAERPHILLY CASTLE, east gate to the outer bailey as seen from the main gatehouse. Note the bridge spanning an inner moat, part of the complex water defences here.

CAERPHILLY CASTLE northern platform curtain and towers, showing the outer moat and north lake water defences.

great corner round towers *inside* the existing curtain wall, which in the early 14th century was then strengthened by the addition of a great gatehouse and flanking towers.

At many other castles throughout the land development took place piecemeal with the addition of gatehouses and flanking towers at the weakest spots on the walls and as a result many castles retained their original motte and bailey layout.

The result of these changes in methods of fortification was that by the early 14th-century castles could at last present a co-ordinated defence to an enemy attacking from any direction. With the bailey walls forming the new main line of defence the castle owner was free to leave his keep, and even the gatehouse, and take up residence in the more spacious comfort of the great hall in the bailey. The whole system of castle defences had been revolutionized.

CORFE CASTLE. The keep and inner bailey are at the summit of the hill with the middle bailey to the left and the outer bailey in the foreground.

6: The Decline of the Castle (1350-1550)

IN the castles of the late 13th, early 14th centuries castle building in Britain had reached its peak and during the remainder of the 14th century there were no major advances in castle design, nor new castles to better those of Edward I, but the Hundred Years War and the resulting threat of invasion along the south and east coasts did lead to the prolonging of the military role of the castle in this century.

The Wars with France placed a continual drain on the manpower of the king and his barons yet produced veteran professional soldiers, and these two factors had their effect on the new castles of the era. The plans of Queensborough (Fig 41) and Bodiam (Fig 42) castles at once illustrate that in the later 14th century the defence systems of castles were greatly simplified, keeping the centre of the castles clear to allow for the rapid movement of the garrison from one point to another. These castles, built to protect the south and east coasts, could therefore be garrisoned by a small body of experienced soldiers, in contrast to the complex defences of Caernarvon, Conway and the like, which had required very large garrisons.

Queensborough, built in 1361 on the Isle of Sheppey, was the finest example of a mid 14th century castle. Employing the circular plan throughout it had only one main gateway, on the west side, with access to the inner ring of defences on the *east* side so that any attacker gaining entry through the outer gate had to make a half circuit of the bailey to reach the inner entrance. On the east side of the outer wall was a small postern gate to allow for sallies by the garrison. Another vital point was the use of cross walls to divide the outer bailey in two and also funnel the attacker up a narrow passageway before being able to turn away, all the time subjected to fire from two towers and the wall. Unfortunately the castle was totally dismantled in the Civil War, which says much for the strength of its defences, but luckily drawings of the castle have survived.

Bodiam Castle dates from 1385. The main gate to the north, and the lesser gate to the south, are machicolated and further protection for the north gate is obtained by the outwork and barbican with two drawbridges which force any attacker to approach the gateway at right angles to the north wall, thus exposing their unshielded side.

Other notable castles of this era include Nunney, Warwick, Farleigh, Donnington and Old Wardour. Nunney (Fig 43) is remarkable in being on the traditional keep and bailey plan with the keep representing almost the whole

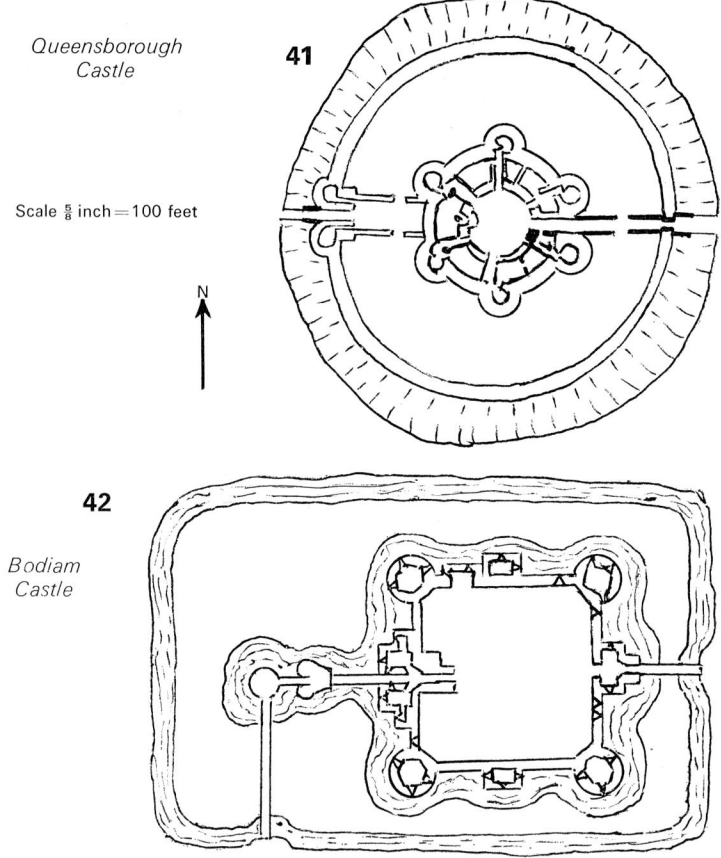

Queensborough
Castle

41

Scale $\frac{5}{8}$ inch = 100 feet

N

42

Bodiam
Castle

strength of the castle. Old Wardour Castle in Wiltshire, built in 1392, has a unique hexagonal plan with alterations made about 1570 in the Renaissance style. The keep and bailey plan is again noticeable here. Tower keeps of this type were popular on the Continent at this date but they are basically a return to the old style of over a century and a half earlier as far as the defensive role is concerned. The low bailey wall and large windows of the tower keep give one the impression that Old Wardour was not seriously designed for warfare yet the castle was besieged by both sides during the Civil War, which led to the western wing being blown up.

Warwick is an example of earlier works being strengthened during this period. The great gatehouse, barbican, north wall of the bailey and its two flanking towers, Guy's and Caesar's, all date from 1370 and present a formidable aspect to the attacker with their great height, double parapets and machicolation. Farleigh and Donnington Castles are of about the same date, 1380 onwards. Donnington has a great gatehouse but a rather weak-looking curtain wall and the defences do not really appear capable of withstanding a long, hard siege, yet the castle underwent just such a siege in the Civil War.

These castles, chosen as being amongst the best fortifications of the period, all show a leaning towards more comfort and in their design the residential part of the castle has been considered by the architect just as much as the effectiveness of the defences. They marked the end of the castle in its predominantly military role and from the late 14th century onwards the defences of the majority of English castles begin to deteriorate, eventually giving way to the fortified manor house.

There were several reasons for the decline of the castle, not least of which was the castle itself. Castles had now become so strong that the only way to bring about their downfall was a long and costly siege which would starve the garrison into submission. Consequently the castle as a focal point of a war was avoided and as a result many of the later castles in England have no military history at all. Wars were now fought well away from the sphere of influence of castles. Shutting oneself up in a castle therefore no longer solved anything and this feeling is reflected in the greater number of gates and posterns in new castles from the end of the 13th century on.

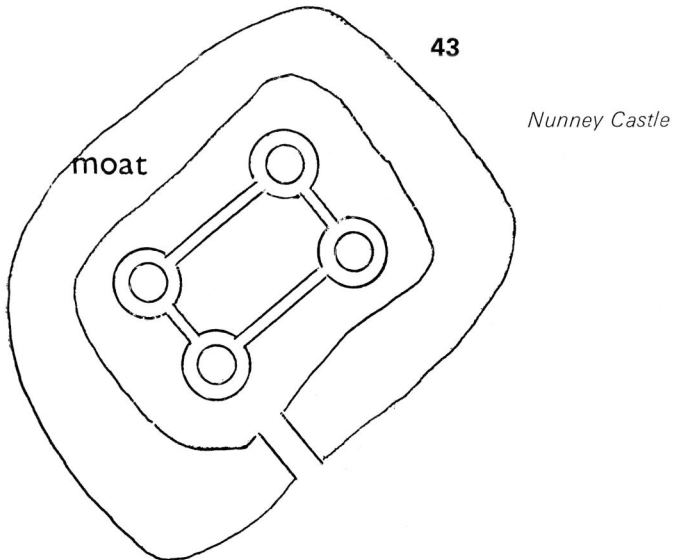

43

Nunney Castle

moat

The invention and development of gunpowder is often stated to be the major cause for the decline of the castle but in fact it was only a contributory reason and not nearly so important as is usually claimed. Gunpowder was not widely used in Britain until quite late on and by the time guns of sufficient power to seriously threaten the castle had been produced, the decline of the castle for the reasons stated above was already well advanced. For many years guns fired stone balls, which had no more effect on stone walls than those hurtled by the mangonel, and iron shot did not come into use until as late as 1480, by which time castles no longer pretended to be fortresses.

FORTIFIED MANOR HOUSES

The unique feature of the castle had always been the dual role of military fortress and private home: the decline of the military role inevitably led to residential considerations becoming predominant and the new 'castles' of the 15th century were no more than fortified manor houses, eventually developing into the moated manor houses of the late Tudor and Elizabethan times.

The fortified manor house was not a new development for buildings of this nature had existed since the end of the 13th century, occupied by lesser

CHESTER CASTLE was built c.1250 but declined over the years and was eventually removed in the late 18th century to make way for other buildings; an unfortunately common occurrence. Only Agricola's Tower (13th century) and the portion of curtain shown here have survived. Note the gunports.

nobility who could not afford castles. Possibly the earliest example is Stokesay Castle in Shropshire. This manor house was fortified in 1291 by the addition of a strong keep or tower and a curtain wall, the latter being destroyed during the Civil War. Acton Burnell, also in Shropshire, is of about the same date and is typical of the early fortified manor house with its rectangular plan, 75 × 54 feet, and four square angle towers. The emphasis on residence rather than fortress is underlined by the lack of a moat, the large windows and three entrances at ground level.

Some of the greatest of these fortified manor houses were Tattershall, Herstmonceux, Ashby-de-la-Zouch and Kirby Muxloe castles. Of these all except Ashby-de-la-Zouch were brick built and it is significant that the return of brick marked the end of the real castle. Ashby-de-la-Zouch is also an exception in being an existing manor house to which was added in 1475 a massive curtain wall and machicolated tower-house. The large windows and ground floor entrance to the tower-house deny the apparent strength of these 'fortifications'. The great machicolated square tower keep at Tattershall Castle, added to an existing castle in 1446, is also an obvious example of comfort being considered before defence.

Herstmonceux Castle is the finest brick 'castle' in England and its position and date, 1441, suggest that it was built to defend the coast, yet here again comfort has been given precedence in the design and the strength of the defences has suffered accordingly. The gatehouse with its machicolated

SKIPTON CASTLE. The great drum towers, built at the end of the 15th century are not seriously designed for warfare despite their apparent strength.

STOKESAY CASTLE, the 13th century moated and fortified manor house, probably the finest of its kind in the country. The keep is on the left.

parapets, crosslet arrow slits and gun ports is set in walls which are too thin and has towers which are too tall and slender to endure sustained bombardment: the architect never seriously considered the likelihood of the defences being tested in war.

Kirby Muxloe, built by the same architect in 1480–84, was unfortunately never finished and only the ruins of one tower and the gatehouse survive surrounded by a deep moat. The gatehouse appears stout enough and the castle is noteworthy as being the first castle in England to be designed for the use of firearms as well as cannon.

The last licence to crenellate, ie, fortify a manor house with battlements etc, was granted in 1533 for the manor house at Cowdray, and here the battlements and towers make no pretence at being genuine fortifications. But by now there was little or no need for every lord to have his own 'castle'. The Wars of the Roses (1455–85) had spelt the end for the private armies of mercenaries maintained by the lords, for Henry VII was the first king strong enough to enforce their disbandment, and as soon as this was accomplished the once powerful nobles no longer had any use for a castle. It followed that the king himself soon had less need for the royal castles: after 150 years of almost continual warfare at home and abroad Britain was at last at peace and life became more settled.

By 1550 the schism between castle and residence was complete, giving rise to the Tudor and Elizabethan country houses on one hand and the military forts of Henry VIII on the other. Many of the castles were incorporated in the town defences, where they were used as the main citadel, armouries, prisons and the like for several centuries. The keeps or flanking towers have often survived to this day because of being used for these purposes, and are often the home of local museums nowadays. By the early 17th century many of the castles were reduced to crumbling ruins. The State Papers for November 1609 (Certificate of His Majesties decayed Castells) list as decayed Rochester, Oxford, Norwich, Guildford, Richmond in Yorkshire, Conway, Colchester,

Beaumaris, Rhuddlan and Caernarvon ; some of the greatest castles of the land.

Yet before saying goodbye to the castle, to a type of fortification which had reigned supreme in Britain for 500 years, we should recall that less than fifty years after this sad report scores of the old castles, and indeed some of the fortified manor houses, were once more armed for war and many put up such stout defences (Harlech held out for seven years!) that when they were finally captured the defences were cast down by the Parliamentarians who wished never to see these fortifications used to such effect again. Much as we may regret this slighting now it was a fitting end to many tough old buildings which were, after all, designed for war.

THE MOATED HOMESTEAD

The moated homestead was the one form of private fortification to survive the 16th century. In its most common form it took the shape of a rectangle with the main dwelling forming one side, barns and sheds the other three, all surrounding an open courtyard in which livestock could be secured for the night. All windows opened on to this yard, as did most of the doors, thus presenting any intruder with a circuit of 'blind' walls pierced only by one, or perhaps two stout doorways. The average area covered by these buildings was 80 to 100 yards by 50 to 80 yards. The whole was surrounded by a wet moat which might be anything from 30 to 80 feet wide with an average depth of about ten feet. Earth excavated to form the moat was thrown inwards to raise the buildings for, being built on lowlying ground in order to obtain the wet moat, these buildings needed to be raised as high as possible to avoid damp and disease.

These moated homesteads were built as early as the 14th century by the Franklins, a new middle class or lesser gentry of small land owners, who lived in open land away from the safety of the towns yet lacked the means to build a fortified manor house. The franklins rose to the peak of their power and numbers during the 15th and 16th centuries.

No royal licence was needed to construct a moat and this encouraged the development of the moated homestead at a time when other more expensive forms of private fortification were becoming impossible or unnecessary. In the 14th century people unable to afford a moat did not build their houses in the open country, but the suppression of the bands of armed retainers of the lords by Henry VII in the 15th century to a large extent made these defences obsolete. From this time on some homesteads now had windows in their outer walls but the majority still clung to their moats, perhaps because of the ingrained custom that each man's home was his castle. By Elizabethan times the need for all private fortifications had ceased to exist and many of the houses were rebuilt outside their moats where there was room to expand and create a more comfortable dwelling.

Like the castles the moated homestead came into its own again during the Civil War and many of them were besieged. However, unlike the castle they were not designed to resist armies, nor the cannon with which they were now armed, and the homesteads were ineffective as fortresses in this context. Those which survived the Civil War slowly decayed until now very little remains to show where they once stood.

It is worth pointing out that the comparatively low but extensive stone walls which still surround the great estates of some of our more important nobles are in fact the last in a long line of obstacles intended to protect the property of the individual and are therefore direct descendants of the castle walls.

7: Scottish and Irish Castles

SCOTLAND did not suffer a Norman invasion but Normans did penetrate her border as immigrants and there are many surviving examples of the typically Norman motte and bailey castle of the period in Scotland, yet not one example of the stone keeps which were also built from the very beginning in England. However, the Normans did not come to Scotland as invaders and they probably had no need for the great keep in the 11th century, yet it is surprising that there appear to have been *no* Norman castles of stone in Scotland. To a certain extent the gap may be explained by the desolation caused by the Wars of Independence, when any castles captured by the Scots were dismantled to prevent them being used by the English, but this is only guess-work.

Only two stone castles built prior to the 13th century have survived, and only one of these may be called Norman. This is Castle Sween (Fig 44) in Knapdale, Argyllshire, built in the middle of the 12th century: the ruins show the angle buttresses and a pilaster, typical of the Norman keep. The second castle, Cobbie's Row on the island of Wyre in the Orkneys, was built about 1145 by a Norse chief and consists of a small rectangular tower within a circular ditch.

Stone castles became common in Scotland during the 13th century and two of the finest surviving examples of this period are Caerlaverock (Fig 45) and Kildrummy (Fig 46) castles. Both are of unusual design. Kildrummy is the most complete example of a 13th-century castle in Scotland with the curtain wall, four rounded towers and great hall all belonging to the original period. Towards the end of the century Scottish castles began to follow the general tendency to concentrate the main strength of the castle in the gatehouse and the great gatehouse at Kildrummy, added during the reign of Edward I, is typical of the period.

During the 14th century the Wars of Independence caused the destruction of many castles and limited the building of new ones. Tantallon Castle (Fig 47),

44

Castle Sween

Scale $\frac{1}{2}$ inch = 50 feet

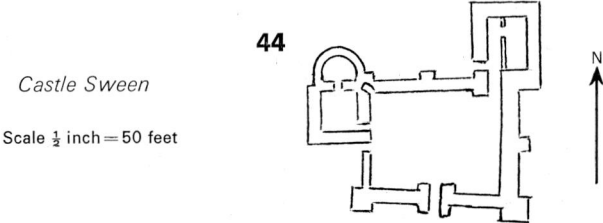

N

Caerlaverock Castle
(Crown Copyright)

45

situated on the rocky coast of the Firth of Forth, was built towards the end of the century with a massive curtain wall and central gatehouse as its main line of defence, its magnificent position rendering further fortification unnecessary. Doune Castle in Perthshire was another fine castle of the same period but these are the exception and the majority of all castles built in Scotland during the 14th century were simple tower keeps, known as peel towers, standing within a small walled courtyard which was called the barmkin and which lacked both gatehouse and flanking towers.

EARLY PEEL TOWERS

These towers were raised all over the northern counties of England and southern Scotland during the 14th and 15th centuries by the lesser gentry who had until now not felt the need for defensive works to protect themselves and their property. Castles were out of the question for these people, nor were they necessary in the circumstances, and the peel tower might well be compared to the earlier broch. The similarity to the keep and bailey of the 12th century is even more pronounced.

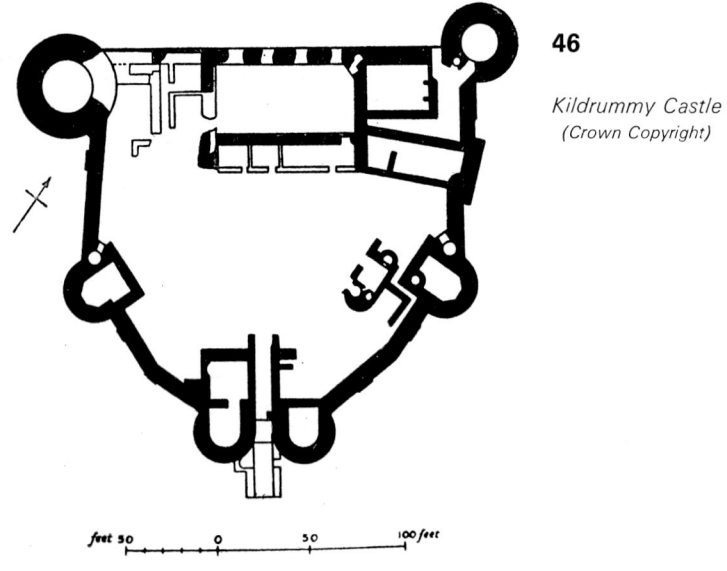

46

Kildrummy Castle
(Crown Copyright)

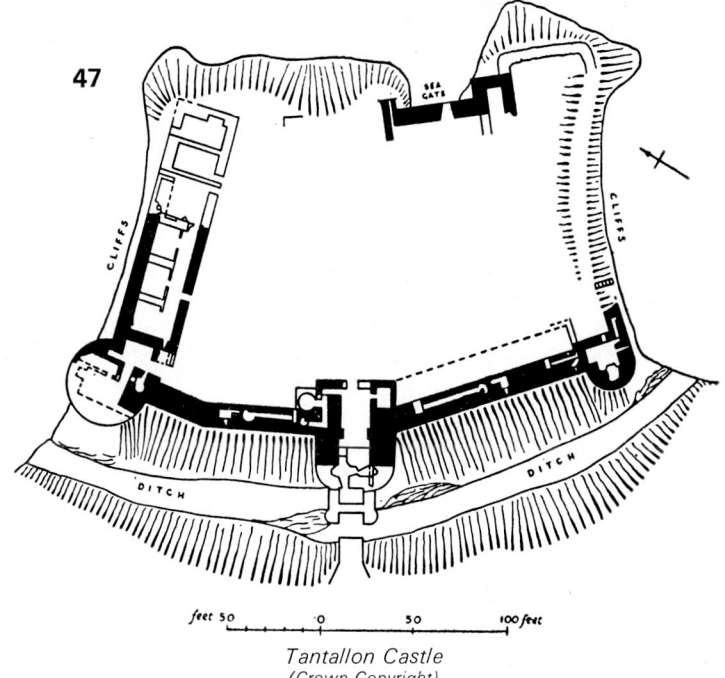

47

Tantallon Castle
(Crown Copyright)

feet 50   ·0   50   100 feet

Two of the finest 14th century peel towers are Lochleven and Threave castles, both built towards the end of the century. Lochleven has five storeys, an entrance on the second floor gained only by means of a ladder, and a well preserved barmkin with a round tower added in the 16th century and equipped with gun ports. Threave, situated on an islet in the River Dee, has four storeys and a barmkin with round towers, loopholed for firearms, which was added in 1513 after the battle of Flodden Field. The main defence

48

Ravenscraig Castle
(Crown Copyright)

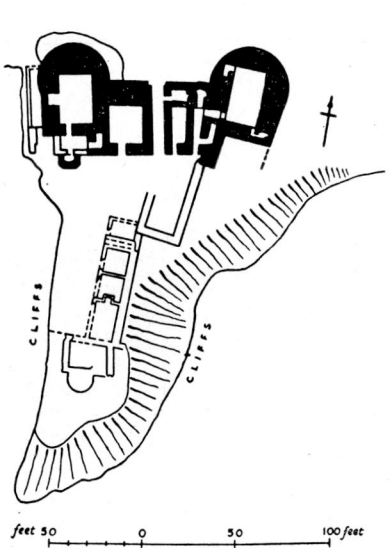

feet 50   0   50   100 feet

KISIMUL CASTLE. The outer walls seen from the top of the tower, with buildings erected against them.

of the towers lay in their height and the thick walls, although there was a crenellated parapet at the top of the building. Machicolation became common in Scotland during the 15th century and was added to the tops of the towers.

As the years passed the occupants began to feel the need for more comfortable quarters and to a certain extent this demand was met by hollowing small closets out of the massive walls, but by the end of the 15th century

CAERLAVEROCK CASTLE, famous for its siege in 1300, is surrounded by a wide moat and guarded by its great gatehouse. Note the machicolation on the gatehouse and other tower visible.

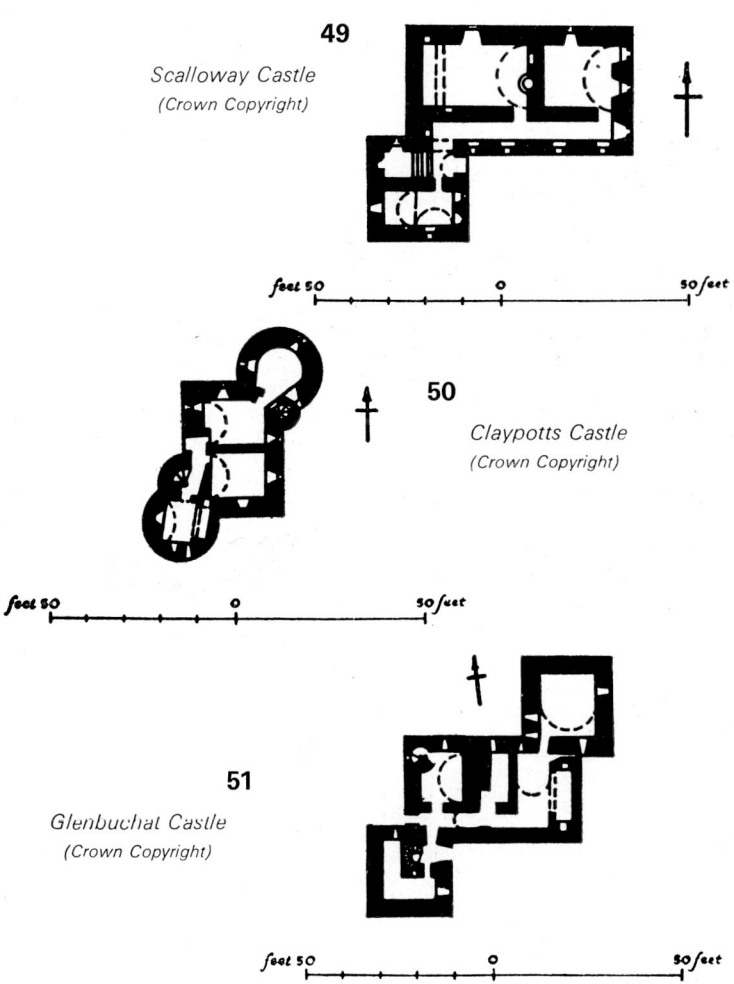

49

Scalloway Castle
(Crown Copyright)

feet 50   0   50 feet

50

Claypotts Castle
(Crown Copyright)

feet 50   0   50 feet

51

Glenbuchat Castle
(Crown Copyright)

feet 50   0   50 feet

the L plan tower had developed, one wing being added to a corner of the main tower. This extra wing solved the problem of more space and comfort for the inhabitants and at the same time made possible the strong defence of a ground floor entrance, set in the angle of the building where the two parts met. Being able to enter their dwelling at ground level must also have been a great step forward in the comfort of the family and its servants.

In 1460 Ravenscraig Castle (Fig 48) was founded by James II as part of a scheme for coastal defence but work was stopped three years later before the royal castle was finished. Ravenscraig is unique in being probably the first castle in Britain to be designed purely for defence by the systematic use of cannon and firearms. Like Tantallon, Ravenscraig also needed only one line of defences, the naturally strong site protecting the other sides. However, Ravenscraig was an exception to the rule and the typical Scottish castle of the 15th century remained the simple peel tower, either of the rectangular or L plan.

LATE TOWER HOUSES

The use of cannon was a royal prerogative in the 15th century and therefore throughout this century the peel towers continued to rely on height and the thickness of their walls for their defence. However, in the 16th century the hand-gun and arquebus became widely available and this changed drastically the whole concept of defence for the peel tower. The old emphasis on height was immediately abandoned and almost at once the extra wing was utilized to provide a flanking fire along two walls of the tower at ground level. Scalloway Castle (Fig 49), built in 1600, is a fine, early example of the wing being used in this way.

The next step was obvious; a second wing was needed to give similar flanking fire to the other two walls of the tower, and this led to the adoption of the Z plan tower house where two wings provided covering fire for the four walls of the main tower house which in return supplied covering fire for the wings. The two wings also provided the extra space for living quarters which the improved standards of living now demanded.

Noltland Castle on the island of Westray in the Orkneys is an exceptional example of a Z plan tower house, begun about 1560 but never finished The square wings, or flanking towers as they might almost be called, have their walls pierced all round with several tiers of gunloops, far more provision for the use of firearms being made here than at any other castle in Britain. Claypotts Castle (Fig 50) near Dundee was built about 1569–88. Note the rounded towers which are corbelled out at the top to form overhanging 'cap houses'. The towers are still roofed and were well provided with gunloops. Glenbuchat Castle (Fig 51) in Aberdeenshire, built with square towers in 1590, is another fine example of the peel tower at the peak of its effectiveness.

More settled conditions in Scotland during the 17th century inevitably led to a decline in fortifications just as had occurred earlier in England and more and more the tower houses were designed purely for comfort. All kinds of ornamentation were affected, though the towers retained their basic L or Z plan, and the building of this period is known as the Scottish Baronial style. It marked the end of the military role of the castle in Scotland.

EARLY IRISH CASTLES

The Anglo-Norman invasion of Ireland began in 1169 and as early as 1170 the motte and bailey castle was appearing in that country. Harryville near Ballymena, overlooking the River Braid in County Antrim, is one of the finest examples of this type of castle in Ireland. The motte here is 140 feet in diameter at the base, 40 feet high and has a diameter at the top of 40 feet. The bailey was rectangular. Dundonald Motte on the outskirts of Belfast rose to about the same height but had no bailey. It was built about 1180. Stone buildings later replaced the original wooden structures on these mottes as had happened in England and the motte and bailey type of castle continued to be built in Ireland until the 14th century.

The first great stone castles were built about 1177–80 and to this date belong the curtain walls of Carrickfergus and Dundrum (Fig 52) castles. The massive keeps of these castles were added early in the 13th century and the outer wards and gatehouses by 1250. The keep at Dundrum Castle has an internal diameter of 46 feet and the walls above the ground level plinth are eight and a half feet thick. The original entrance on the first floor is now a window. The keep at Carrickfergus is 90 feet high with four storeys. This castle is unique in the

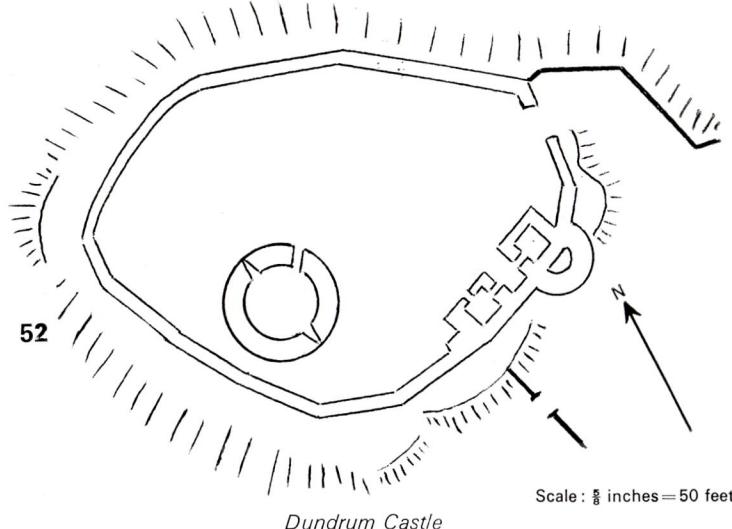

52

Scale: ⅝ inches = 50 feet

Dundrum Castle

history of Ireland, having been continuously garrisoned by English troops for 700 years.

During the 14th century English power in Ireland declined and very few castles were built. Those erected by the Irish princes generally followed the English style.

TOWER HOUSES

The Irish tower house followed approximately the same pattern as those of Scotland, its need being instigated by similar conditions and for the same group of people; the land owners. In 1429 a £10 subsidy was granted to any land owner building a tower 20 by 16 feet and at least 40 feet high and this contributed to the tower house becoming the predominant type of fortification in Ireland during the 15th and 16th centuries. Audley's Castle (Fig 53) is a good example of these earlier tower houses. Overlooking the entrance to Strangford Lough in County Down the tower house measures approximately 30 by 26 feet and has a small barmkin attached. Entrance was at ground level but the doorway was protected by machicolation on the outside and murder holes inside.

This type of tower house continued to be built throughout the 16th century and there are many surviving examples. A lesser number were built in the first half of the 17th century. On the waterfront at Bangor (Fig 54) in County Down is an example built as late as 1637 and, although it was intended to be used as a customs house, it still shows the characteristics of the Scottish tower house.

PLANTERS' CASTLES

Until 1607 Ulster had remained an Irish stronghold but in that year it was thrown open to English and Scottish settlers. Arriving in a more or less hostile area these settlers had need of a defensible home and the so-called Planter's Castle was developed to fill this need. (I say so-called because it was usually no more than a sophisticated tower house).

The tower house had reached its peak in Scotland by this date and the Scottish influence is very obvious in such planters' castles as Derrywoone and Roughan in County Tyrone, there no doubt being many Scottish craftsmen amongst the settlers. Derrywoone (Fig 55) is a typical L plan tower house but Roughan

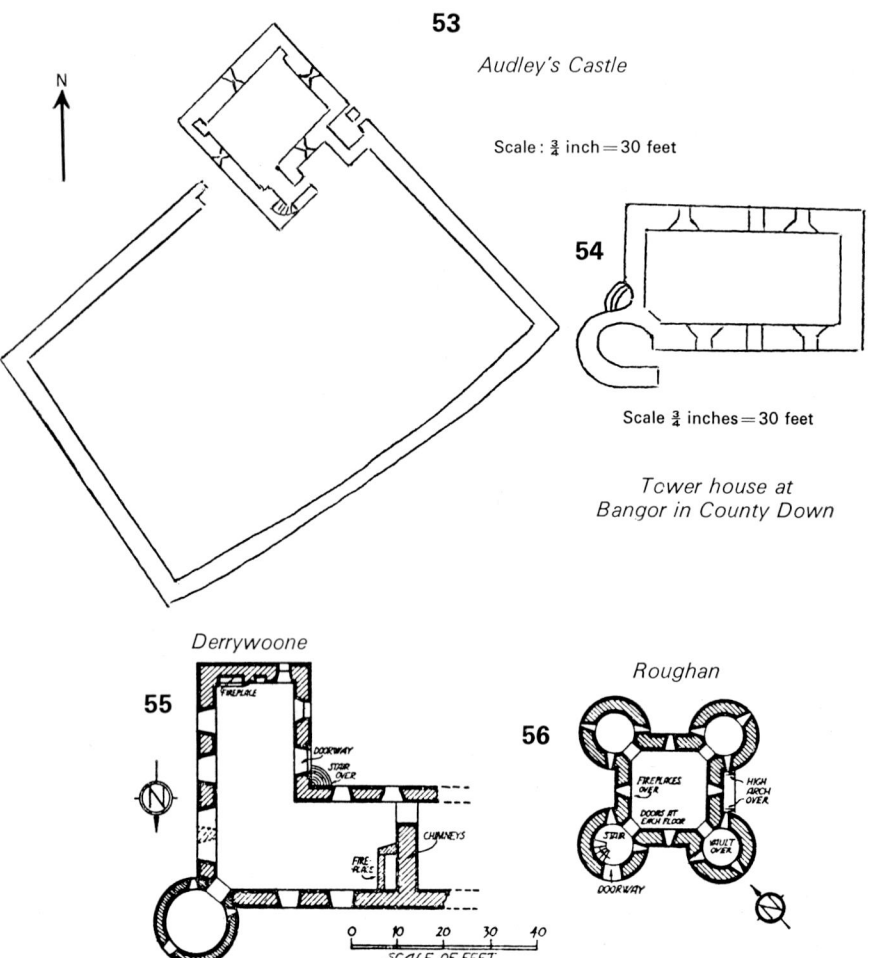

53

Audley's Castle

Scale: $\frac{3}{4}$ inch = 30 feet

54

Scale $\frac{3}{4}$ inches = 30 feet

*Tower house at
Bangor in County Down*

Derrywoone

55

FIREPLACE

DOORWAY
STAIR
OVER

CHIMNEYS

FIRE-
PLACE

Roughan

56

FIREPLACES
OVER

HIGH
ARCH
OVER

DOORS AT
EACH FLOOR

STAIR

VAULT
OVER

DOORWAY

0   10   20   30   40
SCALE OF FEET

(Fig 56), built in 1618, carries the use of the flanking towers to the ultimate conclusion and with its three storeys begins to take on the aspect of a Norman keep.

The London City Companies were granted land in County Londonderry in 1613 and erected their own tower houses, such as Brackfield and Salter's castles, by about 1619. Castle building in England had terminated many years before and again it was the Scottish style which was employed. Although there was no standard pattern laid down for the Companies' tower houses these two examples are remarkably alike. Brackfield had a barmkin wall 62 feet square with a flanking tower 12 feet high; Salter's Castle had a similar rectangular barmkin with a flanking tower. In both these cases the flanking tower was on the south-east corner of the barmkin, flanking the gate on the south wall, and with the tower house itself in the north-west corner. Both castles were well provided with loops for firearms and are amongst the very finest examples of tower houses in Ireland.

8: Medieval town defences

THE walled town was the medieval counterpart of the early British camps and Roman settlements and a logical step forward from the Saxon and Danish fortified towns or *burhs*. The burhs had been maintained by the men farming the surrounding countryside in return for the protection the town could give in times of danger and the Saxon and Danish laws for the period 924–1035 state that all burhs were to be repaired annually by these men. As we have noted earlier, there is now little to be seen of the burhs yet they were quite numerous and sufficiently well maintained to be used into the 11th and even 12th centuries, their effectiveness spanning a period of some 300 years.

However, in the 13th century there was considerable unrest in England which brought about a change in the system. From approximately 1204 to 1225 England was threatened by the possibility of an invasion from France and was torn internally by the Baronial Wars, which began with the struggle for the signing of the Magna Carta and did not begin to abate until the death of Simon de Montfort in 1265. Early in the 13th century therefore the old Saxon burhs began to be replaced by new and more substantial defences of stone which offered greater protection from the weapons of the day.

At first the development was naturally limited to those towns within burhs or those which could utilise old Roman walls, towns such as Chester, Exeter and Colchester, but as the demand for greater security rose Henry III instituted the murage toll. This was a tax levied on a specified range of goods brought into the town for sale and was administered by the towns themselves, the proceeds going towards the cost of constructing new defences. From about 1225 most towns receiving murage grants, i.e., permission to tax certain goods for a set number of years, were towns which had previously had no form of defences.

The 13th century was also the time of the Welsh Wars and nearly 50 per cent of the murage grants in this century went to the Welsh towns. Carmarthen was sacked in 1214, Haverfordwest in 1219, Hay on Wye, Carmarthen, Kidwelly and Montgomery in 1231, the latter again in 1257. Yet surprisingly murage grants were not made to these towns for many years, with the exception of Hay on Wye in 1231. Haverfordwest had to wait until 1264, Montgomery 1267 and Kidwelly 1280. Such long delays can only be attributed to the fact that these towns had castles, although this did not save the towns themselves from the Welsh. Therefore priority must have been given to those towns without castles which, once walled, would provide another secure military base. In other words, the king made sure that those towns raising defences would be of use to him in war time. Town defences such as Beaumaris, Caernarvon and Conway were raised towards the end of the century, with funds direct from the royal purse, specifically to overawe the Welsh.

Early in the 14th century it began to prove difficult to administer the murage tax, collection and collectors were subjected to bribery and many groups such as churchmen, foreign merchants and merchants from neighbouring towns had succeeded in gaining exemption. A new system was therefore instituted at this time whereby the town inhabitants were taxed on the basis of the property they owned within the town, although the old method of taxing goods continued to be used also. Whether it is a coincidence or not is hard to say now, but from this time on there is a slackening off in the construction of town defences and those already built were in many cases allowed to decline.

There were two exceptions to this general decline, the Scottish border and the south-east coast. With the 14th century had come trouble along the Scottish border, caused by Edward I's attempted invasion, and between 1315 and 1321 defences were erected at Berwick, Durham, Hartlepool, Richmond and Lancaster. The Hundred Years War made itself felt at the opposite end of the country in the form of French raids on the coastal towns and during this same period, Dover, Sandwich and Rye had their defences built.

The Wars of the Roses caused the plundering and raiding of many of the richer towns and this re-awakened a general interest in fortification, aided by subsidies from the king who, as we have seen, had his own reasons. However, by the end of the 14th century there was a general reluctance on the part of town councils to spend money on defence, though the king continued to press strategically placed towns to strengthen their walls, and gave many grants for this purpose, so that by the end of the 15th century there were few towns of any importance which did not have walls.

TOWN WALLS AND DITCHES

Even until quite late in the 14th century many towns continued to rely on defences consisting of only a ditch and earthen rampart with a timber palisade. However, such defences could only offer a passive resistance while high walls and towers of stone enabled the towns to fight back. Consequently the use of stone for town walls became common from the middle of the 13th century.

In plan the walls were usually rectangular or roughly circular since this avoided awkward angles which might become weak spots; unlike the bailey wall of a castle the town wall was the first and only line of defence and could not afford to have *any* weak points. Care was also taken to avoid being overlooked by higher ground. Where the lay of the land did not provide a natural advantage deep ditches were dug to provide an outer line of defence which would play a part in keeping the enemy and his siege weapons away from the base of the wall. As in other fortifications of this nature, the weaker the wall or its position the greater the ditch before it and vice versa. Width and height of the wall were usually determined by three factors: the availability of labour, stone and money.

Where a town had grown up 'in the shadow of a castle' the castle was normally incorporated into the defences, sharing a common wall with the town to form a united front. The sections of wall adjoining the castle were usually without a parapet and thinner than the remainder of the town wall: this was a precaution in case the town fell or the townspeople went over to the enemy, and prevented the rampart being used as a 'jumping off' point for an attack on the castle. In some instances it was not possible for the castle to form an integral part of the town defences, such as when it was situated in the centre

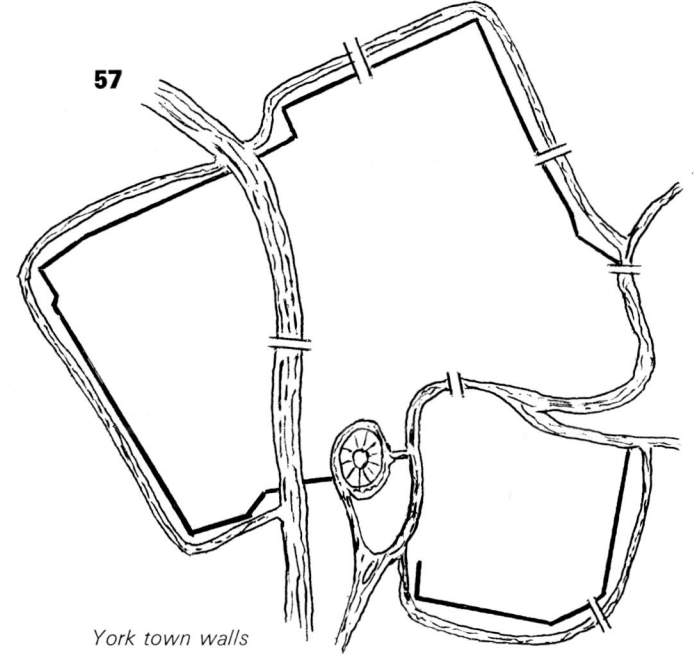

57

York town walls

of the town or, as at Chepstow, separated from the town by a valley. At Chepstow an attempt was made to link the two by means of a wall.

In the majority of town defences the walls were primarily used as a physical barrier to prevent easy access to the town and to link the towers together. Offensive action from these walls could only be taken from the parapets, which were usually crenellated from the earliest examples. This provided the only cover for archers and it was quite impossible to command the base of the wall from the parapet, though hoardings are known to have been used at Carlisle and Berwick in the 14th century and the regular lines of square holes passing through the walls at Chepstow (late 13th century) were probably for the supporting timbers of hoardings. Some town walls did have a second

Canterbury town walls

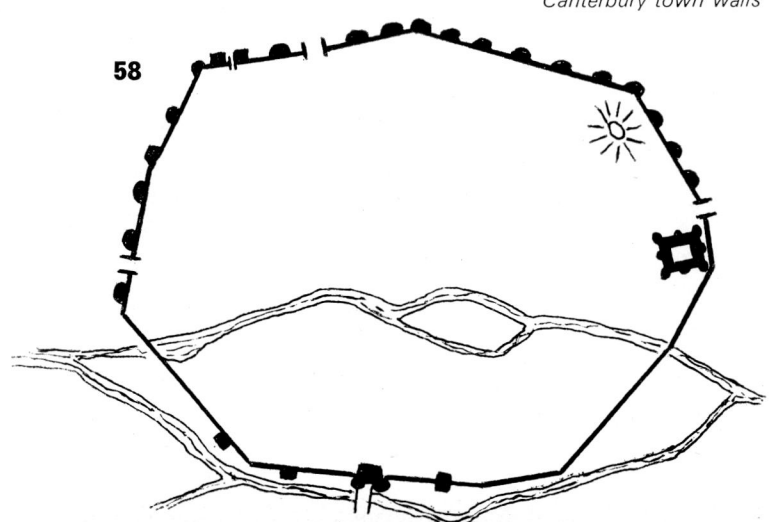

58

row of firing positions at ground level to overcome this disadvantage, notably Tenby, Norwich, King's Lynn, Denbigh and Yarmouth. In each of these examples the wall walk is carried on arches which span the ground level embrasures.

An important factor inside the wall was the *pomerium*, a road which linked the defences immediately behind the walls and thus provided a means of rushing reinforcements, siege engines, supplies and the like from one point to another. Other roads in a well planned town usually ran parallel to each other, cut at right angles by other roads to form blocks for the houses. One such block was left empty to form the market place, normally in the centre of the town, and this was used as a rallying point for the defenders. The main roads connected the market place to the pomerium and the gates.

THE TOWERS

The flanking tower could play a vital part in the defence of a town's walls, just as it did in the defences of a castle, but in the case of towns these towers were often so badly designed and sited that their potential was rarely developed fully. They did provide the necessary flanking fire for the wall, though often from ridiculously few arrow slits, but their role as individual strongpoints and 'circuit breakers' in the wall walk was usually ignored.

Most towers in town walls could be entered only from the wall walk, as for example at Chester and Canterbury where the walk runs *behind* the open backed towers. Thus should a section of the wall fall to the enemy not only were the towers unable to isolate the captured section but they were themselves at once rendered useless. The defences of Caernarvon and Conway, built towards the end of the 13th century by skilled military engineers, are an exception. Here the towers are mutually supporting and can act as individual strongpoints which would isolate and overlook any captured section of wall. Chepstow town wall, built at about the same time, is the only other example known to the author of towers being used in this way in town defences. In this instance the wall walk continues round the inside of the open backed towers, isolating each stretch of wall except via the towers.

The shape of the towers varied considerably, not just from town to town but within the same town. This was to a certain degree due to the long time it took for the defences to be completed because they were financed by an uncertain income in the form of tolls, but there is also a possibility it may have been due to lack of co-ordination in the planning, perhaps different sectors being built by different contractors.

The earliest towers were a half round D shape, presenting a broad face to the front but at the same time permitting flanking fire along the wall. This appears from mid 13th century but towards the end of the century the shape becomes a more pronounced horseshoe shape, giving greater firepower along the walls but presenting a more narrow front to the enemy. It occurs at Caernarvon and Conway and continued in use until almost the end of the 14th century when it was discontinued. Canterbury has many of these towers built about 1390.

The square tower also appears at Canterbury at the same date and this type of tower replaces the round tower everywhere from the end of the 14th century. It is difficult to understand why this happened, when exactly the reverse occurred in castle building. The round tower was less vulnerable to bombardment and mining and the only possible explanation is that square towers were needed in an age when cannon began to be used. Archers and crossbowmen could fit snugly into a round tower but three or four cannon on heavy carriages,

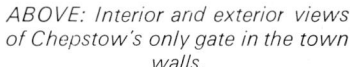
ABOVE: Interior and exterior views
of Chepstow's only gate in the town
walls.

pointing in three different directions and having a recoil, would obviously
need more space.

From the middle of the 14th century towers were also leased out for a small
rent, the occupiers being made responsible for the maintenance of the defences
yet at the same time permitted to make building alterations to increase the
comfort of their accommodation. This inevitably led to the decline of the
military aspect of the tower and this could also have played an important part
in influencing the design of towers: round rooms may appear quaint now, but
in those days they were just inconvenient.

GATEHOUSES

The gate was the most important part of a town's defences and more thought
was given to its design and construction than to any other part. It was often
provided with all the refinements found in the better castles, such as machicolation, murder holes, portcullis, barbicans and drawbridges. Because of its
importance very few examples have survived as built, the original being
constantly improved or repaired, even as late as the 18th and 19th centuries,
while some have been shifted during this century to make room for traffic.

The gates were the first part of the town defences to be built in stone and
in the early 13th century many stone gates were flanked by the old defences
of ditch and earthen rampart. These early gates consisted of the gate itself
flanked by two square or rectangular guard chambers. Those at Caernarvon
and Conway at the end of the 13th century improved on this basic square plan
by adding half-round towers to the front face. This became common practice
and by the mid 14th century had developed into two round towers flanking

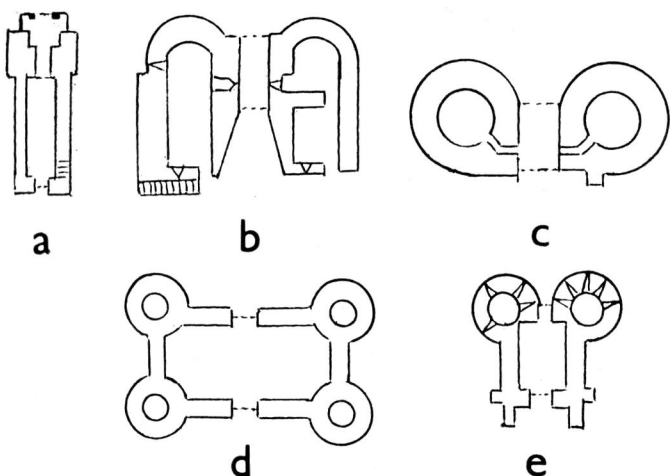

a   b   c

d   e

Town Gates: A: Walmgate Bar, York 12th century: B: Upper Gate, Conway 1283: C: Landgate, Rye 1350: D: Strandgate, Winchelsea 1350: E: Westgate, Canterbury 1380.

a narrow gateway. At Winchelsea the Landgate has four round towers, linked by short stretches of wall. Such gatehouses, providing a defence in depth, became predominant during the century, increasing in size and sometimes having a square building added to the rear which often housed the civic offices. This type of gatehouse reached its highest stage of development by the end of the century. One of the finest gatehouses is the Westgate at Canterbury built in 1380. Here the gatehouse is a large square building, its corners rounded by the two huge towers. This method provided the maximum accommodation space without affecting the military effectiveness.

At this period the gatehouse was at its most impressive, with machicolation making its first appearance in town defences. Paradoxically in this same period

BELOW: Canterbury's Westgate, from the exterior. Note the gunports at all levels, the wide merlons, and the machicolation. RIGHT: Canterbury's Westgate from the interior. Entrance is via the iron bridge to the right, illustrating how this well-designed gateway could be held as a stronghold after the fall of the gates them-selves.

YORK. Walmgate Bar, dating from c.1150–61, is one of the few examples of a barbican added to a town gate.

the round tower was abandoned and the gatehouse became once more a plain square building, as at Winchelsea in 1390. This coincides with the reappearance of square towers on the walls but this time cannot be explained by the advent of cannon as very few gatehouses built after this date make any provision for them. Gatehouses in the late 14th and throughout the 15th century were also used for accommodation, the gatehouses eventually being employed only for the collection of the murage toll, and this reversion to the square plan can only be due to a gradual decline in the military importance of the gatehouse.

Impressive as the gatehouses appeared, they were often as badly designed for defence as were the towers. In many examples once an enemy had broken his way in through the gates there was nothing to stop him climbing to the upper storeys to occupy the entire gatehouse and frequently the gatehouse was linked directly to the wall walk so that the fall of the former led automatically to the fall of the walls. Conway, as might be expected, was an exception, for here the stairs to the upper floors were well defended. The West Gate at Southampton also provides a rare example of military thinking in town defences, there being no connection between the guard chambers and the upper storeys, which are entered from the wall walk.

Town barbicans follow basically the same principles as the simple barbicans for castles. Surviving examples are rare, Walmgate Bar at York and Upper Gate at Conway being perhaps the best.

THE USE OF CANNON

Cannon made little impression on military architecture of the Middle Ages for they had three major disadvantages. Firstly, the vibration they caused within a confined area often did as much damage to the defences as to the enemy; secondly, their line of fire and range was limited; and thirdly, their rate of fire was slow. Most towns appear not to have developed the use of cannon to its greatest possible extent. Exceptions to this are the western arcade at

Southampton and the south-west angle and Westgate at Canterbury where the gunports have been so well sited at different angles and heights that no part of the walls is left uncovered.

Gunports are mainly found in towns where construction of the defences was after the middle of the 14th century and few towns appear to have inserted gunports into existing defences. The early gunports consisted of a round hole topped by a vertical slit, being simply an adaptation of the old arrow slit. The earliest example is at Southampton, dating from 1360, and here the hole is six inches in diameter and the total length vertically is 44 inches. The hole was gradually increased in size, up to a maximum of 11 inches, while the vertical slit grew correspondingly smaller and was finally abandoned altogether in the 15th century.

EFFECTIVENESS OF THE DEFENCES

When assessing the effectiveness of town defences we have to remember that the entire circuit of walls was rarely completed in one go: the defences of Alnwick and Norwich took over 40 years, those at Newcastle 53 years, and those of Coventry 180 years! Also, as we have seen, the defences were badly designed in the majority of cases. There can be little doubt that this last factor was due to the defences being erected by local builders who had no knowledge of military fortifications beyond what they could see from nearby castles, and castle builders did not advertise their methods nor disclose their plans, often being sworn to secrecy by the lord concerned. The exceptions, such as Caernarvon and Conway, which were the first and the last town defences in Britain to be built by military engineers, only serve to emphasize the lack of finesse in the majority of town defences, which were merely amateurish copies of the work of master craftsmen.

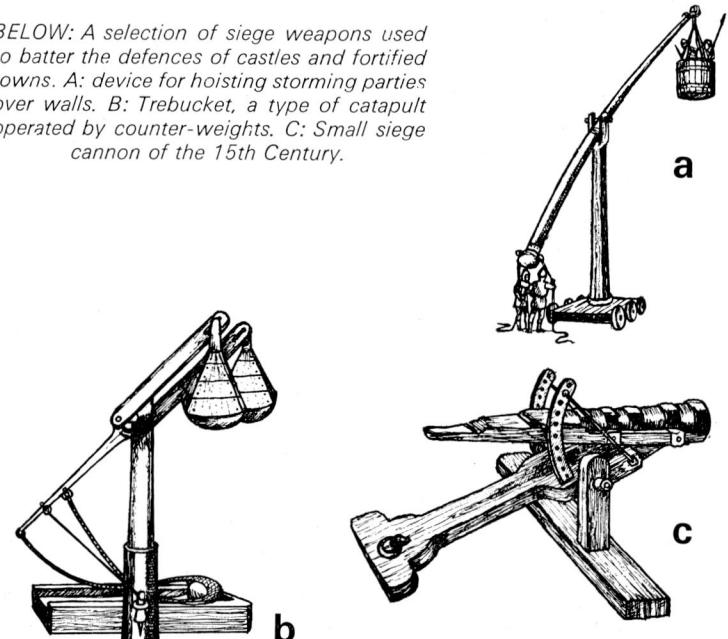

BELOW: A selection of siege weapons used to batter the defences of castles and fortified towns. A: device for hoisting storming parties over walls. B: Trebucket, a type of catapult operated by counter-weights. C: Small siege cannon of the 15th Century.

As a result of these failings town defences were next to useless against a determined assault by an army and they usually fell on the first or second day, though Carlisle successfully held off the Scots for ten days. This in itself may do much to explain the otherwise apparently criminal neglect of the defences and the often ineffectual design. However, it should also be borne in mind that town walls were not designed expressedly to withstand a great siege in the same manner as castles. The defences were not used exclusively for military purposes but played an important part in the economic life of the town, offering a safe market to traders. They were also used to keep out beggars, lepers and the plague, not to mention the peasants of the surrounding country-side in times of unrest. Canterbury's Westgate for example was built at a time when the peasants of Kent had been seething with discontent for some ten years. Wat Tyler's rebellion broke out in 1381 and the rebels broke into the town, despite the new defences, and pillaged it.

Perhaps the most effective role of town defences was that of deterrent; certainly they appeared strong enough to discourage raids by wandering bands and during the Wars of the Roses both sides avoided the larger towns except when they became direct military objectives, as was the case with Ludlow, which was sacked in 1459 because it was an important military base. And over all is the fact that examples of towns actually being besieged in Britain are rare, and this in itself is perhaps indicative of the value of the defences.

TOWN DEFENCES IN IRELAND

There are two major examples of town fortification in Ireland, Carrickfergus and Londonderry, and both are of interest because they were built considerably later than those in Britain.

Londonderry (Fig 59) was first fortified in 1566 with earthworks and was again fortified in 1600, presumably merely repairs and improvements to the existing works. These defences were overrun by the Irish in 1608 and between 1614–18 the now existing town defences were built with a total circuit of 1,708 yards. The wall was 24 feet high and varied in width from fourteen to 30 feet, being faced with stone but having an earth core. There were four tower gatehouses, a ravelin or half moon for cannon being added in front of Bishops-gate in 1689. There was a great square bastion at each corner of the circuit with five more bastions on the west and east sides. The whole was surrounded by a dry ditch, 30 feet wide and eight feet deep. These defences withstood three sieges, in 1641, 1648–9 and 1688–9. The walls survive to almost their full height, as also do three of the gates and five of the bastions. There are also 12 cannon remaining out of a total of 40 which once defended the town.

The walls of Carrickfergus are believed to date from the beginning of the 17th century and replaced an earlier earthen rampart and ditch. There were originally seven bastions and four gates, the whole surrounded by a ditch. Very little of these defences now survives.

ECCLESIASTICAL FORTIFICATIONS

This may seem an unlikely combination but in fact from the earliest days of Christianity in Britain the village church had served as a fortress, primarily because it was the focal point of the small community and the only stone building in the region. In northern counties the churches continued to be used as strongholds long after the last of the Viking raids. The tower of St Michael's church at Burgh-on-Sands, six miles north-west of Carlisle, was in fact a peel tower, built almost entirely of Roman stone. Edward I lay here in

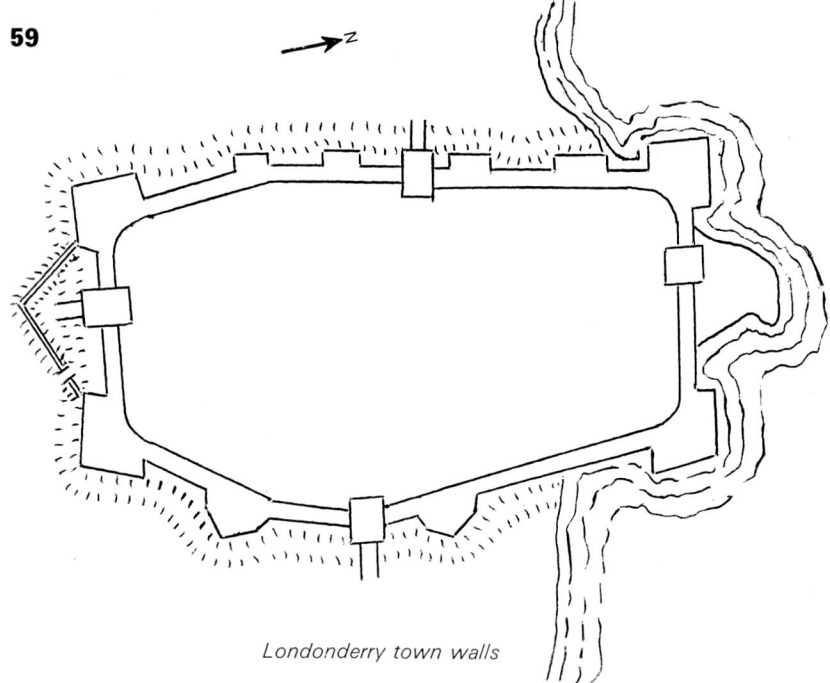

Londonderry town walls

State when he died on his way to attack the Scots. At Bedale in the North Riding of Yorkshire the 14th–15th century church tower had a portcullis which could be lowered to cut off the main body of the church and so isolate the tower as a stronghold. At Great Salkeld in Cumberland, St Cuthbert's church has a massive fortified tower, added to the Norman nave in the 14th century as a refuge from the Scots raiders. Such defensive measures were also taken on the Welsh border and a prime example is Garway Church, just across the River Monnow from Skenfrith Castle in Monmouthshire. Here the square tower is loopholed and stands apart from the main body of the church, looking more like a small keep than a church building.

Walls were also erected to protect communities other than those of towns. St David's Cathedral, 16 miles west of Haverfordwest in Pembrokeshire, was enclosed by a wall as early as 1172, though the existing walls are a reconstruction of the 1300s. Here the wall was designed to protect the cathedral community and also enclosed the Bishop's Palace and canon's residences. Another example in Wales is Ewenny Priory in Glamorgan, where the walls date mainly from the 13th century and still encircle over five acres, complete with their own flanking towers and gatehouse with a portcullis.

Tynemouth Priory, standing on a promontory bounded by the River Tyne and Tynemouth Bay, eight miles east of Newcastle, was first built in the Dark Ages, destroyed by the Danes in 865, rebuilt, abandoned in 1008 and refounded in 1090. With such a turbulent history it is no surprise that when the Scottish troubles began in the 14th century the Priory was encircled by a curtain wall with flanking towers and a gatehouse-keep. After the dissolution of the monasteries these defences continued to be used by the Crown for coastal defence and the walls have some later additions.

9: Fortifications of the 16th, 17th and 18th Centuries

IN Section 6 we saw how the castle had declined in importance until it became totally obsolete in a military role. This did not mean the end of fortification, of course, but simply a complete separation of the residence and the military fortress, the latter now becoming entirely the concern of the Crown. Internal warfare having ceased at last, the Crown naturally turned its attention to the defence of the country's coast line against overseas enemies and the need for strongholds capable of withstanding artillery and placed at strategic points gave rise to a series of fortifications of a nature entirely new to Britain.

At first the invention of gunpowder had not greatly influenced the existing type of fortification as for many years cannon continued to fire stone balls, but the invention of cast iron shot in 1480 at last did away with the great advantage defence had always enjoyed over attack. In the Italian campaign of Charles VIII of France in 1494 the fortresses fell before his guns with startling rapidity and it was not long before stone walls were being protected from the iron cannon ball by great banks of earth. Gradually these earthen ramparts superseded the stone walls but, the high wall having been abolished, some other obstacle was needed to prevent an enemy overrunning the fortifications and this brought back the ditch, ranging from 20 to 30 feet in depth and of varying width. The escarp and counterscarp (the sides of the ditch nearest to and farthest from the parapet respectively) were revetted with masonry and from subterranean chambers within the escarp cannon commanded the bottom of the ditch.

THE COASTAL FORTS OF HENRY VIII

In England this type of fortification is represented by the great series of coastal forts which Henry VIII built from 1539 onwards. This chain of forts, or blockhouses as they are sometimes called, was planned to extend from Hull to Milford Haven, covering every port and possible landing place, but many were never built. Designed purely as artillery emplacements they usually consisted of a central tower surrounded by large circular bastions for the cannon, presenting a low target and rounded surfaces to the enemy guns yet remaining capable of an all-round defence.

The finest surviving examples are St Mawes Castle (Fig 60) in Cornwall and Deal and Walmer castles in Kent. The last two were built to protect the Downs Anchorage within the Goodwin Sands so that the British fleet which

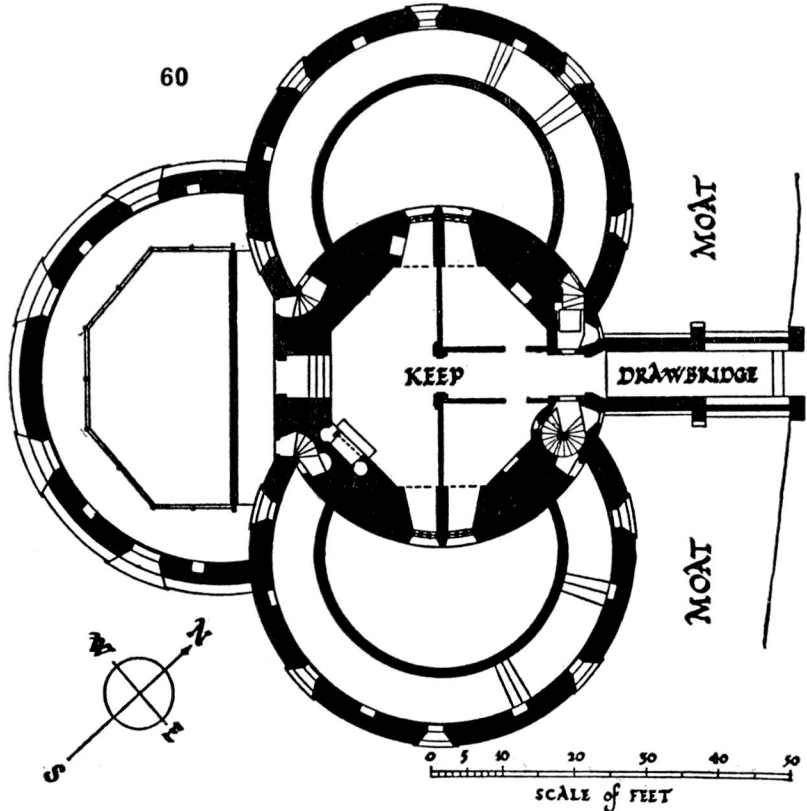

KEEP

DRAWBRIDGE

MOAT

MOAT

N

SCALE of FEET

St Mawes Castle
(Crown Copyright)

was responsible for the defence of the Channel might lay in safety under their guns. Walmer Castle has been the official residence of the Lords Warden of the Cinque Ports since the early 18th century but Deal Castle has been stripped of all the later furnishings and, with its numerous gunports and maze of corridors with their musket loops along the outer walls, it now presents an excellent portrait of what these forts actually looked like in the mid 16th century.

Part of this first national defence scheme has also survived in the Thames Estuary where five artillery blockhouses were built about 1539 : one at Tilbury, one at East Tilbury, two at Gravesend and one at Higham. These consisted of a D shaped bastion with guns at ground level and on the 'roof', with heavier guns mounted on either flank behind earthen ramparts. Higham blockhouse was abandoned in 1553 and its exact position is now uncertain, but the other fortifications were used again during the Napoleonic Wars and several were refortified several times through the centuries.

The scheme was continued under Edward VI right down to the Scilly Isles but already new advances in the art of fortification had made these impressive forts obsolete. The fort at Yarmouth in the Isle of Wight is one of the first to show the influence of the new style, being square in plan with an arrow head bastion, the first of its kind in Britain. The outer defences of the fort at Pendennis, built in 1543 to protect the ports of the Fal estuary in conjunction with St Mawes Castle, were built about 1598 to conform to these new methods with the emphasis on earthen ramparts. At Carisbrooke Castle is one of the earliest and finest examples of this new style of fort, built between 1597 and 1602. It was built by the Italian engineer Federigo Gianibelli who also rebuilt Berwick's defences during Elizabeth's reign. The defences at Berwick, of which three arrow head bastions survive, are the only example of their kind in Britain and amongst the earliest of their type in Europe.

THE STAR FORT

A type of low silhouette fort built of revetted earth and with arrow head bastions was developed in Italy during the first quarter of the 16th century to meet the contingencies of artillery warfare and this star fort began to appear in Britain from the end of the 16th century as we have seen above. It was designed to meet two major needs. Firstly to bring a crossfire to bear on the guns of a besieger, which would be massed at one point of the defences to make a breach, and secondly to provide a plunging and flanking fire along the deep ditch which surrounded the fort.

The arrow head bastion proved to be the most effective for these two needs and it was eventually adopted throughout Western Europe about the middle of the 16th century. If the enemy's artillery attacked the curtain wall it could be met by a direct fire from the curtain wall itself and a crossfire from two of the bastions. For example, if a star fort had twelve guns, one to each curtain wall and two in each bastion, it could bring to bear on any of its four sides a total of five guns, almost 50 per cent of its armament. As a result of this improvement it soon became obvious that the best point at which to attack now was the tip of the bastion for here, in our example, only two guns could be brought to bear properly. Ravelins, that is earthworks of less height than the main curtain wall and chevron in plan, were then built outside the main ditch in front of the curtain walls in order to bring a crossfire to bear on this new attacking position. The ravelins had the effect of giving the fort a double star plan, with the ravelins having their own outer ditches.

As the years passed other lesser works were added to this basic design and defence systems were formed so that a garrison could retire from one line to another, offering resistance at each, and the plans of these later star forts became akin to geometrical puzzles with bastions, ravelins, caponiers (covered passages across the ditch), retrenchments (inner lines of defence usually consisting of a trench and a parapet), hornworks (an advanced work of two half bastions and a curtain wall with two long sides called wings which are flanked by the main defences at the rear), crownworks (a hornwork with double bastions), tenaillons (low outer works between two bastions in the main ditch) and demi-tenaillons.

IRISH FORTS OF THE 17th CENTURY

Despite its strategic position no attempt was made to defend the Irish coast against the possibility of a Spanish attack during the 16th century but the artillery fort does appear in Ireland in the great bastions on the walls of Londonderry (Fig 59), belonging to the early 17th century. Here the massive corner bastions are very similar to the arrow head style of bastion. Charlemont Fort (Fig 61) on the Armagh-Tyrone border overlooking the Blackwater River is another example. Completed in 1624 this fort played an important part in the struggles of the 1640s, surviving until 1921 when the central tower house was burnt and demolished. The surrounding earthworks form a typical star fort with great arrow head bastions. The outer line of defences was added about

61

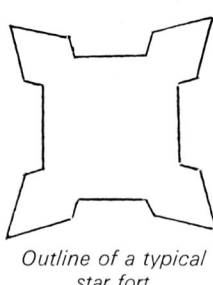

Outline of a typical star fort

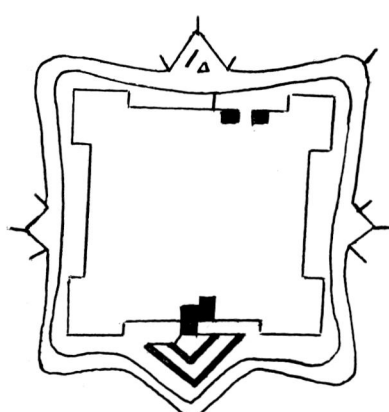

Charlemont Fort 1624, showing the outer defences added in 1673

1673 and is comparable with Civil War earthworks in England with every part of the fort's perimeter now well covered by flanking fire. The gateway is probably an 18th century replacement.

During Lord Mountjoy's campaign of 1600–02 several forts were built at strategic points but these were tall square towers enclosed by a rectangular wall, designed to house a garrison of infantry. Moyry Castle, built to secure the pass from Dundalk to Newry, is typical of this type. Built by a Dutch engineer in 1601 it is three storeys high, 24 feet square, with machicolation over the entrance and musket loops all round the ground floor. The external corners were rounded. Mountjoy Castle on the western shore of Lough Neath was built in 1602. After a turbulent history the square tower house, which had four rectangular angle towers and walls two and a half feet thick, was abandoned in a ruinous state. The fort originally stood in the centre of a large star fort of which no trace now remains and could hold a garrison of 1,100 infantry and a hundred horse.

CIVIL WAR FORTIFICATIONS

The operations of the Civil War made a greater mark on the landscape of Britain than had been made at any time since the building of hundreds of motte and bailey castles in the 11th century, not only because of the long duration of the war and the wide area covered by the fighting, but also because for the first time in Britain cannon were used extensively and, needing fortifications which could protect them from counter battery fire and infantry attack, brought about a revival of earthworks and entrenchments. However, it should be borne in mind that the cannon used at this time were still quite small and consequently not much remains of these new works, either because of cultivation, or because the areas in which they were built have become densely populated, or because the fortifications themselves were only on a small, temporary scale. As a result the majority of the 'Civil War' fortifications visible today are not those which were built during that war but are earlier works which were re-occupied, restored and in the end often destroyed to prevent them being used as strongholds again. In fact as far as fortifications are concerned, the Civil War might be said to be marked more by what was destroyed rather than by what was built.

As has been mentioned in the earlier sections on castles, many castles became the scene of a long and bitter siege between the opposing forces. Harlech, Corfe, Pontefract, Queenborough, Chepstow, Old Wardour, Donnington, Caerphilly and Colchester castles are but a few of those which were besieged. Some held out for only a few days, others held off the attackers for a year or more, as at Beeston Castle in Cheshire and at Scarborough, the only Royalist port on the east coast. But castles could only hold out for long periods where no heavy artillery was brought to bear on them: once siege guns arrived on the scene it was a different story. Brampton Bryan Castle in Herefordshire held out for a whole summer and the siege was abandoned for the winter, but the next year heavy guns were used, the defensive outerworks which had been added to the original fortifications were broken down, and the castle itself was reduced to ruins by the bombardment. Donnington Castle, which commanded the important Oxford-Newbury road, held out for two years but once heavy artillery was brought to bear the castle was soon reduced to ruins and only the main gate and part of the walls survived the bombardment.

Many of the castles captured by the Parliamentarians were blown up or dismantled to prevent them being used again and of their surrounding earthworks little remains to be seen today. Colchester for example endured a siege lasting twelve weeks in 1648 and although many sections of earthen ramparts are still standing these belong to previous centuries and scarcely any sign remains of the less grandiose earthworks of the Civil War period.

The same may be said of the fortified manor houses, large numbers of which were also re-fortified. Lathom House held out for three months, the garrison of 300 losing only half a dozen men while the Parliamentarians under Fairfax lost 600 or more out of a force of 1,000. The siege was raised on the approach of a relieving force under Prince Rupert. Raglan Castle, which had been converted into a Tudor mansion, was able to hold out for ten weeks in 1646. The great hexagonal tower house was hardly damaged by 20 pound cannon balls which were fired at it at the rate of 60 a day and the castle was finally taken by undermining the tower house. Moated homesteads were also occupied as strong points on occasions and proved highly effective against infantry attacks but they stood no chance at all once artillery was brought against them.

Perhaps the most effective of these re-occupied fortifications of earlier centuries were those which had the most in common with the 17th-century earthworks: the prehistoric hill forts. Some of these were occupied during the course of the war, including Badbury Rings, Castell an Dinas and Hambledon Hill. The latter was held in 1645 by 2,000 Clubmen (armed countrymen who fought both sides in an attempt to stop the war destroying their livelihood) and had to be stormed to remove the threat they posed.

One other type of adapted fortification was the village church. For centuries these buildings were the only stone-built, and therefore the only defensible buildings in the countryside and some were 'sandbagged' with bags of wool and held as strong points during the course of battles. The earthworks surrounding many of these village churches are often attributed to the Civil War period but are in fact of much earlier origin, usually dating from the time of the Saxons and Danes or even earlier, for the early Christian missionaries frequently occupied Roman sites in order to use the dressed stone for their churches and the old ramparts and ditch for defence in a still barbarous land.

Medieval town defences were also put to good use by both sides, strategically placed towns and cities having a garrison installed in order to control the lines of communication and the surrounding countryside. Newark, Chester, Reading

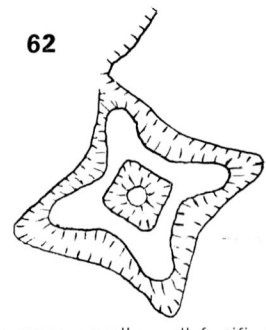

and other towns occupied by the Royalist forces were usually well fortified in the contemporary manner, for the King was able to employ experienced military engineers from the Continent. First a deep ditch was dug round the town, with every so often an arrow head bastion protruding outwards, and the earth was thrown up on both sides. The earth thrown up on the inside was made into a raised platform for artillery, protected by a parapet of earth and stakes; that thrown up on the outside was made into a rampart with a parapet for musketeers and presenting a long sloping glacis towards the enemy. In front of the glacis was erected a line of pitfalls and a stake palisade; behind it was a 'covered way', a narrow berm running round behind the rampart which allowed troops to move from one point to another without being exposed to enemy fire. Of the series of defences built to defend Newark-on-Trent only a star fort known as the Queen's Sconce (Fig 62) has survived. This originally formed the north-west angle of the defences.

At the beginning of the war the Parliamentarians were less fortunate. After Edgehill the City of London was hastily fortified by digging a series of earthworks to command the various approaches, these being roughly linked by an inadequate system of banks and ditches. Cannon were placed at every gate and concealed behind barricades in the main streets, and armed ships were brought up from the docks to protect the Houses of Parliament. At Liverpool the city's weak mud walls were padded with hundreds of bags of wool and managed to withstand an artillery bombardment for five days before falling, but an improvised citadel at Leicester was breached after only three hours of bombardment by six great guns. Later in the war the Parliamentarians were capable of constructing fortifications on a par with those of the Royalists and strongholds such as Lyme Regis and Plymouth successfully resisted assaults and bombardment by Royalist forces.

Such complex fortifications meant that the besiegers often had to resort to the construction of a similar line of fortifications right round a town in order to provide cover for their guns and for mining or sapping operations. The latter were usually in the form of a three-foot deep trench which took a zigzag course towards the chosen part of the defences so as to prevent the defenders being able to enfilade the trench. The excavated earth was heaped on the side nearest the town to provide additional cover. At Newark the Parliamentarians and Scots erected a complex system of siege works round the town, which was besieged three times between 1642 and 1646. Little remains of these works but one of the besiegers drew a plan of the lines and parts of this are reproduced here (Fig 63) to illustrate some of the types of earthwork constructed during this period.

Field works other than those round towns were built on occasions but were

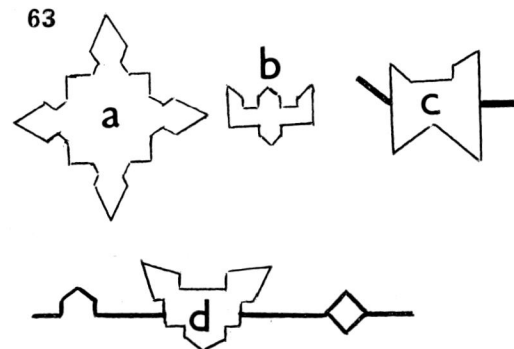

Siege works at Newark: A The HQ of the Scots Army: B the Redoubt at Crankley Point: C a hornwork at Winthorpe: and D Crawford's Sconce and redoubts.

63

seldom of a large scale. Perhaps the largest to survive is a well preserved example of an artillery star fort at Earith in Huntingdonshire, known as The Bulwark (Fig 64). This is 250 feet across with bastions which project nearly a 100 feet. The rampart is 20 feet wide in places and the whole fort is surrounded by a ditch 30 to 40 feet wide with a low breastwork on the counterscarp side. Other field works used to be visible in a field by Holman's Bridge in Buckinghamshire, where the so-called Battle of Aylesbury was fought in 1642. Most notable was a zigzag line of entrenchments running along the top of the high ground. The rampart stood four to five feet high and every 20 yards or so was a gap for a cannon.

The Cromwellians also adapted any existing mounds available to take their artillery and examples occur of tumuli and Norman mottes being used in this way. Cambridge castle (Fig 65) was so used, the old walls and towers of the bailey being cleared away and the greater part of the ditches filled in in the process. A star fort was then superimposed on the site, all but obliterating the earlier fortification.

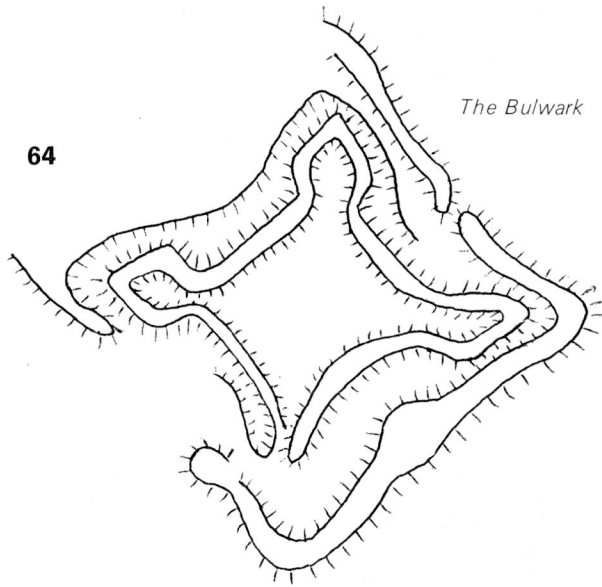

The Bulwark

64

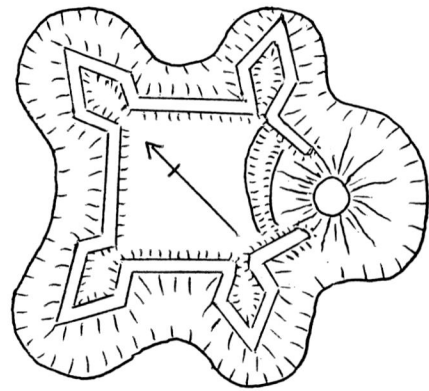

*Cambridge Castle with the
star fort of 1645
superimposed*

DEFENCES AGAINST THE DUTCH

By the 17th century Henry VIII's system of coastal forts had fallen into considerable disrepair. After the Restoration some attempt was made to strengthen the defences but in 1667 the Dutch fleet bombarded Sheerness and sailed up the Medway, although they were driven off at Dartmouth where the old 15th and 16th century works had been regularly improved and repaired during the 16th century and were armed with some 160 guns.

In 1670 Charles II ordered the construction of many new fortifications along the coast and repairs to the existing ones. Mount Batten Castle, built on an island in the Plymouth roadsteads, and the Citadel at Plymouth both date from about this time.

The star fort was perfected by the French military engineer Vauban in the latter half of the 17th century and most artillery fortifications were still of this design. Tilbury Fort, built on the site of an earlier fort, is a rare and very fine example of English fortification of this period. It is pentagonal in plan with large bastions at the angles and a double ditch surrounds it, with additional earthworks beyond the ditch. It was completed about 1682. Another example of the fortifications of the period may be seen at Fort Charlotte overlooking Lerwick Harbour in Shetland. The massive walls are roughly pentagonal in plan with projecting bastions at each angle. It was begun in 1665, burned by the Dutch in 1673 and repaired in 1781.

THE '15 AND THE '45

The Jacobite rebellions provoked the building of new fortifications in Scotland during the 18th century. Fort Augustus in Inverness-shire was built in 1730 but taken by the Jacobites in 1746 and demolished. Ruthven Barracks, three-quarters of a mile south-east of Kingussie, also in Inverness-shire, was built in 1719 to check the flood of Jacobite disloyalty. This has survived although much ruined, having been captured and burnt by Prince Charles in 1746. The barracks were designed to hold a garrison of one company of infantry in two blockhouses, the whole being encircled by a wall with flanking towers.

Fort George, west of Nairn, is the finest relic of this period of British military history. Built after the rebellions it consists of a very strong bastioned fort with outworks, all of which have survived more or less intact and unaltered to this day. The fort, said to be one of the finest if not *the* finest example of 18th century artillery fortification in Europe, is still garrisoned by a battalion of infantry.

10: Fortifications of the 19th Century

FORTIFICATIONS OF THE NAPOLEONIC PERIOD

WHEN Britain declared war on France, Napoleon assembled an invasion fleet at Boulogne. The Battle of Trafalgar changed his mind but until then feverish attempts were made to prepare the coastal defences of Britain. One of the major military works of this period to survive is the Royal Military Canal which was dug from Hythe, through Lympne and Appledore to Rye, isolating Dungeness and the Romney Marsh. Remains of coastal forts may also be found here and there along this stretch of the coast; at Chatham, the Western Heights at Dover, and the Redoubt at Eastbourne. There are also remains of forts on Berry Head, east of Brixham in Devon, and a complex of signal stations and fortifications on the outer island of the Mumbles at the western end of Swansea Bay.

The defences of the Thames were also strengthened. The artillery blockhouses of 1539, improved in the 17th century, were refortified once more and new forts were built at Coalhouse Point, Lower Hope and Shornemead. These latter were quite small, earthen fortifications, pentagonal in shape and each mounting four 24 pounder guns. They were abandoned at the end of the Napoleonic Wars.

However, the most well known and common survival of this age is the Martello Tower. These towers were originally 30 to 40 feet high with walls eleven feet thick on the seaward side, and were surrounded by a deep ditch. Entry was by a small door at the rear, at the top of a twenty foot ladder. The basement held the powder magazine and stores, the first floor the living quarters for a garrison of 24 men and an officer, and on the top platform was mounted either a 68 pounder gun or two howitzers, with sometimes a swivel gun added for close work.

The towers are said to have been first built by Charles V in Italy for coastal defence and named after one at Cape Mortella on the island of Capraia off the north-east coast of Corsica, which British troops under Hood had great difficulty capturing in 1794. When the threat of a French invasion of these shores came, the Duke of York, as C-in-C of the Army, recommended this type of construction for the British coastal defence and many were erected on the most vulnerable stretch of the English coast from Beachy Head to Hythe in 1804. Examples may be seen at Dymchurch, Eastbourne, Hythe and at many other parts of this coast line. In all 74 Martello towers were built along the south coast and round the east coast of Kent.

Presumably at about the same time many towers were also built in the Channel Islands. On Guernsey and Jersey every bay has one or more of these towers, together with remains of batteries and forts of the same date. In L'Ancresse Bay in Guernsey there are no less than five towers, the shore here being lower than usual. These towers appear to have been built with square apertures on two levels, an unusual feature not seen on the English coast, though it is possible the walls were thus pierced at a later date. Fort Regent, on Mont de la Ville overlooking the harbour of St Helier, was built in 1806 and garrisoned until 1926.

There is a Martello tower and battery at Magilligan Point, west of Coleraine in County Londonderry, guarding the entrance to Lough Foyle. As far as is known to the author this is an isolated example of the Martello tower in Northern Ireland.

Between the years 1810 and 1812 the line of towers was extended by the addition of the 'East Anglian Line', a series of 29 Martello towers stretching up the east coast. Examples may be seen at St Osyth, Beacon Hill and Walton-on-the-Naze in Essex, and at Hollesley, Slaughden and Felixstowe in Suffolk.

After the Napoleonic Wars the towers began to lose their value as naval guns became more and more powerful and they were taken over by the revenue officers in an attempt to reduce smuggling. Some are now private homes, others have been utilized as navigational aids, and at the seaside resorts several have been restored and opened to the public. The Wish Tower at Eastbourne is a good example of this last class, and here it is possible to study the interior arrangements, though much of the original tower has been altered or restored.

VICTORIAN FORTIFICATIONS

Up to the end of the Napoleonic Wars a fortress had been a stronghold surrounded by a continuous line of fortifications but when peace finally came to Europe artillery had been developed which could breach fortifications at a range of 800 yards and the art of fortification was therefore forced to undergo a radical change. In order to keep the enemy's guns at a sufficient distance a line of detached forts were needed about a mile in advance of the main fortress, and from this development sprang the independent redoubt. However, most artillery fortifications still followed basically the star shape which had for so long fascinated military engineers with its geometrical symmetry.

After 1859 rifled artillery began to come to the fore and during the next ten years the effective range of siege guns increased to about 4,000 yards. Despite this advance military engineers clung to traditional methods of fortification until the siege of Paris in 1870, which finally proved the uselessness of such defences against the new artillery. Thereafter the tendency was to reduce the size of forts to as small a unit as possible and provide cover from artillery fire by the use of iron cupolas and concrete bunkers.

The fortifications of the British Isles had been allowed to fall into disrepair during this period, and in any case by this date they were obsolete. However, it was argued that the Royal Navy was still Britain's first and main line of defence and the country did not need massive concrete and iron fortresses, since an enemy could not land large numbers of siege guns, nor those of the heaviest calibre.

Under Victoria this situation was rectified to a certain extent by a new system of coastal defences designed to protect the ports and naval bases. The improvements to the fortifications on the Western Heights at Dover are part of this scheme, and work was also carried out at Portsmouth and other large bases. The collection of forts known as Palmerston's Forts on Portsdown Hill and the

Gosport Peninsula, a series of complex moated forts which are for the most part still in the hands of the Armed Services, are the finest examples of this last great coastal defence system. Fort Brockhurst looks like nothing so much as a moated castle of the early 15th century but Fort Wallington, above Fareham, is vastly impressive with provision for 50 guns. Fort Widley is another of these massive forts on Portsdown Hill, in the hands of the Portsmouth Corporation and therefore available for inspection by the public.

The network of fortifications on Alderney in the Channel Islands is also of this period. Costing £1½ millions they were designed for the protection of a British fleet, Cherbourg being only twenty miles away, but they were never completed. A small garrison was maintained there until the 1930s, backed up by the Militia of the island. Fort Albert, the largest and most impressive of the forts, could hold a garrison of 2,000 men.

In the late 1840s and early 1850s the Shornemead and Coalhouse Point forts in the Thames Estuary were again rebuilt and equipped with thirteen 32 pounder smoothbore guns. Barrack blocks were also erected. These forts, together with the Gravesend and Tilbury Forts, were again refortified about 1866, when they were armed with fourteen 11 inch rifled guns housed in D shaped casements of granite and armour plate, together about 25 inches thick, and protected by rifle loops in the barracks block on the landward side. Soon after 9 inch rifled guns, firing an armour piercing shell, were added in open batteries on the flanks of the forts.

During the 1880s a plan was drawn up for a line of entrenchments, redoubts and fortified storehouses to be built for the defence of London in case of a landing on the vulnerable south-east coastline. The line was to run eastwards from Guildford, along the top of the chalk escarpment to Knockholt near Sevenoaks in Kent, then northwards along the ridge west of the River Darent towards Dartford and on into Essex. The line was to be manned by Volunteer units but of this plan only fifteen storehouses were built. An example has survived at Farningham (A20 road) near Eynsford Castle in Kent and this consists of an underground system of store rooms covered by an earthen mound and surrounded by a deep ditch and a metal palisade. The entrance is on the west side and is protected by a wall and a rifle parapet behind the ditch. To the rear of this is a 'lodge', presumably accommodation for the small garrison. It is brick built with large windows, covered on the inside by steel shutters pierced by loopholes. A similar 'lodge' has survived almost at the top of Box Hill in Surrey and may be seen when making the ascent from the west side. The scheme was abandoned soon after the turn of the century.

Towards the end of the century, and into the beginning of the 20th century, it was believed that any attack on British harbours would most likely be in the form of torpedo boats and that therefore coastal fortifications should be armed with quick firing guns, there still being no need for great concrete structures or armoured shields. This is contradicted by the 19th century fortifications at Hurst Castle, one of the last military works of the century. Stuck out on a two and a half mile spit into the Solent near Milford-on-Sea, the fort here is faced with granite and the gun batteries are protected by thick armour plating.

11: Fortifications of the 20th Century

WORLD WAR 1 COASTAL DEFENCES

BEFORE the outbreak of World War 1 Britain had the most formidable navy in the world and, because the huge fleet was regarded as sufficient to deter any serious threat of invasion, no attempt was made to provide the country with a comprehensive system of coastal defences. In fact in 1911 the Committee of Imperial Defence concluded that invasion by a force exceeding 70,000 men was impossible and at the same time recommended that no defences be erected at the Fleet Anchorage of Scapa Flow: the Royal Navy, by taking offensive action from a series of bases, would form the main line of defence and complex land fortifications were therefore not considered essential for the protection of the country.

As early as 1909 the War Office had been carrying out experiments to see if it was possible to shift troops to the coast by motor transport in order to concentrate a large force at any point where an invading army might land, and by the time war broke out most counties had a Motor Volunteer Corps whose job it would be to transport reservists, veterans and invalided ex-soldiers to any invasion point. By 1917 this Territorial Force had some 500,000 members and it was considered that together with the 150,000 men home from the front each month this force would be sufficient to deal with any invading army.

For these reasons there was never a complete network of fortifications round the British coast line during World War 1. In 1914 Scapa Flow had no coastal artillery, no searchlights, no anti-submarine booms or nets and the Fleet at anchor was wide open to attack. Rosyth and Cromarty had batteries for defence against surface shipping but no defence against submarines. These discrepancies were remedied as soon as possible. Other focal points were the fleet bases of Sheerness, Portsmouth, Plymouth and Milford Haven: the ports of the smaller forces of light cruisers, destroyers and submarines, such as Harwich, Dover and the mouths of the Forth, Tyne and Humber: and the lesser patrols which operated from smaller ports such as Hartlepool, Ramsgate and Yarmouth. About 100 guns were positioned to guard these installations on the west and south-west coasts, another 100 guarded the Channel ports, and about 120 were spaced out along the east coast between Dover and Aberdeen. These guns ranged from 4 inch to 9·2 inch, but they were there primarily to defend the bases of the Royal Navy, and no serious attempt was made to link them so that they would be capable of repelling an invading army.

Because of this there are few fortifications which can be attributed to the World War 1 period. On Gosport peninsula may be seen the concrete artillery forts of Gilkicker, Browndown, Gomer and Blockhouse which helped to guard the Solent ports, while at the mouth of the Humber are Fort Haile Sand and Fort Bull Sand, perhaps the best examples of large scale fortification of the time, although they were in fact not completed until some time after the war.

The plans for these two forts originated in 1913–14 but building was not actually begun until 1915. Fort Bull Sand was built south-west of Spurn Head lighthouse on sand 120 feet deep, with a great circular foundation of interlocking steel piles in the form of caissons. These were connected by further piling to give a cell-like effect to the plan, then the outer compartments of the caissons were filled with concrete and the inner part with sand, the whole structure then being capped with concrete so that it resembled an inverted bucket of concrete and steel enclosing a cylinder of sand. The foundation had a diameter of 107 feet and on this were built a basement and three other floors with a diameter of 82 feet, rising 45–50 feet above high water level and faced with armour plate twelve inches thick on the seaward side. Some 40,000 tons of concrete and steel were used in the construction, including many 100 ton blocks of concrete which were placed on the bed of the river to prevent the sand being scoured away by the tides.

The fort was armed with four 6-inch guns as well as small and rapid fire weapons and had a garrison of 200 men. Facilities included an electricity generating plant, air conditioning, fresh water drawn from 600 feet below, baths, recreation rooms, etc.

Fort Haile Sand was of similar design but on a slightly smaller scale, and being on a foundation of clay and chalk, on the Sandhaile Flats two miles south of Cleethorpes, did not need such a complex base. Both forts are now in the care of the Humber British Transport Docks Board.

WORLD WAR 2 FORTIFICATIONS

By the end of June 1940 the whole of Western Europe was occupied by the forces of Nazi Germany and for the first time in almost 150 years Great Britain found herself seriously threatened with an invasion; at a time when her coasts were particularly vulnerable. During the 20th century the rapid development of weapons had caused the art of fortification to undergo a change more radical than ever before and the old forts dotted sparsely around Britain's shores were hopelessly inadequate for the defence of the coastline against a modern invasion force, especially one so well equipped, well trained and successful as the Wehrmacht.

France's Maginot Line had been built over a period of ten years at a cost of many millions of pounds and, despite the outflanking of the Line, had proved this type of fortification could be successful, for many forts in the Maginot Line had held out during the battle for France and did not surrender until several days after the rest of the French Army had lain down its arms, and only then on the orders of General Weygand. But in June 1940 Britain had no time to build a Maginot Line, even had her extensive coastline lent itself to such a scheme. Germany's Siegfried Line on the other hand was based on the theory of defence in depth and consisted of a wide band of more than 3,000 mutually supporting pill boxes and gun emplacements, with a screen of obstacles and lightly held posts in front. The first line of defence was designed only to delay the initial enemy advance and destroy the element of surprise. Once the enemy's attack began to gain momentum this first line would be abandoned and the main brunt of the assault taken by the main line of defences. Behind this main line were held highly mobile reserve divisions and once the enemy's assault began to lose impetus these fresh divisions would be launched in a counter-

Improvised beach defences on the South Coast of Britain, 1940

attack to drive the enemy back. The principle had worked with Finland's Mannerheim Line, holding up the Russian Army for several months, but only because of the narrow front and the correspondingly great depth of the defences. In 1940 this defence in depth seemed to be the only possible form of defence for Britain, but with only a few weeks in which to construct the main line of fortifications.

In the case of Britain the first line of defence was, as always, the Royal Navy. Because of the important role given to aircraft in the German Blitzkrieg, and the need for air supremacy over the Channel, the RAF and a system of anti-aircraft guns formed the second line of defence. Many anti-aircraft batteries were housed in or around the forts of World War 1 and the 19th century, such as those which overlooked Portsmouth and Dover and guarded the estuary of the Humber; others had nothing but revetted earth and sandbags. Many new anti-aircraft gun sites of concrete and steel were built as soon as possible, with supplies and quarters in underground bunkers, such as those on Wimbledon Common which guarded one of the bombing runs on London, and at Pitney Lock near Cleethorpes, close by RAF Northcote with its Blenheim bombers.

Machine gun post sited to cover beach, South Coast, 1940

ABOVE: Horse Sand Ford in the Solent. This was one of the three different types of sea fort installed all around Britain's coastline throughout World War 2.

THE SEA FORTS

Along the east coast, as far out as a line drawn from Margate to Felixstowe, a revolutionary form of fortification also made its appearance during those anxious months: the sea fort. These consisted of a hollow pontoon base measuring 168 by 88 feet with two hollow towers each 24 feet in diameter and 60 feet high, topped by a gun deck, an upper deck, and a central tower unit. The tower 'legs' were divided into seven floor levels for accommodation and stores, two 4·5-inch guns were mounted on the main gun deck, two 40mm Bofor guns and four Lewis machine-guns on the upper deck, and the central tower was topped by a radar scanner. At one end was a landing jetty supported by a steel framework and equipped with a crane for the hoisting aboard of stores. Fully manned, these forts were towed out to key positions, the base flooded, and thus converted into permanent fortifications capable of engaging aircraft and U-boats alike. The Army was responsible for three of these forts in the Thames Estuary, in a line stretching out seawards from between the Isle of Sheppey and Southend. The Royal Navy had four more, forming an outer line, and these were referred to as His Majesty's Forts. HMF Roughs guarded the approach to Harwich, HMF Sunk Head lay out beyond Clacton, HMF Knock John was on the sand banks off Foulness, and HMF Tongue Sand was on the sand bank north of Westgate-on-Sea, on Kent's northern coast. For

BELOW: Another type of AA fort manned by both Army and Navy personnel.

ABOVE: A third type of AA fort just after it has been positioned in the Channel. Thirty minutes after launching, one of this type of fort was in action.

some years after the war these forts were a common sight from the east coast holiday resorts.

ARTILLERY EMPLACEMENTS

The third line of defence was the coastal artillery, guarding the key naval bases, the lesser ports, river estuaries and eventually any open stretch of coastline where an invading force might attempt to land. At first, because of the lack of guns and munitions, this third line was restricted to the old World War 1 and earlier forts, which were usually at the main naval bases. At Portsmouth the old forts on the Gosport peninsula and at Portsdown Hill came back into their own, as did the defence works above Dover, Forts Haile and Bull at the mouth of the Humber, and the ancient Thames Estuary forts, some of which dated back to the Napoleonic Wars. Perhaps fortunately for Britain the expected invasion did not come in the summer of 1940 and by the following summer most of the gaps in the coastal artillery defences had been plugged.

Along the south coast the ports of Falmouth, Plymouth, Dartmouth, Portland, Southampton, Portsmouth, Newhaven and Dover were heavily armed with approximately 120 large calibre guns, mainly 9·2 and 6 inch, 12 and 6 pounders. Between Dartmouth and Portland the coastline was also dotted with what were known as beach batteries, batteries of smaller calibre artillery with often nothing more than revetted earthworks or sandbags for protection. From the important Solent ports of Southampton and Portsmouth, which were protected by 36 guns, as far east as Dover, the coast was guarded by an almost continuous line of these batteries, supplementing and connecting the fire plans of the larger guns. Dover itself, gateway to England, had two 14-inch guns, six 9·2 inch, sixteen 6 inch, two 4 inch, three 12 and three 6 pounders, all installed in the mass of fortifications on the high ground round the town. More beach batteries linked Dover to Ramsgate and Ramsgate to the forts of the Thames Estuary, which had 23 large guns between them.

North of the Thames Estuary the east coast was protected by 98 guns, distributed at Harwich, Lowestoft, Yarmouth, the Humber, Hartlepool, Sunderland and the mouths of the Tyne and Blyth. Round the bulge of the East Anglian coast beach batteries formed a continuous line as far as The Wash, with a few more bridging the gap between Boston and the Humber.

Scotland had 50 large calibre guns, centred at the Forth and Clyde, Dundee, Aberdeen and Invergordon. The naval base at Rosyth had 29 of these guns, and Scapa Flow in the Orkneys was equipped with 40 guns, eleven of them 6 inch. Down the west coast there was less protection, with only eight 6 inch guns shared between Barrow and the Mersey, but along the south coast of South Wales, overlooking the Bristol Channel, eighteen large guns were emplaced between Milford Haven and Newport, with a battery of two 6 inch guns at Avonmouth on the English side of the Channel. A series of beach batteries lined the north coast of Somerset and Devon between Avonmouth and Appledore. Ulster had eight 6 inch guns and a 12 pounder, six 6-inch guns being at Belfast.

Not a great deal remains to be seen of all the fortifications which housed these large batteries, although most of the pre-1940 forts at the key naval bases remain. These have been dealt with under earlier headings and include Forts Haile and Bull at the Humber; Forts Blockhouse, Gomer, Gilkicker and Browndown in the Portsmouth area; the Palmerston forts of Wallington, Southwick, Widley, Brockhurst and Rowner, also round Portsmouth; and the forts in the Thames Estuary at Coalhouse Point, Tilbury, Gravesend and Shornemead.

BELOW: 6 pdr beach battery at Druridge Bay manned by the Royal Artillery. Note the sandbagged addition to the main concrete emplacement which probably housed the gun's crew when they were off duty.

The smaller guns of the various beach batteries were removed soon after the war and those which had only sandbag and corrugated metal shelters have long since disappeared, but a surprisingly large number of small emplacements have survived. Examples may be seen at Dartmouth Castle, above Cefn Sidan beach near Pembrey in Carmarthenshire, at Pett Level near Hastings, at Puckpool Point and the Culver downs on the north-east and south-east coasts of the Isle of Wight, at Gorleston-on-Sea in Norfolk, Canvey Island in Essex and Heysham Harbour in Lancashire.

The example at Pett Level, on the inland side of the road, is a two-storied building of red brick. The bottom section is now occupied by sheep but a metal ladder has survived to give access to the upper floor. The emplacement at Heysham is on the south-west slopes of Heysham Head Pleasure Gardens, by the north side of the road from Heysham village to Heysham harbour, and is now incorporated in a mock castle advertising the gardens. Its position covers the entrance to the harbour. The utilization of old fortifications for amusement purposes seems to be a British trait, for the large emplacement at Puckpool on the Isle of Wight is also used for amusements, housing an aquarium and aviary amongst other things.

Two 6-inch guns were housed in the emplacement on the cliffs of Gorleston-on-Sea and although the site has now been levelled the underground works still exist. A dummy site was also built at nearby Hopton in an attempt to confuse German Intelligence. Underground works of emplacements are also to be seen in the Grimsby area. One is situated in the dock estate, on land to the side of the Drewery Brothers fish factory, on the north wall. Another is situated further along the sea wall, at the old Admiralty slip. A third may be seen near Suggitts Lane railway crossing at Cleethorpes.

There are two emplacements to be seen on Canvey Island, one on the sea wall at a place known locally as The Lobster Smack, after a nearby public house, and the other a mile east of this, behind Fielders Holiday Camp. The former is of brick with a metal top and overlooks the Thames. The second is a larger work, consisting of a number of pill boxes embedded in the sea wall and facing the Kent coast, and two large towers which held the guns, facing out to sea. Above the gun emplacements are what appear to have been observation posts.

Small artillery emplacements were also constructed at strategic points

BELOW: Hidden coastal defence at Berwick upon Tweed. The picture sequence shows a 6-inch Naval gun emerging from a 'hide' made of wood and canvass to represent a factory building.

ABOVE: Anti-tank defences at Tentsmuir being built by Free Polish troops. Visible in the foreground are anti-tank obstacles with, in the background emplacements for heavy artillery.

further inland, mainly in the south-east 'invasion corner' of England. Examples may be seen at Pevensey Castle in Sussex, on the west side of Box Hill in Surrey, and in the Tilford-Farnham area of Surrey. There are no less than seven surviving gun emplacements in the last-named area, all sited to cover the approach to the natural barrier formed by the River Wey. Construction of the seven emplacements is so varied that they were probably built for the Home Guard by local builders, rather than by Royal Engineers. All are of brick, two having concrete roofs and another an inner 'skin' of concrete. Each held one gun, but the number of rifle apertures varies from none to six and their plans range from the six sided pill box shape to square, oblong and even irregular outlines, best described by the drawings.

PILL BOXES

The pill boxes built during World War 2 for the defence of Britain may be generally divided into two classes: those which linked and supported the main coastal defences and were manned by front line troops for the most part; and those which were built inland and were often allocated to the local Home Guard unit. The coastal pill boxes were usually built of reinforced concrete, but were sometimes of brick with concrete roofs. Although many were blown up by the Army after the war, or have fallen from cliffs with the erosion of the

117

Standard octagonal pill-box, with infantry patrol.

land, examples are still very numerous and may frequently be seen in strings of half a dozen or more, their fields of fire forming a continuous and overlapping curtain along their front. Such lines still exist at Landguard Point near Felix-stowe, on the cliffs between Llantwit Major and St Donats in Glamorgan, along the coast at Hartlepool (although these are now ruined), along the coast between the entrance to Portsmouth harbour and Lee-on-Solent to the west, in the Barrow-in-Furness area where they guarded the approaches across the low tide sand flats, and between Minehead and Blue Anchor on the Somerset coast. The last named were faced with pebbles from the beach to assist in camouflaging them and at some seaside resorts, particularly Morecambe, the pill boxes along the front were disguised as promenade seat shelters. It is

ABOVE: Octagonal pillbox disguised as part of a church in Edinburgh.

interesting to note that in many cases the pill boxes were erected close by earlier fortifications built to protect the same part of the coast, like the string of pill boxes along the River Adur near Shoreham Airport, fulfilling the role once taken by nearby Bramber Castle, built in the 11th century.

Inland the quality of pill box construction was usually inferior, the majority being built of brick with concrete roofs, though they were often protected and to a certain extent camouflaged by the heaping of earth round the lower courses and sometimes even on the tops. These pill boxes were strung across the countryside in chains, placed at strategic points such as rail, road and river bridges, behind the 'moats' of rivers, streams and land drainage ditches, and looking down on the main roads which ran through the gaps in the Downs from the coast towards London.

Many of these pill boxes were destroyed after the war but almost as many were put to peace time uses such as sheltering livestock, the storing of agricultural implements, or serving as changing rooms when built by playing fields. Good examples of chains of these pill boxes may be seen along the Bridgwater-Taunton canal, along the River Wey in the Farnham-Tilford area of Surrey, along the south side of Box Hill, also in Surrey, and at Pevensey Castle where

BELOW: 6 pdr emplacements camouflaged as part of a fairground on the beach.

ABOVE: An octagonal emplacement covering a railway line disguised as a stack of logs by clever painting.

the boxes were camouflaged to blend with the old fortifications.

The most common design of pill box was six sided, with or without a steel door at the rear, or with a T shaped internal barrier. Wall thickness seems to have averaged 15 inches with the roof a foot thick. Each face of the box was about seven feet in length, and the average height of the boxes is seven feet three inches. Apertures are usually a foot high, with a ten inch opening on the exterior, splayed to 32 inches on the inside. As shown by the illustrations, these boxes normally had five and seven apertures.

Variations to this basic plan were numerous, oblong or square with three apertures and an L shaped wall to cover the rear entrance, or octagonal. The latter had four main faces, each having a large aperture for a light machine-gun, flanked by two smaller apertures for rifles, and four angled corners with a single rifle aperture in each. Two other variants, both probably of Home Guard

BELOW: Two standard octagonal pillboxes one with disruptive camouflage painting and the other concealed inside a haystack.

ABOVE: Standard trench manned by an infantry section on exercise.

origin, were built entirely of metal. In Sheephatch School playing field at Tilford in Surrey is a pill box constructed of sheets of corrugated iron, forming a double circle with the gap between them filled with concrete. This example has three apertures for rifles and a small entrance. The other variant is on the south side of the first railway bridge over the line between Iver and Langley in Buckinghamshire. This is of a most unusual construction, being in the form of a circular metal 'igloo' with a hole at the top, probably originally housing a Blackie Bombard mortar, as issued to the Home Guard.

TRENCHES

The great strength of defensive systems in depth, based on trenches, barbed wire, interlocking arcs of machine-gun fire and artillery supporting fire, had been amply illustrated in World War 1 but it was not until World War 2 that this form of defensive entrenchment was put to any great use in Britain. As we have seen, pill boxes were built at many vulnerable points along the coast and at tactically important points inland, and these were often strengthened and linked by some form of entrenchment. As may be expected, none of these modern earthworks have survived, but in the following paragraphs the basic points of trench construction have been outlined to give some idea of what these works looked like.

Trenches may be divided into fire, communication and support trenches. Support trenches contain the reserve troops and serve as a rallying point if the first line is driven back: they have a parapet at front and rear to provide protection against the blast and splinters of high explosive shells and are between 200 and 400 yards to the rear of the fire or front line trench. Connecting the support trench to the fire trench is the communication trench, which consists of a plain trench approaching the front line diagonally or in a zigzag fashion so as to be covered from enemy fire, and which allows reinforcements to move up to the fire trench whilst remaining under cover.

Fire trench for an infantry platoon with revetment, firestep, and duckboards.

The siting of the fire trench is dictated by three important factors: it must have a clear field of fire; it must be concealed from view as much as possible; and there must be easy access for the reinforcements. When defending high ground there are three possible positions for the fire trench: at the foot of the forward slope, just forward of the crest, or on the reverse slope. A position near the crest of the hill gives a good view of the enemy, easy reinforcement, and the defenders feel safe on the high ground, but against these points are the disadvantages of plunging fire, which is not so effective as level fire, and artillery support for the attacking infantry right up to the last minute. A position at the foot of the hill gives a good field of fire but sacrifices efficient reinforcement. However, with a fire trench on the reverse slope support is easy, there is concealment from the enemy and cover from his fire, and attacking infantry may be met at close range with a withering fire from rifles, bolstered by a crossfire from machine-guns stationed on each flank.

Since the direction of an attacker's fire would not always be from the front, trenches were not long and straight but were protected from enfilade and oblique fire by making the lines irregular, the trenches following the contours of the land to gain the maximum cover. Any straight lengths of trench were broken into sections of eight to ten yards by means of traverses, or earthen banks.

A parapet four and a half feet high is standard for men firing in a standing position. The trench itself would never have been less than two feet in width three feet being more usual, since this allows the men to crouch down for cover if necessary. The thickness of the parapet would have been between two and three feet, sufficient to stop a rifle bullet, the inner face being revetted with sandbags, sods or timber. Head cover was added by building up the parapet another 18 to 24 inches with sandbags, leaving loop holes for rifles. The loop

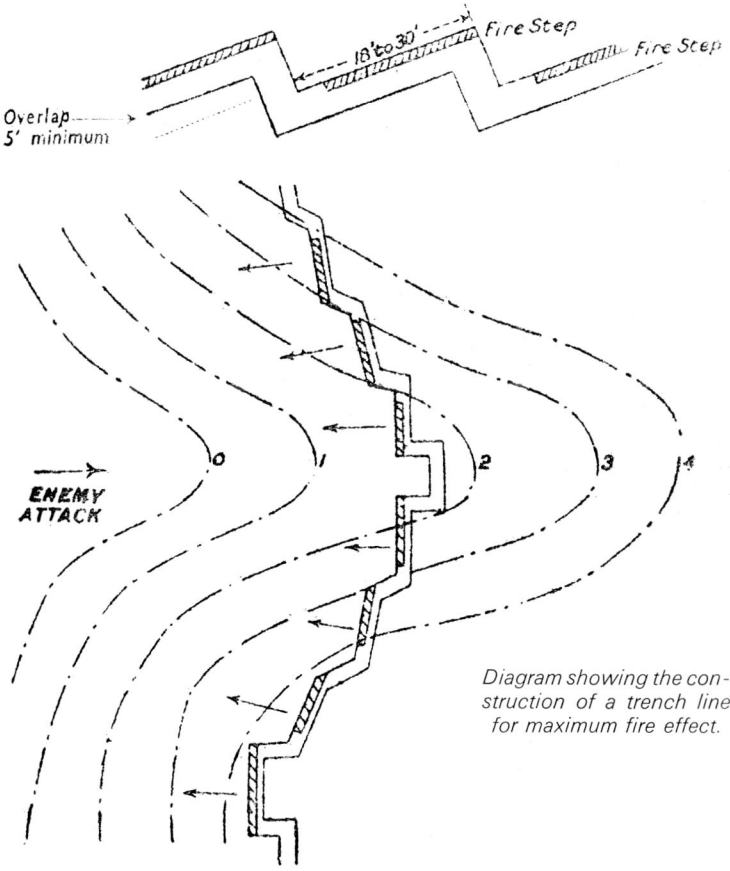

Overlap
5' minimum

18' to 30'

Fire Step

Fire Step

Fire Step

ENEMY
ATTACK

0   1   2   3   4

Diagram showing the con-
struction of a trench line
for maximum fire effect.

holes were splayed, narrow ends outwards, and were usually ten inches high, six inches wide outside and 20 inches wide on the inside.

Dug outs for headquarters and casualty stations, etc, were constructed every so often along the fire trench or immediately behind it, and these were usually topped with timber or metal and two feet of earth so that they were proof against bullets and shrapnel. Machine-gun posts were essential for adequate defence of a trench line and were sited so that their arcs of fire interlocked to form a cross-fire at the places most likely to be assaulted. Sometimes the machine-guns were placed in a small sap slightly in advance of the fire trench, serving rather like the medieval flanking tower, and from here they could rake the face of the front line if the enemy managed to pierce the cross-fire.

OBSTACLES

In 1940 the main highways leading inland from the south-east coast were straddled at strategic points by dragon's teeth and barbed wire barricades. Great anti-tank ditches and various forms of anti-tank traps, some illustrated by the drawings in this section, were dug or erected across the countryside,

Trench covering cross-roads, manned by Home Guard.

stretching for mile after mile. All these lesser types of defence works were also used on the coast, supplementing the larger works. There were numerous other minor precautions. Attack was to be expected from the air as well as from the sea. Government buildings and other important centres of organization were sandbagged and barricaded with barbed wire barriers, armed sentries checked those entering and leaving: Britain had seen what had happened to Holland and Norway. Road signs were removed, railway station names painted out, and place names on buildings obliterated to confuse any enemy gaining the shore. The Local Defence Volunteers, later the Home Guard, was formed, at first armed with shotguns and pitchforks for there were only 70,000 rifles in the country, and weekly magazines carried do-it-yourself articles on how to destroy a German tank from your bedroom window or cut off the head of a German despatch rider with wire stretched across the street. 'Take one with you' was the popular slogan. Recently it has been revealed that steps had even been taken to form a resistance movement in case the invasion was successful and the men selected for this role, split into perhaps 500 or so small

Home Guard unit manning a fortified town gate of an earlier age, 1941.

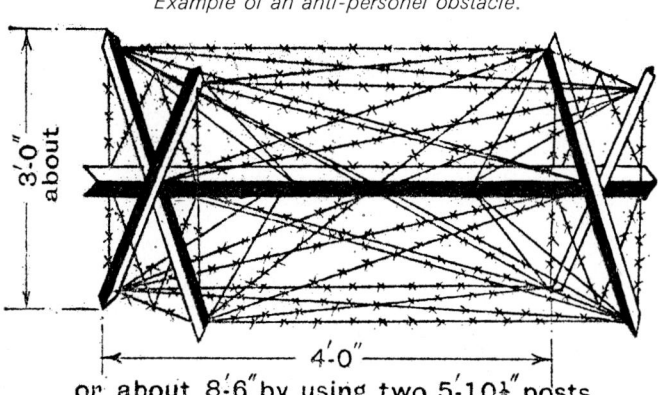

The fortified gate seen from inside; this is a typical example of old defence works pressed into new use during World War 2.

groups of hand picked men, were provided with underground bunkers in which they were to lie low for the first weeks of the occupation. The bunkers were of reinforced concrete, entered by a camouflaged manhole, and contained beds, arms, ammunition and stores. Their sites are not known.

All these lesser defences, except the underground bunkers, were of a very

Example of an anti-personel obstacle.

3'-0" about

4'-0"

or about 8'-6" by using two 5'-10½" posts.

temporary nature and as soon as the need for them disappeared they were removed. Cultivation, intensified to encompass every scrap of land during the lean years, obliterated most of the anti-tank ditches and traps, while the barriers on the roads in the south could not have survived past 1944 when all roads were urgently needed to shuffle the vast D-Day armies to their embarkation ports. However, examples of tank traps and dragon's teeth may still be found.

THE CHANNEL ISLANDS

No book on the fortifications of the British Isles would be complete without a summary of those works built in the Channel Islands during World War 2, but there is a sting in the tail here. Being situated near France and having already been heavily fortified in the preceding century, the Channel Islands probably have more remains of fortifications per acre than any other part of the British Isles. However, the World War 2 fortifications here were not built by the British but by the Germans. It is ironic that the first (Celtic Iron Age hill forts) and the last fortifications in the British Isles were erected by invaders.

Many of the Napoleonic and other 19th-century fortifications built by the British Governments of the time were adapted and reinforced by the Germans. In Petit Bot Bay on the south coast of Guernsey an old Martello tower was converted into a machine-gun emplacement: Saumarez Fort on the north-west coast, an old Napoleonic fort, had a German tower added: Prévoté Tower, again on the south coast, was also fortified by the Germans. On Jersey, Castle Cornet and Elizabeth Castle, the former dating from the 13th century, were both strongly fortified during the occupation, while at Corbiere, the south-west point of the island, extensive fortifications were built in the cliffs and a former observation tower has now been converted into a radio station.

But the greatest works are those built by the Germans from scratch on Jersey. St Lawrence Military Underground Hospital was constructed by Russian slave labour and took two and a half years to build, still being only half finished then although 14,000 tons of rock had been removed and 4,000 tons of concrete used to line the interior. St Peter's Bunker is an underground bunker of seven rooms, built in 1942 by the Todt Organization, again using slave labour. It was a strongpoint to guard the important cross roads leading to the west of the island and the airport. The bunker held 33 men and could be sealed off against gas attacks, being equipped with its own air conditioning unit.

ST PETERS. French tank turret used as a machine gun post on top of one of the entrances to the bunker there.

Gazetteer

ACCESS to the sites listed in the gazetteer may be roughly divided into classes.

1 On common land and therefore open at all times to everyone. No comment has been made with these entries.

2 On private land, not normally open to the public. This type of site has only been listed when necessary, and then only if the ruins may be seen from the road or other public land. However, permission can usually be obtained from the owner for a closer inspection if permission is sought before the visit. This has been stated when necessary.

3 On private land but open to the public for a small charge and at set times. Hours have been listed with each entry in this class.

4 Sites in the care of the Department of the Environment, open at set hours, usually for a small fee. Standard hours for England and Wales are:

March-April	9.30 to 5.30	Sundays 2 to 5.30	
May-Sept.	9.30 to 7	Sundays 2 to 7	
October	9.30 to 5.30	Sundays 2 to 5.30	
Nov.-Feb.	10 to 4.30	Sundays 2 to 4.30	
Scotland	April-Sept. 9.30 to 7	Sundays 2 to 7	
	Oct-March 10 to 4.30	Sundays 2 to 4.30	

Closed Christmas and Boxing Days throughout the British Isles.

Any variations to these hours are listed with the individual entries. All entries in this classification are marked In care of Dept of Environment.

1: England

BEDFORDSHIRE

FLITWICK CASTLE Remains of motte and bailey castle NW of village church.
MEPPERSHALL HILLS Remains of motte and bailey castle SW of village church.
TEMPSFORD Danish camp, sometimes called Gannock's Castle, near junction of Ouse and Ivel to W of village.
WILLINGTON Danish camp four miles E of Bedford by the Ouse.

BERKSHIRE

ALFRED'S CASTLE Iron Age earthwork on Swinley Down, near Ashbury.
BADBURY RINGS Iron Age earthwork on 500 foot hill, one mile N of Great Coxwell.
BLEWBURTON HILL Iron Age camp on hill E of village.
CAESAR'S CAMP Iron Age Camp covering some 20 acres, one mile S of Easthampstead. Probably used in Roman times also.
DONNINGTON CASTLE Late 14th century castle with extensive earthworks of Civil War period, one mile N of Newbury. In care of Dept of Environment, hours standard.
GRIM'S BANK Earthwork near Aldermaston, still standing up to eight feet high in places, probably dating from the 5th century and perhaps built by Britons to keep out Saxons.
SEGSBURY CAMP Iron Age fort, sometimes called Letcombe Castle, covering about 26 acres on Segsbury Down near Letcombe Bassett. Rampart originally faced with stone blocks.
UFFINGTON CAMP Iron Age hill fort with single rampart and ditch on White Horse Hill (856 feet) two miles S of village.
WALBURY HILL Largest Iron Age camp in the county, covering 80 acres of hill (974 feet high). Near Combe.
WALLINGFORD A Roman settlement later occupied and fortified by Saxons. Destroyed by Danes in 1006 but parts of rampart still stand 25 feet high with ditch 20 feet wide.
WINDSOR CASTLE Largest inhabited castle in the world, covering 13 acres. Mainly built in middle of 13th century. Admission to Round Tower limited to 11 to 4, April to Sept, closed when Royal Family in residence.

BUCKINGHAMSHIRE

CUBLINGTON Remains of Saxon *burh* round the old village, especially noticeable on NW side. The lord's motte also survives, named The Beacon.

GREAT MISSENDEN Various earthworks near the town, all scheduled for preservation as ancient monuments : Grim's Ditch near Woodlands Park, Rook Wood and Redding Wick.

HOGGESTON Remains of rampart and ditch of Saxon *burh* surrounding village.

CAMBRIDGESHIRE

CAMBRIDGE CASTLE Scant remains of Norman motte with gun platform of Civil War period built on top.

DEVIL'S DITCH 7 miles of earthwork between Reach and Ditton Green on Suffolk border, probably erected by Saxons as boundary between East Anglia and Mercia. Best part is on Newmarket Heath.

FLEAM DYKE Second of set of three dykes separating East Anglia from Mercia in Saxon times, straddling the Icknield Way near where it fords the Cam.

ROMAN WAY Third dyke, part of boundary marked by Devil's Ditch and Fleam Dyke.

WANDLEBURY Iron Age fort on top of Gog Magog hills outside Cambridge.

CHESHIRE

BEESTON CASTLE Castle dating from early 13th century. Dismantled after long siege in Civil War but considerable remains. Two miles W of Bunbury. In care of Dept of Environment, hours standard, Sundays 9.30 May to Sept.

BOSLEY CLOUD Remains of Roman fort on Bosley Cloud hill, Bosley Reservoir.

CHESTER City walls almost complete, following line of earlier Roman walls. Remains of Roman walls may be seen along the N side and by Newgate. Of Chester Castle only Agricola's Tower remains (c.1246) and part of the wall overlooking the Dee.

EDDISBURY Part of Saxon *burh*, sometimes called the Old Pale, covering over 12 acres near Delamere.

MAIDEN CASTLE Iron Age earthwork north of Malpas off A41.

CORNWALL

CARN BREA Iron Age fort on hill SW of Redruth.

CASTLE-AN-DINAS Probably the best Iron Age hill fort in the county, with three rings of defences including stone ramparts. On 700 foot hill off B3311, 2½ miles E of St Columb Major.

CHUN CASTLE Formidable Iron Age hill fort, 1½ miles NW of Lanyon Quoit.

KELLY ROUNDS Iron Age hill camp two miles NE of Wadebridge.

LAUNCESTON 12th-13th century castle, slighted after Civil War, with cylindrical keep on tall motte. In care of Dept of Environment, standard hours. Bailey walls formed main part of the medieval town walls, of which only the magnificent South Gate survives.

PENDENNIS CASTLE Part of Henry VIII's coastal defences, built 1543 to protect ports of Fal Estuary with St Mawes Castle. One mile SE of Falmouth, in care of Dept of Environment, hours standard, Sundays 9.30 May to Sept.

PIRAN ROUND Iron Age hill camp 1¾ miles NE of Perranporth.

RESTORMEL CASTLE Norman motte and bailey castle with shell keep c.1200. In care of Dept of Enviromnent, standard hours, Sundays 9.30 May to Sept.

ST MARY'S POOL 16th century fort, known as Harry's Walls, built to command harbour. ¼ mile NE of Hugh Town, Scilly Isles. In care of Dept of Environment.

ST MAWES CASTLE Coastal fort of 16th century, two miles E of Falmouth. In care of Dept of Environment, hours standard, Sundays 9.30 May to Sept.

ST MICHAEL'S MOUNT Began life as a monastery in 1044, taken over by Crown in 1425. Much rebuilding in 17th century and since. Access by boat at high tide, by causeway at low tide. Guided tours only.

TINTAGEL CASTLE Remains of mid 12th century castle, ½ mile NW of Trevena. In care of Dept of Environment, hours standard, Sundays 9.30 May to Sept.

TRENCROM HILL Iron Age fortifications on the hill, three miles S of St Ives.

TRESCO King Charles's Castle, 16th century castle with Civil War fortification added, ¾ mile NW of New Grimsby, Scilly Isles. Cromwell's Castle, a round tower of 17th century for cannon to command haven of New Grimsby. Altered in 18th century, The Old Blockhouse, a 16th century fortification for artillery at southern end of Old Grimsby Harbour. All in care of Dept of Environment.

TREVALGEY HEAD Well sited Iron Age camp, on a small island separated from the mainland by a 20 foot chasm, some two miles E of Newquay. There are three ramparts and ditches on the island, another four lines on the mainland.

CUMBERLAND

BIRDOSWALD Roman fort on Hadrian's Wall, covering 5 acres near village of Gilsland. East gate and wall well preserved. Interior in private ownership, permission to enter at farmhouse.

BURGH-ON-SANDS St Michael's fortified church, 6 miles NW of Carlisle.

CARLISLE Castle founded 1092, enlarged later. Keep 12th century with later alterations. In care of Dept of Environment, standard hours, Sundays 9.30 May to Sept. None of gates of medieval town walls survive, but large stretches of walls may be seen, notably West Wall and in Bitts Park.

CARROCK FELL Remains of stone ramparts, surrounding 5 acres on very steep hill, of Iron Age hill fort. East of Keswick, north of A66.

DACRE CASTLE 14th century fortified house, later converted into farmhouse, NW of Penrith. See also Hutton-in-the-Forest and Hutton John.

GREAT SALKELD 14th century fortified tower attached to St Cuthbert's Church.

HADRIAN'S WALL Built AD 121-126, runs from Wallsend in Northumberland to Bowness, a distance of 73½ miles. Forts on or close by the wall include Birdoswald, Chesters and Housesteads.

HARDKNOTT CASTLE Roman auxiliary fort of 2¾ acres established *c*. AD 103. At W end of Hardknott Pass, 800 feet up on head of Eskdale.

HUTTON-IN-THE-FOREST 14th century peel tower near Penrith. Open by appointment only, apply Head Gardener.

HUTTON JOHN Peel tower with later manor house near Penrith. Open by appointment only.

DERBYSHIRE

CODNOR CASTLE Early 13th century castle. Part of bailey wall and the round towers remain. Preservation work being undertaken.

FIN COP Remains of Iron Age fort, 1½ miles NW of Ashford-in-the-Water.

MAM TOR Iron Age camp covering 16 acres near top of 700 foot high tor close to Edale.

MELANDRA CASTLE Roman fort covering two acres, one mile WNW of Glossop.

PEVERIL CASTLE Castle protected on three sides by lay of land. Keep dating from 1175 guards main entrance, N and W curtain late 11th early 12th century. In care Dept of Environment, hours standard, Sundays 9.30 May to Sept.

DEVON

BAYARD'S COVE CASTLE 16th century fort covering entrance to inner haven at Dartmouth.

BERRY POMEROY CASTLE Late 13th, early 14th century castle, restored in mid 16th century but now in ruins. Three miles NE of Totnes. Hours as advertised.

BLACKBURY CASTLE Iron Age camp 1½ miles SW of South Leigh with single rampart and ditch and complex entrance on S side.

BRIXHAM Remains of Napoleonic Wars forts on Berry Head, one mile E of town. To W of harbour is cliff named The Battery, originally a fortification stood here to work in conjunction with those on Berry Head.

CLOVELLY DYKES Iron Age hill fort ¼ mile S of Clovelly, probably used again in Roman times.

COMPTON CASTLE 14th to 16th century fortified manor house near Marldon. Open April to Oct on Mon, Wed and Thurs 10 to 12 and 2 to 5.

CRANBROOK CASTLE Iron Age hill fort S of Drewsteignton.

CROFT CASTLE Norman motte with rampart still standing round top, near Winkleigh.

DARTMOUTH CASTLE 15th century fort, added to end of 16th century, guarding estuary mouth S of town. In care of Dept of Environment, hours standard, Sundays 9.30 May to Sept. Brick emplacement, built in 1940, still standing.

EXETER Town walls, mainly 13th century with 15th century repairs, following line of Roman walls, much of which still survive. Best seen in car parks off Paul Street and Southernhay and Northernhay Streets. 11th century gatehouse of Exeter Castle also survives.

GRIMSPOUND Bronze Age camp surrounded by well preserved wall with a magnificent entrance of granite slabs on S side. Three miles NW of Widecombe.

HEMBURY FORT Iron Age camp inhabited from 200 BC to 75 AD. One mile SE of Broadhembury.

HOLNE CHASE CASTLE Iron Age hill fort three miles W of Ashburton.

LYDFORD CASTLE Late 12th century keep and bailey within a Saxon earthwork.

MOUNT BATTON CASTLE Thirty foot tower built 1665 on island in Plymouth Harbour. Admission once a month, by appointment with Officer Commanding RAF Plymouth.

OKEHAMPTON CASTLE 11th century castle, largely rebuilt in 14th century and dismantled 1539. In care of Dept of Environment, hours standard, Sundays 9.30 May to Sept.

PLYMOUTH CITADEL Fortification raised against Dutch after Restoration. Admission by appointment with Officer Commanding. Gate in care of Dept of Environment, hours standard.

TOTNES CASTLE Motte and bailey castle founded soon after Conquest with shell keep and bailey curtain wall added in early 13th century. In care of Dept of Environment, hours standard.

DORSET

ABBOTSBURY CASTLE Iron Age hill fort covering 4½ acres, 1½ miles NW of Abbotsbury.

BADBURY RINGS Iron Age earthwork enclosing 14 acres near Wimborne, consisting of three concentric rings of massive ramparts and ditches, the centre rampart 40 feet high and a mile in circumference.

BOKERLEY DYKE   Four mile long defensive earthwork built by Romano-British against Saxons. Forms part of Dorset-Hampshire border near Cranborne.

CORFE CASTLE   Castle dating from Conquest and 14th century, slighted after siege in Civil War.

EGGARDON   Iron Age hill fort on 800 foot hill SE of Powerstock village.

HAMBLEDON HILL   Iron Age hill fort, 623 feet up, ½ mile SE of Child Okeford, complementing Hod Hill fort where Stour meets the Iwerne.

HOD HILL   Iron Age hill fort with triple ramparts, ditch 40 feet deep. Roman or Romano-British camp constructed in NW corner and known as Lydsbury Rings. SW of Hambledon Hill.

MAIDEN CASTLE   Most famous of all Iron Age earthworks, covering 115 acres above Dorchester. Most of the visible remains were constructed in the first century BC and comprise three lines of ramparts and ditches with cunningly protected entrances. Stormed by Romans in AD 43.

PILSDON PEN   Iron Age earthwork on top of 909 foot hill.

POOLE   Scant remains of medieval town walls in Thames Street, comprising postern, steps to rampart and crenellations of wall.

PORTLAND CASTLE   Fortification of Henry VIII, added to in 17th century, overlooking Portland Harbour. In care of Dept of Environment, hours standard, April to Sept only.

SHERBORNE CASTLES   Ruins of keep, walls, towers and gates of 12th century castle. The new castle was built by Raleigh in 1594 with additions in 1625. Old Castle in care of Dept of Environment, hours standard.

WAREHAM   Earthworks round the town are mostly Norman and Cromwellian, though following line of Saxon *burh*. Best seen on W side. Ramparts originally 55 feet wide and now stand about 17 feet high.

WOODSFORD CASTLE   Mainly 14th century fortified manor house, 2½ miles NE of West Stafford.

DURHAM

BARNARD CASTLE   Castle first built about 1150, present remains date from 14th century mainly, including the cylindrical keep. In care of Dept of Environment, hours standard.

THE CASTLES   Remains of stone walled camp overlooking Bedburn Beck, one mile N of Hamsterley village, built after end of Roman occupation.

HARTLEPOOL   Unique Sandwell Gate, only remnant of medieval town walls.

HYLTON CASTLE   Early 15th century keep-gatehouse guarding ford on the Wear against the Scots. 3¾ miles W of Sunderland. In care of Dept of Environment, hours standard.

LUMLEY CASTLE   Late 14th century castle now belonging to University College. Admission by appointment.

PIERCEBRIDGE   Roman fort covering almost 11 acres guarding Dere Street where it crossed the Tees. Built about 297 to hold 1,000 cavalry.

RABY CASTLE   Castle first built here 1016, appears now as stood in 14th century. One mile N of Staindrop. Admission May to Sept, Wed, Sat and Bank Hols. 2 to 5.

SOUTH SHIELDS   Roman supply base at N end of Baring Street. Built under Hadrian, covering 4½ acres.

ESSEX

AMBRESBURY BANKS   Iron Age earthwork in Epping Forest.

BEACON HILL   Here, and on the beach at St Osyth, are three Martello towers, part of the E. Anglian defence line.

BRADWELL   Roman fort of the Saxon shore, three miles from village via a footpath along sea wall.

CASTLE HEDINGHAM   Keep dating from 1140, standing about 100 feet high and one of most impressive in England. In village of same name. Open May to Sept, Tues, Thurs, Sat, 2 to 6.

COAL HOUSE FORT   Victorian fort at East Tilbury, built 1866.

COLCHESTER   A large Celtic and Belgae centre, remnants of the defences can be seen when leaving by the Lexden Road, namely Grymes Dyke, Half Moon Dyke and Triple Dyke. Of the later Roman walls most remain standing, preserved in the medieval town walls. The Balkerne Gate is the original Roman gate on the road to London. The three surviving bastions on the wall are medieval. Colchester Keep is the largest keep built in Europe and dates from 1085.

GREAT EASTON CASTLE   Remains of motte and bailey castle near church in the village.

HADLEIGH CASTLE   Castle first built 1231 but most of ruins date from mid 14th century. ½ mile S of Hadleigh village. In care of Dept of Environment, hours standard, Sundays 9.30 May to Sept.

PLESHEY   Small village surrounded by earthwork which formed the outer bailey of a 12th century castle. Large moated keep survives on a motte 50 feet high. Admission a.m. only, key at cottage.

RING HILL   Remains of Iron Age hill fort, 1½ miles W of Saffron Walden.

TILBURY FORT   Fortification built about 1670 for defence against Dutch and French raiders.

WALTON-ON-THE-NAZE Along the coast here is a Martello tower, also the Naze Tower, built as a beacon in 1720.

GLOUCESTERSHIRE

BERKELEY CASTLE Mostly 14th century castle, with Norman shell keep. Open April to Sept, 2 to 5.30 daily.

ST BRIAVELS CASTLE Early 12th century castle overlooking Wye Valley, of which only the gatehouse and twin towers survive, remainder of more recent construction. Now used as a Youth Hostel, admission on request.

SUDELEY CASTLE Parts dating from 12th and 15th centuries. Open April to Sept daily, 2 to 5.30.

ULEY BURY Iron Age camp near Uley village, off B4066. Used again during Roman times.

HAMPSHIRE

BEACON HILL Iron Age camp on 858 foot high hill near Burghclere village.

BUCKLAND RINGS Iron Age earthworks with triple ramparts, one mile N of Lymington.

BURY HILL Iron Age camp one mile SW of Andover.

CAESAR'S CAMP Iron Age fortification with double ditch and rampart NE of Crondall village. Reoccupied in Roman times and c. AD 600.

CALSHOTT CASTLE Henry VIII fort two miles SW of Fawley. View from outside only.

CARISBROOKE CASTLE Extensive motte and bailey castle of late 11th century with Norman curtain wall and shell keep. 1¼ miles SW of Newport, Isle of Wight. In care of Dept of Environment, hours standard, Sundays May to Sept 2-5.30.

CHRISTCHURCH CASTLE Rectangular tower keep on Norman motte, dating from c.1160. In gardens of King's Arms Hotel. In care of Dept of Environment, hours standard.

DANEBURY RING Iron Age fort NW of Stockbridge covering 27 acres and with multiple ramparts. Key from Danebury Stables.

GRIM'S DYKE Still formidable defensive work of Saxons extending for almost whole length of the Chilterns and forming more or less the S boundary of Salisbury Plain. Probably divided Saxon villages of the Icknield Way from kingdom of East Saxons.

HURST CASTLE Complex blockhouse built by Henry VIII near Milford on Sea. Added to in 18th and 19th centuries, the latter fortifications being especially impressive. In care of Dept of Environment, open a.m. only.

ODIHAM CASTLE Remains of 13th century octagonal keep, the only one of its kind in the country.

PALMERSTON'S FORTS Series of mid 19th century forts built to defend Portsmouth and Gosport naval bases. Mostly in hands of Armed Services, who may grant permission to view: Fort Widley on Portsdown Hill is property of Portsmouth Corporation, admission on application.

PORTCHESTER Large Roman fortress of late 3rd century with most of walls and bastions still standing. In the NW corner is a Norman castle. In care of Dept of Environment, hours standard, Sundays 9.30 May to Sept.

PORTSMOUTH Portsmouth Round Tower is part of the 14th century fortifications, the square tower being added in the late 15th century. Two gates also survive, dated c.1665; King James' Gate and Landport Gate, both at entrances to recreation grounds of Forces and visible from the street.

QUARLEY HILL Iron Age hill fort on 560 foot height just off edge of Salisbury Plain by village of Quarley.

ST CATHERINE'S HILL Iron Age hill fort, one mile S of Winchester.

SILCHESTER Celtic centre, later used as Roman settlement, with very complete circuit of walls enclosing about 100 acres. Four main gates, two posterns and ramparts in places still 20 feet high.

SOUTHAMPTON Considerable remains of medieval town walls. Of 29 towers and 7 gates, 13 towers and 4 gates have survived, Bargate being the finest. Walls on N and W sides are almost complete.

WINCHESTER Parts of the medieval walls survive, mainly Westgate, King's Gate and stretches of wall between the latter and the Eastgate site. Westgate is the finest part, dating from 13th and 14th centuries.

WINCHESTER HILL Iron Age hill fort on 650 foot height, 2½ miles NW of Corhampton.

WINCKLEBURY CAMP Iron Age earthwork covering about 20 acres, 1½ miles NW of Basingstoke.

WOLVESEY CASTLE Remains of early 12th-century castle, including square keep. In care of Dept of Environment but not yet open to public.

WOOLBURY CAMP Iron Age hill fort covering 20 acres on Stockbridge Down, one mile E of Stockbridge.

YARNMOUTH CASTLE Ruins of fort built by Henry VIII, having first arrow head bastion in England. Situated on W side of Isle of Wight. Cowes and Sandown also have forts of same period, but of different design.

HEREFORDSHIRE

BRIERLEY HILL Iron Age hill fort ½ mile from Wharton.

COXWALL KNOLL Iron Age camp on 400 foot hill, known locally as site of last battle between Caractacus and Romans. N of Brampton.

CROFT CASTLE 14th and 15th century walls and towers with 16th and 17th century alterations. Open April to Sept Wed, Thurs, Sat, Sun, 2.15 to 6. In castle estate, N of the park, is an Iron Age camp covering about 24 acres. Occupied 400 BC to AD 50. Near Leominster.

EWYAS HAROLD CASTLE Motte and earthworks of pre-Conquest Norman castle in Golden Valley.

GARWAY CHURCH Fortified tower belonging to church, standing just across River Monnow from Skenfrith Castle, on Welsh border.

GOODRICH CASTLE 12th century keep with other parts of castle dating from 13th and 14th centuries. Three miles SW of Ross. In care of Dept of Environment, hours standard, Sundays 9.30 May to Sept.

HEREFORD A few remnants of the medieval walls, once possessing 17 towers and 6 gates.

HEREFORDSHIRE BEACON Famous Iron Age hill fort on summit of Malverns on Herefordshire-Worcestershire border, three miles SE of Corwall. There are a series of ditches and ramparts covering 44 acres with a citadel of thick stone walls in the centre. Owen Glendower is said to have rallied his forces here in 1405.

KILPECK CASTLE Ruins of motte and bailey castle of great size. In village of same name.

MIDSUMMER HILL Iron Age hill fort on summits of Midsummer Hill and Hollybush, three miles E of Eastnor village

MUCH MARCLE Iron Age hill fort $1\frac{1}{2}$ miles W of village.

RAVENSBURGH CASTLE Iron Age hill fort covering 22 acres, SW of Barton Hills. Double ditch on W side, entrance at NW corner.

RICHARD'S CASTLE Earthworks of pre-Conquest Norman castle on Vinnall's Hill $3\frac{1}{2}$ miles S of Ludlow on B4361.

SNODHILL CASTLE Remains of 12th century round towers and 14th century bailey on high motte with earthworks covering 10 acres. One mile S of Dorstone.

VOWCHURCH Iron Age hill fort about a mile from the village, later used in Roman times.

HERTFORDSHIRE

BERKHAMSTEAD CASTLE Remains of large motte and bailey castle of the 11th century. Little remains of the round keep. In care of Dept of Environment, standard hours.

ST ALBANS Remains of Roman walls standing to 12 feet can still be seen here, also some of the bastions.

HUNTINGDONSHIRE

EARITH BULWARK Civil War earthworks, including arrow head bastions, in field near Ouse bridge, Earith village.

KENT

CANTERBURY Medieval town walls originally enclosing 100 acres, over half the defences still standing. 17 towers remain, and the fine Westgate of 1380. Of the Norman castle only the keep remains, dating from 11th century. Attempts to slight the keep after the Civil War were thwarted by the solidity of the structure.

CHATHAM In town gardens behind the Town Hall are remains of a fort of the Napoleonic Wars.

DEAL CASTLE Coastal defence fort built in 1530s. In care of Dept of Environment, hours standard, Sundays 9.30 May to Sept.

DOVER Great Norman keep within double curtain walls, one of the largest and most important castles in England. Within the castle is a Roman lighthouse. In care of Dept of Environment, hours standard, Sundays May to Sept, from 10 a.m. to sunset. On the Western Heights are a series of fortifications built in the Napoleonic Wars and Victorian times.

DYMCHURCH Martello tower in care of Dept of Environment, hours standard. Nearby stand two more of these towers.

EYNSFORD CASTLE 12th century castle in care of Dept of Environment, hours standard.

HEVER CASTLE Fortified farmhouse of 13th century, converted into crenellated manor house in 15th century and restored this century without altering the exterior. Three miles SE of Edenbridge. Open April to Sept, Wed, Sun and Bank Hols, 2 to 7.

IGHTHAM MOTE Fine and rare example of moated manor house, built in 14th century. Open April to Oct, Fri 2 to 5, Nov to March, Fri 2 until dusk.

LYMPNE Roman fort of the Saxon shore on edge of Romney Marsh, built 3rd century AD. Near Hythe is a fortified manor house of the 14th century, restored 1905 but retaining original character. Open April to Oct, Wed, Sun and Bank Hols, July to Sept daily except Mon, from 10 to 12.30 and 2.30 to 6. Passing through Lympne is the Hythe to Rye Royal Military Canal, constructed during the Napoleonic Wars.

RICHBOROUGH Roman port and fortifications, scene of first landing in AD 43 and last embarkation of Roman troops from Britain. On Deal road from Canterbury, down a small lane to your left. In care of Dept of Environment, hours standard, Sundays 9.30 May to Sept.

ROCHESTER Great Norman keep c.1130 within bailey walls. NW angle of wall and keep rebuilt 1215 after siege. In care of Dept of Environment, hours standard. Remains of Roman and medieval walls can also be traced, in Corporation Street mainly. Castle probably part of the circuit to SW. Roman walls were repaired at end of 12th century, other parts added in mid 13th century.

SALTWOOD CASTLE Norman castle, rebuilt 1160, 14th century gatehouse, restored in Victorian times. ½ mile N of Hythe. From here the knights rode to assassinate Becket. Open as advertised.

SANDWICH Remains of medieval town defences, most impressive at SE corner. Two gates also survive, Fishergate of 15th and 16th centuries and the Barbican, mid 14th century.

SCOTNEY OLD CASTLE Ruins of moated Tudor manor house, with massive tower built 1378. The new Scotney Castle was built in 1837. One mile SE of Lamberhurst. Open April to Oct, Wed, Sat and Bank Hols, 2 to 6.

SHARE FARM Moated farmhouse with unusual concentric moats, near Horsmonden.

TONBRIDGE CASTLE Ruined Norman castle in centre of town with massive gatehouse and shell keep of early 14th century and bailey walls of 12th century. In care of Tonbridge Council and open all year at normal hours.

UPNOR CASTLE Fortified manor house c.1560, one of number of fortifications to protect Medway against Dutch. Altered later to present pointed bastion to river. In care of Dept of Environment, hours standard.

WALMER CASTLE Henry VIII coastal fort of 16th century, residence of Lords Warden of Cinque Ports. Along beach from Deal. In care of Dept of Environment, hours standard, Sunday 9.30 May to Sept.

LANCASHIRE

BLEABERRY HAWS Iron Age fortification on hill W of Torver, Coniston Water.

LANCASTER CASTLE Large square Norman keep built c.1170. Curtain and gate added by King John. Used for assize courts, open subject to court sessions.

RIBCHESTER Roman fort covering 6 acres, only part on view. Probably had multiple ditches, part of which traced.

TURTON TOWER 12th century peel tower with top storey added in 15th century and east wing in 16th century. 4½ miles N of Bolton. Open all year, Wed and Sat, 2 until dusk.

LEICESTERSHIRE

ASHBY-DE-LA-ZOUCH CASTLE Great tower of 1474 with ruins of 12th century Norman manor house around it. In care of Dept of Environment, hours standard.

BREEDON BULWARKS Iron Age encampment on hill top outside village of Breedon-on-the-Hill.

BURROUGH HILL Iron Age hill fort near Somerby, off A606.

KIRBY MUXLOE CASTLE Moated fortified manor house of late 15th century, four miles W of Leicester. In care of Dept of Environment, standard hours, closed Sundays.

LINCOLNSHIRE

BOLINGBROKE CASTLE Hexagonal shaped castle, probably 13th century, 4 miles W of Spilsbury. In care of Dept of Environment, not yet open.

GREAT CASTERTON Roman fort of 2nd century AD, extended in 4th century. On Grantham road beyond Stamford.

HORNCASTLE Roman fort of 3rd century AD in centre of small town of same name. Walls still visible, part built into Library.

LINCOLN Lincoln began life as a Celtic settlement, occupied by Romans later and the Newport Arch is a Roman gate of 3rd century AD. Traces of medieval walls remain, following old Roman walls. Stonebow Gate dates from 15th century. Lincoln Castle founded 1068 on site of Celtic fort, parts survive. Cobb Hall dates from 14th century.

TATTERSHALL CASTLE Fortified manor house of 1445, on site of 13th century castle, with great quadrangular tower keep in brick. 3½ miles SE of Woodhall Spa. Open all year 9.30 to 7, Sundays 1 to 7 or dusk.

LONDON

Little remains of Roman London but one of the most notable parts of the old defences to survive is the bastion and section of wall in the General Post Office, St Martins le Grand. The West gate of the Roman fort may be seen at the Guildhall Museum between 12 and 2 and sections of the walls may be seen at the Barbican, in the gardens of St Alphage's Church and on the East side of Trinity House Square.

Much of the medieval walls were merely rebuilding of the Roman structure and hardly any medieval work has survived. St Alphage's church gardens contain Roman wall with medieval battlements of 1476, and there is a section of medieval wall parallel to Cooper's Row, including loopholes.

The Tower of London was built in 1078, an inner wall and towers being added in the 13th century, and an outer wall at the end of the 14th century. The complex defences form one of the best examples of a medieval castle in the world.

NORFOLK

BACONSTHORPE CASTLE Moated fortified house of the 15th century, half a mile N of village of same name. In care of Dept of Environment, hours standard.

133

BURGH CASTLE One of a chain of Roman fortresses guarding the East coast against Saxon raiders. Three miles SW of Great Yarmouth. In care of Dept of Environment, hours standard.

CAISTER Remains of small Roman town, part of wall and S gate, $\frac{1}{2}$ mile NW of Caister-on-Sea. In care of Dept of Environment. One mile inland from Caister-on-Sea is Caister Castle, fine example of a 15th century castle. Open May to Oct, daily from 10 to 6.

CASTLE ACRE Of this great castle little remains but the earthworks, though these are excellent. The 13th century N gate to outer bailey survives across the village street. Open any time.

CASTLE RISING Massive keep of mid 12th century with gatehouse of inner ward and outlying earthworks. In care of Dept of Environment, hours standard.

GREAT YARMOUTH Remains of medieval town walls, mostly altered or obscured by modern buildings. However, so much of the walls remain that some is worth seeing, and there are 11 towers of the original 13.

KING'S LYNN Fragments of medieval town walls, East gate an 18th century reconstruction, but South Gate dates from c.1520 and is still used.

NORWICH Twelve towers of medieval town defences survive, of particular interest being the boom towers on the banks of the River Wensum. The great keep of c.1160 is an excellent example of a Norman keep.

THETFORD CASTLE Great motte of a castle demolished in 1173 and once the seat of the early East Anglian kings.

NORTHAMPTONSHIRE

BOROUGH HILL Iron Age camp on 650 foot high hill N of Daventry.

ROCKINGHAM CASTLE Norman castle and royal fortress of early Kings of England, now mainly an Elizabethan house within Norman walls. Eight miles N of Kettering. Open April to Sept on Thurs and Bank Hols, 2 to 6.

NORTHUMBERLAND

ALNHAM Several Iron Age earthworks round a small village.

ALNWICK CASTLE Walls, keep and towers of 14th century castle with fine example of a barbican. Interior altered in 19th century. Open April to Sept daily except Fri and Sat, 1 to 4.30. Of the medieval town walls only fragments remain, notably the Bondgate of c.1450.

AYDON CASTLE Fortified manor house of late 13th century with 14th century curtain wall, two miles NE of Corbridge. In care of Dept of Environment, not yet open to public.

BAMBURGH CASTLE Fine 12th century Norman keep, remainder of castle much restored in later centuries. Open April to Sept daily, 2 until 8.

BEADNELL PEEL TOWER Peel tower of 1460, now part of the Craster Arms, in Beadnell.

BEWCASTLE Roman fort north of Hadrian's Wall, designed to act as an outpost to give warning of an attack in terrain advantageous to surprise assaults. North of Birdoswald.

BYWELL CASTLE Good example of 15th century tower house in village of same name.

CALLALY CASTLE 15th century peel tower incorporated in a later manor house. Two miles from Whittingham. Open weekends and Bank Hols. only.

CHESTERHOLM Roman garrison fort for Hadrian's Wall, founded by Agricola and covering $3\frac{1}{2}$ acres. South of the wall, near Bardon Mill.

CHESTERS Fine example of a Roman fort on Hadrian's Wall, covering $5\frac{3}{4}$ acres and housing a garrison of 500 cavalry. Close by Chollerford. In care of Dept of Environment, hours standard.

CHEW GREEN Two Roman forts in Cheviot Hills on the Dere Street leading into Scotland. Four miles NE of Byrness, Redesdale. A mile N on Brownhart Law was a signal station, 1,664 feet up.

CORBRIDGE Cavalry fort for Hadrian's Wall, originally built AD 79. Enlarged to take 500 cavalry and 1,000 infantry, abandoned c. AD 120. Reconstructed c. AD 203 and became supply base for wall. In care of Dept of Environment, hours standard, Sundays 9.30 May to Sept.

DODDINGTON Ruined peel tower built 1584, now enclosed in farmyard.

DOD LAW Two Iron Age forts on 654 foot height S of Doddington.

DUNSTANBURGH CASTLE Early 14th century castle, strengthened later in same century. N of village of Craster, on high cliffs above the sea. In care of Dept of the Environment, hours standard.

EMBLETON Peel tower dated c.1415, incorporated in vicarage, typical Northumberland tower of the period.

FARNE ISLANDS Peel tower c.1500 now HQ of bird observatory. By boat from Bamburgh.

FEATHERSTONE CASTLE 14th century peel tower with Jacobean mansion added. Now part of a holiday centre for young people. Situated three miles N of Haltwhistle, where another peel tower is incorporated into the Red Lion.

HADRIAN'S WALL Built AD 121–126, runs from Wallsend to Bowness in Cumberland, a distance of $73\frac{1}{2}$ miles. Forts on or close to the wall include Birdoswald, Chesters and Housesteads.

HOUSESTEADS Roman fort on Hadrian's Wall, N. of Chesterholm. In care of Dept of Environment, hours standard, Sundays 9.30 May to Sept.

HUMBLETON HILL   Iron Age fortifications on hill one mile from Wooler.
KETTLE'S CAMP   Iron Age camp 2½ miles from Wooler.
LANGLEY CASTLE   Good example of 14th century tower house, restored 1900 and now a girls' school. 1½ miles SW of Haydon Bridge.
LORDENSHAW'S CAMP   Iron Age fort and beacon site on 1,000 foot high hill overlooking Chillingham.
MAINS RIGG   Roman signal tower north of Hadrian's Wall, linking the Stanegate forts of Throp and Nether Denton.
NEWCASTLE   Remains of 13th century town defences, including eight towers. Of the Norman castle built c.1172 the keep and Black Gate survive, now housing museums. Open weekdays 10 to 5, 2 until 5 on Mondays, during summer only.
NORHAM CASTLE   Border castle with ruins of Norman keep. built c.1160 and altered in succeeding centuries. On Tweed eight miles W of Berwick.
PIKE HILL   Roman signal tower near Nether Denton fort on Hadrian's Wall.
PRUDHOE CASTLE   Extensive remains of castle first built c.1150, curtain wall added late 12th century, strengthened 13th century, barbican added in 14th century. Keep ruined by Parliamentarian bombardment. Half mile NW of Prudhoe village.
ROBIN HOOD'S BUTT   Roman signal station near summit of Gillalees Beacon flanking the Roman road from Birdoswald to Bewcastle.
ROWTING LINN   Iron Age earthwork 3½ miles N of Doddington.
TYNEMOUTH PRIORY   Curtain wall, towers and gatehouse-keep of 14th century, constructed for defence of Priory. In care of Dept of Environment, hours standard, Sundays 9.30 May to Sept.
WARKWORTH   North gate and bridge of 14th century town defences, most of rest of town protected by loop of River Coquet and the castle. Of the latter the earliest remains are of the 12th century, but keep and most of other defences date from late 14th, early 15th centuries. In care of Dept of Environment, hours standard, Sundays 9.30 May to Sept.
WHITTINGHAM   15th century peel tower.
WHITTON   Peel tower, now a children s home, just across river from Rothbury. At nearby Tosson and Hepple are other peel towers.

NOTTINGHAMSHIRE

NEWARK   Ruins of castle dating from 12th century, of which only North gate and SW tower survive. East of the Devon River is the Queen's Sconce, part of the siege works erected during the Civil War.

OXFORDSHIRE

DYKE HILLS   Remains of Iron Age earthworks enclosing 114 acres, near Dorchester.
OXFORD   Of the medieval town defences five half round, open-backed towers and parts of the crenellated wall survive in New College garden and at the NE angle of the town.

SHROPSHIRE

ABDON   Three Iron Age hill forts at Abdon Burf, Clee Burf and Nordy Bank, eight miles NE of Ludlow.
ACTON BURNELL   Fortified manor house of late 13th century at E end of village, open any time. In care of Dept of Environment.
CAER CARADOC   Iron Age Celtic hill fort on Caradoc range near Cardington, supposed site of Caractacus' last stand against the Romans.
LUDLOW CASTLE   Remains of large Norman castle, first built here 1085 on site of earlier Saxon fortifications.
MORETON CORBET CASTLE   Early 13th century keep and shell of Elizabethan mansion. In care of Dept of Environment, hours standard.
OLD OSWESTRY   Iron Age fort of great strength, abandoned c. AD 250. N of the town on 540 foot height.
SHREWSBURY   Castle dating mostly from 12th century with 13th century additions. Normally open at usual hours, but subject to use by courts. Of the medieval defences a tower remains near English Bridge and part of the walls may be seen within the Library building at Riggs Hall.
STOKESAY CASTLE   Finest example of a 13th century fortified manor house in Britain, gatehouse added in 16th century. ¾ mile S of Craven Arms on Shrewsbury–Ludlow road. Open daily all year, summer 9 to 6, winter 9 to dusk.
TITTERSTONE CLEE HILL   Iron Age camp covering about 70 acres on flat summit of 1,749 foot high hill. Basalt blocks used in rampart construction.
WAT'S DYKE   Probably an earlier version of Offa's Dyke, running about three miles E of Offa's Dyke and in a few places equalling or surpassing that dyke in size.

SOMERSET

BATH   Of the medieval town walls, originally enclosing 23 acres, only the East Gate has survived.
BRENT KNOLL   Iron Age fort on 457 foot high hill, later used by Romans and Anglo-Saxons.

CADBURY CASTLE Stone Age and Iron Age hill fort, later used by Romans, Britons during 5th and 6th centuries, and Anglo-Saxons about 1010. Supposed site of Arthur's Camelot, traces of timber hall of late 5th century discovered. Approach up a lane from South Cadbury. Excavation taking place usually in July and August, when a guide will show you round.

CADBURY HILL Iron Age earthworks, reoccupied later. East of Yatton.

CASTLE NEROCHE Impressive Norman earthworks 900 feet up on Blackdown Hills.

DOLEBURY Iron Age hill fort on W edge of Mendips with stone-faced ramparts.

DUNSTER Castle mainly dating from 16th century on but founded in 1070 and continually inhabited since. Open June, Wed and Thurs, July to Sept Tues, Wed, Thurs, 10.15 to 12.40 and 2.15 to 4.40. In Dunster Park are Gallox Hill and Bat's Castle, two Iron Age forts.

FARLEIGH CASTLE Castle of the late 14th century in Farleigh Hungerford. In care of Dept of Environment, hours standard.

GLASTONBURY Centre of lake villages with examples scattered all round. There is little to see for the layman, but in the town's court house is a museum specializing in finds from these sites.

LYNG Remains of Saxon *burh*, originally a bank and ditch across the landward side of a spit of land projecting into marshes. St Bartholomew's Church stands on the line, which is clearly marked by a dip in the road.

MEARE Little trace of the lake village which occupied the marshy lake here, although finds from the site are on show in the Taunton Museum.

NUNNEY CASTLE 14th century castle of unusual design. In care of Dept of Environment, hours standard.

STOKE SUB HAMDON Remains of hill fort, possibly Iron Age, later used by Britons.

WORLEBURY Iron Age fort with stone-faced ramparts at N end of Weston-super-Mare. Finds in town museum.

STAFFORDSHIRE

CASTLE RING Iron Age camp covering some 18 acres NE of Cannock.

KINVER EDGE Iron Age hill fort on promontory at N edge of Kinver Edge, overlooking town of Kinver.

TAMWORTH CASTLE Norman keep with Tudor and Jacobean additions on motte built on site of a Saxon fortification. Open March to Oct, weekdays 10 until 8 or one hour before sunset, Sundays 2 until 8. Nov to Feb, daily except Fri, 10 to 4, Sundays 2 to 4.

TUTBURY CASTLE Remains of castle on isolated rock, successor to a series of fortifications going back to the Iron Age. 14th century gatehouse survives and the S tower, where Mary Queen of Scots was held for many years.

SUFFOLK

DEVIL'S DITCH 7 miles of earthwork between Reach and Ditton Green on Cambridgeshire border, probably erected by Saxons as boundary between East Anglia and Mercia. Best part is on Newmarket Heath.

FELIXSTOWE Martello tower S of the Beach Station.

FRAMLINGHAM CASTLE Fortified manor house developed into a castle in early 13th century. In care of Dept of Environment, hours standard, Sundays 9.30 May to Sept.

HOLLESLEY Martello tower, one of the string of east coast towers built between 1810 and 1812. Others may be seen along this stretch of coast between Slaughden and Lowestoft.

LANDGUARD FORT 16th century fort built to guard the entrance to Harwich Harbour, rebuilt during 17th and 18th centuries.

ORFORD CASTLE Only the cylindrical keep remains from the late 12th century castle built here, but is well worth a visit, being of unique design and 90 feet high. Half mile NW of Orford Quay. In care of Dept of Environment, hours standard, Sundays 9.30 May to Sept.

SURREY

ANSTIEBURY Iron Age hill fort NE of Leith Hill, traditionally said to have been built in the time of the Saxons and the scene of a great Saxon victory over the Danes in 851. Private land, but access by footpaths.

FARNHAM CASTLE Motte and bailey castle with impressive shell keep. Most of castle dates from 15th to 17th centuries. Keep open daily at standard hours, in care of Dept of Environment, but remainder a training college and only open on certain days.

GUILDFORD CASTLE Norman keep built on site of earlier Saxon fortifications, part of which may be seen in corner of the gardens round the keep.

SUSSEX

BODIAM CASTLE Castle built 1385, slighted during Civil War but restored this century and exterior has appearance of the original. Three miles S of Hawkhurst. Open all year, weekdays 10 to 7, Sundays the same but April to Sept only.

CHANCTONBURY RINGS Iron Age camp on highest point in area, near village of Washington. Later used by Saxons.

CHICHESTER Remains of the Roman and medieval town walls, standing up to 20 feet high except on W side. Bastions are Roman as is much of the wall but due to repairs through the centuries it is no longer possible to tell where Roman ends and medieval begins.

CISSBURY RINGS Iron Age hill fort between Worthing and Findon, occupied 5th century BC to 1st century AD and later by the Romans. Covers 60 acres, excavation from time to time.

EASTBOURNE By the Lifeboat Museum is The Wish Tower, a Martello tower, and further along the front, travelling E, is The Redoubt, a fort of the Napoleonic Wars period. Both open at normal hours, April to Sept.

HERSTMONCEUX CASTLE Moated castle built of brick in 1440, twice restored but the exterior little changed. Interior not open to public except by prior application to Royal Observatory.

HIGHDOWN HILL Iron Age hill fort three miles NW of Worthing.

LEWES CASTLE Norman shell keep on motte and remains of Norman gatehouse, with fine 14th century barbican. Open normal hours all year on weekdays, except for interior of barbican.

MOUNT CABURN Small but very strong Iron Age hill fort on Downs directly E of Lewes. Name comes from the Celtic *Caer Bryn*, hill fort.

PEVENSEY CASTLE Roman fort of the Saxon shore with extensive remains of gates, walls and many bastions. Open at all times. At the E end a Norman keep was built in the 11th century, curtain walls and towers being added in the 13th century. In care of Dept of Environment, hours standard. Various alterations and additions were made to the defences during the Civil War, the Napoleonic Wars and World War 2. Many parts of the defences of the latter period survive.

RYE Few remains of medieval town defences, the Landgate being the major object of interest. Also Ypres Tower, built in 13th century as the town fort, now used as museum. Below this tower is Gun Garden, once a gun battery.

THE TRUNDLE Stone and Iron Age hill fort on South Downs overlooking Goodwood race course, covering 12 acres.

WINCHELSEA Medieval town defences, parts of rampart and ditch, but mainly three gates, Strand, New and Landgate. First two date from 13th century, the latter from early 15th century.

WARWICKSHIRE

BAGINTON Roman fort overlooking the River Sowe, at present being excavated. Also in the village are the ruins of a 14th century castle.

COVENTRY Of the medieval town defences two gates, Cook Street and Priory Gates, and several towers survive.

KENILWORTH CASTLE Large and impressive castle, earliest parts dating from mid 12th century. Slighted in 1649. In care of Dept of Environment, standard hours, Sundays 9.30 May to Sept.

WARWICK CASTLE Originally a motte and bailey castle, earliest parts to survive date from 13th century. Conducted tours only, open all year, weekdays April to Oct, 10 to 5.30, Oct to March 10.30 to 4.

WESTMORLAND

ARTHUR'S ROUND TABLE Iron Age earthwork, one mile S of Penrith.

ASKHAM HALL 14th century fortified tower in village of same name.

BROUGH CASTLE Remains of keep of c.1170 and curtain and tower of early 13th century, within earthworks of a Roman fort. Off main road to Barnard Castle. In care of Dept of Environment, hours standard.

BROUGHHAM CASTLE Norman keep of c.1170 within Roman fort on S bank of River Eamont 1½ miles E of Penrith. In care of Dept of Environment, hours standard.

GALAVA FORT Roman fort built on site of an earlier one *c* .AD 79. In Borrans Park, Ambleside.

MAXSTOKE CASTLE Castle built 1345, restored 1440 and modern times, with polygonal towers and curtain wall.

MAYBURGH Iron Age earthwork covering an area 300 feet across with rampart of earth and stone. One mile S of Penrith.

SIZERGH CASTLE Peel tower built 1340 and added to during 15th, 16th and 18th centuries. Open April to Sept, Wed only, 2 to 5.45. Three miles S of Kendal.

WILTSHIRE

BARBURY CAMP Iron Age hill fort covering 12 acres along ancient Ridgeway track over the Downs between Swindon and Marlborough.

BATTLESBURY Iron Age hill fort with great ramparts, near Warminster.

BRATTON CASTLE Large Iron Age camp, one mile SW of Bratton.

CASTERLEY CAMP Iron Age assembly camp covering over 5 acres, reoccupied in 1st century AD. SW of Upavon, on Salisbury Plain.

CHISBURY CAMP Iron Age camp covering 15 acres, 576 feet up, SW of Great Bedwyn.

FIGSBURY RING Large and strong Iron Age assembly camp on ridge overlooking Bourne Valley and enclosing about 15 acres. Four miles NE of Salisbury.

LIDDINGTON CASTLE Iron Age earthwork with rampart 40 feet high, one mile to S of village of same name.

LUDGERSHALL CASTLE   Norman castle of motte and bailey plan, in ruins but worth visiting. Open any time, in care of Dept of Environment.

OGBURY CAMP   Iron Age assembly camp near Durnford.

OLDBURY CAMP   Iron Age camp S of Calne. On private land but access by footpaths.

OLD SARUM   Extensive earthworks of 11th century on site of Iron Age and Saxon fortifications. Also few remains of later castle. Small museum on the site. In care of Dept of Environment, hours standard, Sundays 9.30 May to Sept.

OLD WARDOUR CASTLE   Hexagonal fortified manor house built 1392, altered at end of 16th century. In Wardour Park. In care of Dept of Environment, hours standard.

WANSDYKE   British fortification of the late 5th, early 6th centuries, constructed to keep out the Saxons. Runs from Portishead on the Bristol Channel to Salisbury Plain and on to Berkshire.

WHITE SHEET HILL   Iron Age hill fort N of Mere, on ancient track known as The Hardway.

WICK CAMP   Iron Age hill fort in Dinton Park. Prior application to YWCA.

WINDMILL HILL   Stone Age and later earthwork of three concentric lines, built c.2500 BC originally. 1½ miles NW of Avebury.

WINKLEBURY CAMP   Iron Age earthwork with 40 foot rampart near Berwick St John and Dorset border.

YARNBURY CASTLE   Iron Age hill fort with triple ditches and complex entrances, on the Downs above Chitterne.

WORCESTERSHIRE

BREDON HILL   Iron Age camp covering 11 acres built last century BC. Near village of Bredon.

DUDLEY CASTLE   Norman castle with barbican, drum towers and curtain of 14th century, now in ruins.

WYCHBURY HILL CAMP   Iron Age earthwork one mile NE of Hagley Hall, near Kidderminster.

YORKSHIRE

ALMONDBURY   Important hill fort of the Brigantes, converted into a castle during reign of Stephen. S of Huddersfield.

BEDALE   14th century church tower, fortified against Scots raiders.

BEVERLEY   Of the medieval town defences only the North Bar survives, built 1409.

BOWES CASTLE   Large keep of c.1187 with a Roman fort. Four miles W of Barnard Castle. In care of Dept of Environment, open normal hours.

CASTLE DYKES   Small Roman fort, south of the wall, using lay of the land extensively. Three miles N of Ripon.

CAWTHORN CAMPS   Four Roman practice camps, probably built by the IX Legion from York. Four miles N of Pickering.

CONISBROUGH CASTLE   Circular keep of 1185 with curtain wall and solid towers of a later date. In care of Dept of Environment, hours standard.

DANES' DYKE   Double line of entrenchments isolating the cape of Flamborough Head, constructed by either the Saxons or Danes c.950.

GOLDSBOROUGH   Roman signal station of late 4th century. 4½ miles NW of Whitby off A174.

HELMSLEY CASTLE   Keep, curtain wall and towers of late 12th century with earthworks. In care of Dept of Environment, hours standard.

INGLEBOROUGH   Stronghold of the Brigantes, built with stone blocks c.300 BC and occupied until AD 100. Three miles NE of Ingleton.

KNARESBOROUGH CASTLE   Norman castle, rebuilt 1310–1340, with 14th century gatehouse. Slighted during Civil War.

MALTON   Roman fort built AD 79 of turf, later replaced by stone. NE of York on A64.

MARKENFIELD HALL   Fine example of fortified manor house, built 1310 with 16th century gatehouse. Three miles S of Ripon. Open May to Sept on Mon, 10 to 12.30 and 2.15 to 5.

MIDDLEHAM CASTLE   Good keep of c.1170 within defences of 13th century and with 14th century gatehouse. Dismantled in Civil War but keep remains to almost full height. Two miles S of Leyburn. In care of Dept of Environment, hours standard.

PICKERING CASTLE   Remains of late 11th, early 12th century castle with shell keep on a motte. Curtain wall and towers mostly 14th century. In care of Dept of Environment, hours standard.

PONTEFRACT CASTLE   Ruins of late 12th century keep, slighted at end of Civil War.

RICHMOND CASTLE   Castle with earliest parts dating from 1071, the keep being of special interest. Overlooking Swaledale. In care of Dept of Environment, hours standard, Sundays 9.30 May to Sept.

SCARBOROUGH CASTLE   Remains of 12th century castle, dominating town. The square keep dates from 1160, curtain wall from c.1130. An Iron Age camp once occupied the site and a Roman signal station is enclosed by the castle walls. In care of Dept of Environment, hours standard, Sundays 9.30 May to Sept.

SHERIFF HUTTON CASTLE   Ruined castle of 14th century, replacing earlier one of 12th century, and important centre during Wars of the Roses.

SKIPSEA CASTLE   Earthworks of a typical Norman motte and bailey castle, demolished *c.*1220. Five miles N of Hornsea. In care of Dept of Environment, but open any time.

SKIPTON CASTLE   Gate of early castle survives, but remainder dates from 14th century. Open all year, weekdays 10 to sunset, Sundays 2 until sunset.

STANWICK   Huge earthworks of the Brigantes covering 850 acres with an inner citadel of 17 acres. Built *c* AD 69–72 and scene of last stand against Romans. Ramparts still almost continuous, ditch originally 40 feet wide and 16 feet deep, cut in rock. In care of Dept of Environment but open any time. 6½ miles N of Richmond, near Forcett.

TEMPLEBOROUGH   Remains of Roman fort, 1½ miles SW of Rotherham. Finds in museum at Clifton House, Clifton Park.

TICKHILL CASTLE   Remains of 12th to 15th century castle, including curtain wall, gatehouse and 75 foot high motte.

WINCOBANK   Iron Age hill fort covering 2½ acres, occupied 1st century BC to 1st century AD. 2½ miles NE of Sheffield.

YORK   Of the Roman fortress here only a multangular tower remains, though this is one of the finest Roman buildings in Britain. It may be seen in the Museum Gardens. The medieval town walls have been much rebuilt over the centuries but mainly date from the 13th century. Four gates have survived. Clifford's Tower is a 13th century keep built on the motte erected by William the Conqueror *c.*1068. This last item is in care of Dept of Environment, hours standard, Sundays 9.30 May to Sept.

2: Scotland

ABERDEENSHIRE

CASTLE OF DUNIDEER   Ruins of 13th century castle within ramparts of a vitrified Iron Age hill fort.

CORGARFF CASTLE   16th century tower house, converted into a garrison post in 1748 and enclosed within a star fort. Half mile SW of Cockbridge on A939. View of exterior only.

GLENBUCHAT CASTLE   Z plan tower house of 1590, 14 miles W of Alford. In care of Dept of Environment, view of exterior only at time of going to press.

HUNTLEY CASTLE   Ruins of 15th century castle on site of Norman castle. On E side is a ravelin, probably dating from Civil War. In care of Dept of Environment, hours standard.

KILDRUMMY CASTLE   Most complete example of a 13th century Scottish castle. In care of Dept of Environment, open at all times.

MITHER TAP   Iron Age hill fort on 1,698 foot high summit of Bennachie, SSE of Oyne.

PEEL RING OF LUMPHANAN   Major earthwork with small amount of stone work on summit, dating from 11th century. Half mile SW of Lumphanan.

TOLQUHON CASTLE   Rectangular tower house with 16th century mansion added, noted for its gatehouse and gunloops. In care of Dept of Environment, hours standard. Three miles from Pitmedden, N. of Aberdeen.

ANGUS

AFLECK CASTLE   Late 15th century tower house of L plan type, at Monikie. In care of Dept of Environment, admission at any reasonable hour on application to custodian.

BRECHIN   One of the two round towers in Scotland, dating from *c.*1000 and now attached to a 13th century cathedral. Spire added 14th century. May be viewed from churchyard.

BROUGHTY CASTLE   16th century dwelling with battlemented top in Broughty Ferry. In care of Dept of Environment, weekdays except Fri 11 to 1 and 2 to 5, Sundays 2 to 5 only.

CATERHUNS   Brown: Iron Age hill fort with four concentric ramparts and ditches, near Menmuir village, open at all times. White: Iron Age hill fort with massive stone ramparts and ditches, the ramparts reinforced at intervals with horizontal and vertical timber lacing which indicates 9th century BC. Also near Menmuir village, open all times.

CLAYPOTTS   Late 16th century tower house, fine example of the Z plan. 3½ miles E of Dundee. In care of Dept of Environment, hours standard.

EDZELL CASTLE   Early 16th century tower house with mansion added later in same century. One mile W of Edzell. In care of Dept of Environment, hours standard.

ARGYLL

CASTLE SWEEN   Earliest stone castle in Scotland, probably mid 12th century. Destroyed 1647. In care of Dept of Environment but open at any time. On E shore of Loch Sween.

DUNADD FORT   Well preserved hill fort identified as capital of Dalriada, the kingdom of the Scots in the Dark Ages.

DUNSTAFFNAGE CASTLE   13th century castle in good condition on S shore of Loch Etive. View from outside only.

KILCHURN CASTLE   Tall square tower of the mid 15th century with outer defences added in 17th century to form a castle. Two miles W of Dalmally, view from outside only.

AYRSHIRE

DUNDONALD CASTLE   Large tower house of late 14th century, built on to remains of 13th century gatehouse. Off A759 to Troon. In care of Dept of Environment, not yet open to public.

LOCH DOON CASTLE Unusual castle having eleven sides, built late 13th, early 14th centuries. On the shore of Loch Doon, having been 'transplanted' from the centre of the Loch some years ago because of a rising water level. In care of Dept of Environment, but open at all times.

BANFFSHIRE

AUCHINDOUN CASTLE Massive ruin on isolated hill, enclosed by Iron Age earthwork. Central tower was built in the 15th century, other buildings in 16th century. In care of Dept of Environment but not yet open. Two miles from Dufftown.

BALVENIE CASTLE Earliest parts date from early 14th century but most of the existing castle dates from the 15th-16th centuries. In Dufftown. In care of Dept of Enviromnent, hours standard.

BERWICKSHIRE

BERWICK Of the castle built here in the 12th century only the W wall and three towers remain. The medieval town walls of the 14th century were mostly destroyed by the construction of artillery defences in the 16th century, but the NW wall and Bell Tower survive from these earlier defences. Of the Elizabethan artillery defences Cowport gate and three arrow head bastions still exist. In the late 18th century the walls along the river were rebuilt once more with gun emplacements to overlook the river mouth. The guns were removed for scrap in World War 2.

EDINSHALL BROCH One of 10 known brochs in the Lowlands, this one is very large and was originally defended by a series of outworks. Situated on the NE slope of Cockburn Law, 4 miles from Grantshouse. Open all times.

GREENKNOWE TOWER L plan tower house of 1581, $\frac{1}{2}$ mile W of Gordon on A6105. In care of Dept of Environment, open at all reasonable hours.

BUTESHIRE

BRODICK CASTLE Part of the present castle dates from the 14th century, the remainder from 1652 and 1844. Open May to Sept daily 1 to 5 except Sundays. In Brodick, Isle of Arran.

LOCHRANZA CASTLE Remains of 16th century castle, first recorded in 14th century. In care of Dept of Environment, admission by application to Post Office, Lochranza, Isle of Arran.

ROTHESAY CASTLE Fine example of 13th century castle, plan being unique in Scotland. Curtain walls reach a height of 30 feet. In care of Dept of Environment, hours standard. In Rothesay centre, Island of Bute.

DUMFRIESSHIRE

BIRRENSWARK HILL Roman fortifications apparently encircling an Iron Age hill fort, clearly marked on S side. Two miles N of Ecclefechan, Annandale.

CAERLAVEROCK CASTLE Remarkable triangular castle of the 13th and 15th centuries, famous for the siege by Edward I. 7 miles SSE of Dumfries. In care of Dept of Environment, hours standard.

EAST LOTHIAN

THE CHESTERS Good example of Iron Age hill fort with multiple ramparts, one mile S of Drem.

DIRLETON CASTLE Rare example of a 'clustered' donjon, a group of 13th century towers, within later works from 14th century onwards. Besieged by Edward I in 1298. In care of Dept of Environment, hours standard.

NORTH BERWICK LAW Ruins of Napoleonic Wars watch tower on summit N of Berwick.

TANTALLON CASTLE Famous castle of the Douglases in magnificent position, with great frontal curtain wall flanked by towers and with a central gatehouse, all 14th century. Earthworks before the castle date from 1526 and Civil War period, erected as defence against cannon. In care of Dept of Environment, hours standard. Three miles E of North Berwick.

FIFE

ABERDOUR CASTLE Ruins of 14th century tower and later buildings overlooking Aberdour harbour. In care of Dept of Environment, hours standard.

FALKLAND PALACE Hunting lodge of Stuarts in Lomond Hills, built 1542 to replace earlier castle. Front pierced with gunloops and iron grilles on windows. Open April to Oct, weekdays 10 to 6, Sundays 2 to 6.

RAVENSCRAIG CASTLE Built 1460 and probably the first British castle to be built for defence by firearms. On coast at N end of Kirkcaldy. In care of Dept of Environment. Work in progress, open during these hours.

SCOTSTARVIT TOWER Five storey turretted tower house of c.1579, two miles S of Cupar, off the A916. In care of Dept of Environment, open all reasonable hours.

INVERNESS-SHIRE

FORT GEORGE Best example of an 18th century fort in Western Europe. Begun 1748 as

result of Jacobite rebellion, survives almost unaltered. Houses museum of Queen's Own Highlanders. 6½ miles W of Nairn. In care of Dept of Environment, hours standard.
GLENELG BROCHS Two brochs, Dun Telve and Dun Troddan, now ruined but still standing up to 30 feet high in places. 1½ miles SE of Glenelg.
INVERLOCHY CASTLE Good example of 13th century castle with largest tower forming the keep. In care of Dept of Environment but not yet open to public. View from outside only. 1½ miles NE of Fort William.
KISIMUL CASTLE 15th century castle of the Macneils of Barra, now largely restored. In Castlebay, Island of Barra. Open May to Sept on Sat, 3 to 6. Apply Post Office, Castlebay for boat.
RUTHVEN BARRACKS Built 1719 and designed to hold a company of infantry. Captured and burnt 1746. ¾ mile SE of Kingussie, off B970.
URQUHART CASTLE Began as a motte and bailey castle but most of building now dates from after 1509. Blown up after Jacobite rising of 1689. On W shore of Loch Ness. In care of Dept of Environment, hours standard.

KINROSS-SHIRE

BURLEIGH CASTLE Tower house of c.1500 with curtain wall. ½ mile E of Milnathort on A911. Open all reasonable hours, keyholder at farm opposite. In care of Dept of Environment.
LOCH LEVEN CASTLE Oblong tower of late 14th, early 15th century, with 16th century curtain wall. At one angle is a projecting tower with gunloops. On island in Loch Leven, ferry run by Kinross Council. Open daily in summer 10 to 6, Sundays 2 to 6.

KIRKCUDBRIGHTSHIRE

BORGUE CASTLE Remains of a great Iron Age fort, built amongst the rocks above the shore, three miles W of village of same name.
CARDONESS CASTLE Well preserved 15th century tower house, one mile SW of Gatehouse of Fleet on A75. In care of Dept of Environment, hours standard.
CARLSUITH CASTLE 16th century tower house with L plan, three miles SSE of Creetown on A75. In care of Dept of Environment, open all reasonable hours.
DRUMCOLTRAN TOWER Mid 16th century tower house, 4½ miles NE of Dalbeattie amongst farm buildings. In care of Dept of Environment, open all hours.
MOTE OF URR 12 century earthwork 500 feet long and 80 feet high, two miles NW of Dalbeattie.
ORCHARDTON TOWER Unique cylindrical tower house of mid 15th century at Old Orchardton. In care of Dept of Environment, open all reasonable hours.
THREAVE CASTLE Late 14th century tower with outer wall of 1513 with flanking towers and loops for firearms. On Threave Island in River Dee. In care of Dept of Environment, open April to Sept standard hours but closed Thur.

LANARKSHIRE

BOTHWELL CASTLE 13th century castle with cylindrical keep sited on a steep bank overlooking the Clyde. At Uddingston, in care of Dept of Environment, hours standard.
CRAIGNETHAN CASTLE Early 16th century tower house, 4½ miles WNW of Lanark. In care of Dept of Environment, hours standard.
COULTER MOTTE HILL Example of early motte, originally moated. By Coulter railway station, open at all times.
CROOKSTON CASTLE Remains of early 15th century tower within earthwork. One mile SE of Crookston. In care of Dept of Environment, hours standard.

MIDLOTHIAN

CASTLE LAW FORT Small Iron Age hill fort on summit of Castle Knowe, W of A702 and one mile NW of Glencorse. Prior permission needed from Dept of Environment, Argyle House, 3 Lady Lawson Street, Edinburgh.
CRAIGMILLAR CASTLE 14th century tower enclosed by 15th century curtain wall, 2½ miles SE of Edinburgh centre. In care of Dept of Environment, hours standard.
CRICHTON CASTLE 14th century tower house with later additions on lofty site overlooking Tyne 2¼ miles SSW of Pathhead. In care of Dept of Environment, hours standard but closed Fri, Oct to May.
EDINBURGH CASTLE Most famous of all Scottish castles, the bulk of the building dates from the 17th and 18th centuries. Half Moon Battery encloses the remains of the Great Tower, destroyed by cannon in 1573. In care of Dept of Environment, hours June to Sept 9.30 until 6, Sunday 11 to 6. Winter hours are generally shorter.

MORAY

BURGHEAD Iron Age hill fort where the Celtic timber and earth method of building ramparts has been employed.
DUFFUS CASTLE Finest example of motte and bailey castle in Scotland. The great tower and curtain wall were built c.1300. Three miles NW of Elgin, open at any hour.

NAIRNSHIRE

ARDCLACH BELL TOWER   Square tower of two storeys built 1655 and equipped with square gunloops. S of Nairn off A939. Open all reasonable hours.

ORKNEY

COBBIE'S ROW CASTLE   Probably the earliest Scottish castle, c.1145, consisting of a small rectangular tower enclosed by a ditch. Isle of Wyre. In care of Dept of Environment, open at all times.
GURNESS BROCH   Broch now ruined but still surrounded by secondary buildings and deep rock-cut ditch. On coast at Aikerness, near Evie. In care of Dept of Environment, hours standard.
MIDHOWE BROCH   Broch and walled courtyard on promontory on W coast of Rousay. In care of Dept of Environment, open all reasonable hours.
NOLTLAND CASTLE   Ruin of Z plan tower house built mid 16th century with tiers of gunloops. Half mile WNW of Pierowall, Isle of Westray. In care of Dept of Environment, open all reasonable hours.

PERTHSHIRE

ABERNETHY   One of two remaining Irish type round towers in Scotland, dating from end of 11th century. In care of Dept of Environment, open all reasonable hours.
DOUNE CASTLE   One of the best preserved medieval castles in Scotland, built in 14th century but much restored in 1883. Open daily 10 to 1, 2 to 6. Closed Thur and all Dec.
ELCHO CASTLE   16th century fortified manor house well equipped for defence by firearms. On S bank of Tay, 3½ miles SE of Perth. In care of Dept of Environment, hours standard.

RENFREWSHIRE

NEWARK CASTLE   16th and 17th century turretted manor house incorporating an earlier tower house. Port Glasgow. In care of Dept of Environment, hours standard.
WHITE MOSS   Roman fort at W end of Antonine Wall, guarding the exposed flank. S side of Clyde Estuary, Bishopton.

ROSS AND CROMARTY

CARLOWAY   Most perfect Iron Age broch in Scotland, SW of village on Lewis. Still standing to height of 30 feet, one side being broken down and giving a good view of the plan within the hollow walls.
KNOCKFARRILL   Remains of Iron Age vitrified fort, 720 feet up on narrow ridge known as the Cat's Back, 1¼ miles E of Strathpeffer.

ROXBURGHSHIRE

HERMITAGE CASTLE   Vast ruin with earliest parts dating from 14th century but much restoration in 19th century. NE of Newcastleton. In care of Dept of Environment, hours standard.
NEWSTEAD   Roman fort built by Agricola and later extended to cover some 50 acres. Strongest fort in the Lowlands. Near Melrose.
SMAILHOLM TOWER   15th century square tower, 6 miles from Kelso. Entry at any reasonable time, apply keyholder at nearby Sandyknowes Farm.
WODEN LAW   Roman earthwork on site of older camp on 1,388 foot height of this name, 4½ miles S of Hownam.

SHETLAND

CLICKHIMIN FORT   Late Bronze Age hill fort fortified c.500–300 BC with stone ramparts and 'blockhouse'. Occupied until c. AD 700. ¾ mile SW of Lerwick. In care of Dept of Environment, open all reasonable hours.
FORT CHARLOTTE   Pentagonal fort with projecting bastions begun 1665 to protect Sound of Bressay. Overlooking Lerwick Harbour, open at all times.
JARLSHOF   Stone, Bronze and Iron Age settlement inhabited for over 3,000 years. Iron Age broch of fine condition and also wheelhouses. On Sumburgh Head, S of Lerwick. In care of Dept of Environment, hours standard.
MOUSA   Best example of an Iron Age broch, standing to over 40 feet high. On W shore of island of Mousa, open at all times.
MUNESS CASTLE   Late 16th century tower house on Z plan at S end of Unst Island. In care of Dept of Environment, open all reasonable hours on application to Mr Peterson, Castle Cottage.
NESS OF BURGI   Iron Age stone structure similar to broch on coast at tip of Scatness, S end of mainland of Shetland. Open all times.
SCALLOWAY CASTLE   Fortified manor house built 1600. In Scalloway, in care of Dept of Environment, open all reasonable hours.

STIRLINGSHIRE

ROUGH CASTLE Roman fort and part of wall of Antonine Wall. One of most important Roman sites in Britain. 1½ miles E of Bonnybridge. In care of Dept of Environment, open all times.

SEABEGS WOOD Section of the Antonine Wall, 1½ miles SW of Bonnybridge.

STIRLING CASTLE Strategic centre of Scotland, the castle has been frequently destroyed. The fine gatehouse belongs to late 15th century, the outer works to the 16th, 17th and 18th centuries. Still in hands of Armed Services, parts are open April to Sept 10 to 6.45, Sundays 11 to 6. Oct to March, 10 to 4, Sundays 1 to 4.

SUTHERLAND

DUN DORNADILLA Iron Age broch, 120 feet in circumference and standing to height of 20 feet. 10 miles NW of Altnaharra.

INCHNADAMPH Ardvreck Castle built in late 16th century with rectangular keep. In ruins.

WEST LOTHIAN

BLACKNESS CASTLE 15th century fortress, much altered, but with strong oblong tower In good state of preservation. Four miles NE of Linlithgow. In care of Dept of Environment, hours standard.

WIGTOWNSHIRE

BARSALLOCH FORT Iron Age fort of horseshoe shape on hill above road at Barsalloch Point, W of Monreith. Ditch is 33 feet wide by 12 feet deep.

3: Wales

ANGLESEY

BEAUMARIS CASTLE Finest example of the concentric castle in Britain and still almost intact. In care of Dept of Environment, hours standard, Sundays 9.30 May to Sept.

CAER GYBI Small Roman fort on cliff at Holyhead, dating from late 3rd, early 4th centuries AD. Open any time.

CAER LÊB Earthwork of double rampart and ditch occupied from 3rd century AD. 1½ miles WNW of Llanidan. Open any time.

CAER Y TWR Iron Age hill fort on summit of Holyhead Mountain.

CASTELL BRYN-GWYN Neolithic defensive site, twice rebuilt and altered, last time in 1st century AD. 1½ miles WNW of Llanidan.

BRECKNOCKSHIRE

BRECON GAER Roman fort founded *c.* AD 75 and rebuilt in stone early 2nd century. Four miles W of Brecon. In care of Dept of Environment, open any time except May to July.

BRONLLYS CASTLE Early 13th century round tower on a 12th century motte. ¾ mile NW of Talgarth.

CASTELL DINAS Iron Age hill fort with 11th century Norman motte inside. N of Crickhowell, ½ mile E of A479.

TRETOWER CASTLE Cylindrical keep of mid 13th century built within remains of a Norman castle. In care of Dept of Environment, hours standard, apply custodian Tretower Court.

CAERNARVONSHIRE

CAERNARVON Most impressive of the Edwardian castles, built on the site of a Norman motte and bailey castle. In care of Dept of Environment, hours standard, Sundays 9.30 May to Sept. Of the town walls much still stands with a circuit of walls 28 feet high and two gates and 8 towers.

CONWAY Edwardian castle 1283–89 in care of Dept of Environment, hours standard, Sundays 9.30 May to Sept. Town walls with circuit of 1,400 yards are probably the finest example in Britain and survive almost intact.

CRICCIETH CASTLE Dating mainly from early 13th century, this castle was altered by Edward I towards the end of the century. In care of Dept of Environment, hours standard, Sundays 9.30 May to Sept.

DINAS DINLLE Iron Age hill fort with double ramparts on a mound by the sea about one mile from Llandwrog, formerly connected with Segontium by a causeway. Inland, past Pontllyfni and Nantlle lake are two more hill forts, Craig y Dinas and Caer Engan.

DOLBADARN CASTLE Massive round tower of early 13th century on rocky hill commanding entrance to Llanberis Pass. In care of Dept of Environment, hours standard, April to Sept only.

DOLWYDDELAN CASTLE Late 12th century keep with early 13th century curtain wall, one mile W of village of same name. In care of Dept of Environment, hours standard, Sundays 9.30 May to Sept.

SEGONTIUM Roman auxiliary fortress connected to Chester, once the Roman centre of power in Wales. Founded c. AD 80 for 1,000 men. Close by Caernarvon. In care of Dept of Environment, hours standard.

TRE'R CEIRI Dry stone hill town of 2nd century AD covering more than 5 acres, overlooking Llanaelhaearn. Defences are best seen on NW side.

CARDIGANSHIRE

ABERYSTWYTH Iron Age hill fort on summit of Pen Dinas, just S of the town.

CARREG-Y-FRAN Iron Age hill fort ½ mile NE of Tregaron.

CILGERRAN CASTLE Mid 13th century castle on promontory site of great strength above River Teifi, 2 miles SE of Cardigan.

CARMARTHENSHIRE

CARREG CENNEN CASTLE Late 13th century castle on fine site above River Cennen, 4 miles SE of Llandilo. In care of Dept of Environment, hours standard.

KIDWELLY Earthwork dating from early 12th century with inner ward built c.1275 and an outer curtain wall added in early 14th century. In care of Dept of Environment, hours standard. Of the medieval town defences only a 14th century gatehouse survives, near the castle entrance.

LLANSTEPHAN CASTLE Norman castle of 12th century but remains mainly late 13th century. Above mouth of River Towy, SW of Carmarthen.

DENBIGHSHIRE

CAER CARADOC Celtic hill fort 1,367 feet up on Pen-y-gaer hill near Cerrigydrudion, traditionally where Caractacus sought refuge from the Romans and was betrayed by local ruler.

DENBIGH Castle built 1282–1322, on site of Welsh castle destroyed by Edward I. The medieval town defences date from the same period and the Burgess Gate and most of the circuit is still complete. In care of Dept of Environment, standard hours, Sundays 9.30 May to Sept. Conducted tours of castle and walls.

DINAS BRAN Celtic hill fort probably of Iron Age, although site re-used in 5th–6th centuries AD for Celtic resistance to Saxons. 900 foot hill overlooking Vale of Llangollen.

DINORBEN Iron Age fortifications near Abergele with rampart still over 40 feet high. In 2nd century AD Romans added stone parapets and gates.

MOEL FENLLI Fortified town of 2nd century AD in Clwydian Hills near Denbigh, the most southerly of a series of such sites.

FLINTSHIRE

EWLOE CASTLE 13th century Welsh castle with typical round towers. One mile NW of Hawarden. In care of Dept of Environment, hours standard, April to Sept only.

FLINT CASTLE Great Edwardian castle of 1277–84 with keep in form of a detached round tower of exceptional strength. In care of Dept of Environment, hours standard.

RHUDDLAN Fine example of concentric castle begun 1277. The town walls were built 1281–2 and are still visible at the NW corner. In care of Dept of Environment, hours standard, Sundays 9.30 May to Sept.

GLAMORGAN

CAERPHILLY CASTLE Concentric castle built late 13th century, noted for its extensive water defences. In care of Dept of Environment, hours standard, Sundays 9.30 May to Sept.

CARDIFF CASTLE Built on the site of a Roman fort, the original Roman work survives in parts. Much of the castle was restored during the 19th century but the Norman motte remains, topped by a Norman keep. Open March to Oct, weekdays 10 to 12 and 2 to 4 (till 8 in summer), Sundays 2 to 4.

CASTELL COCH Small castle of the 13th century, beautifully restored in 1875 to its original splendour. Five miles NW of Cardiff. In care of Dept of Environment, hours standard, Sundays from 9.30 May to Sept.

COITY CASTLE Inner ward and keep of late 12th century within other works of the 14th century. Two miles NE of Bridgend. In care of Dept of Environment, hours standard.

COWBRIDGE Remains of large circuit of medieval town walls, best seen from the surviving South Gate to the SW corner.

EWENNY PRIORY Fortified wall and gateways of the late 12th, early 13th centuries, protecting priory of 1141. 1½ miles S of Bridgend. In care of Dept of Environment, work in progress and admission only during working hours.

GELLY GAER Small Roman fort covering 3½ acres, built AD 105–112 with stone-faced ramparts. On private land.

LLANTWIT Probably Iron Age hill camp, with Roman fortifications built in 2nd century AD and occupied until 4th century. Commanding entrance to creek, once port of Llantwit. S of Cowbridge.

THE MUMBLES Complex of signal station, storehouses and fortifications of late 18th century, built on the outer island of the Mumbles peninsula.

NEWCASTLE Norman gate and part of curtain wall and keep of 12th century on spur above Bridgend.

OGMORE CASTLE   12th century rectangular keep enclosed by early 13th century curtain wall. Three miles SW of Bridgend.

OYSTERMOUTH CASTLE   Castle dating from 1287 with very high curtain wall without flanking towers. In care of Swansea Corporation.

PENRICE CASTLE   13th century castle with tower keep, abandoned in the 16th century and now in ruins. In park behind Nature Reserve at Oxwich Bay. The village is W of this and here may be seen the motte of the first Norman castle at Penrice.

SWANSEA CASTLE   14th century castle at present hidden by later buildings and not yet open to the public. Best part visible so far is the arcaded parapet on the S side. In care of Dept of Environment, work in progress.

WEOBLEY CASTLE   Late 13th, early 14th century fortified manor house, W of Swansea. In care of Dept of Environment, hours April to Sept, 10 to 7, Sundays 1 to 7, Oct to March 10 to 4, Sundays 1 to 4.

MERIONETHSHIRE

CAER DREWYN   Iron Age dry stone hill fort overlooking Corwen. Later used by Owain against Henry II (1165).

CASTELL Y BERE   Remains of 13th century Welsh castle, 8 miles NE of Towyn. Open any time.

HARLECH CASTLE   Well preserved concentric castle, built by Edward I 1283-90. In care of Dept of Environment, hours standard, Sundays 9.30 May to Sept.

PENNAL   Roman fort, sometimes called Cefn Gaer, off the road from the village of Pennal towards Marchlyn.

TOMEN-Y-MÛR   Roman auxiliary fort of 1st century AD holding the S flank of Snowdonia. Much of earthworks visible probably date from medieval times, William Rufus c.1095 perhaps.

MONMOUTHSHIRE

CAERLEON   Remains of Roman fortress, two miles NE of Newport. The SW corner has been exposed, showing rampart, ditch, bastions and barracks. In care of Dept of Environment, hours standard.

CAERWENT   Roman fortified town, strengthened in 3rd century AD with stone facing, bastions and parapet. In village of Caerwent, limited access, in care of Dept of Environment, but surrounded by farming land.

CHEPSTOW   The Bulwarks, Iron Age hill fort, above the town at new village of Bulwark and overlooking the River Wye. The castle on the river dates from Norman times with additions in the 13th century. In care of Dept of Environment, hours standard, Sundays 9.30 May to Sept. Of the medieval town walls much remains standing with seven towers and one gate, the latter much restored.

GROSMONT CASTLE   Castle dating mainly from 1201–43 with additions in the early 14th century. Very deep moat. In care of Dept of Environment, hours standard.

LODGE HILL   Iron Age hill fort encircling height NW of Caerleon. On private land, permission from Mr Till, Lodge Farm, Caerleon.

MONMOUTH   Medieval town walls survive partially, incorporated into later buildings. Of the four gates only the fortified gate on the bridge over the River Monnow still stands.

RAGLAN CASTLE   15th century castle with hexagonal keep and large curtain wall. Half mile N of Raglan. In care of Dept of Environment, hours standard, Sundays 9.30 May to Sept.

SKENFRITH CASTLE   Small 13th century castle with early cylindrical keep, 6 miles NW of Monmouth. Open at all times.

USK CASTLE   Main gate and square keep, with a round tower and portions of the Great Hall are all that remain of this castle on a hill above the town. Some parts are well preserved, but becoming overgrown.

WHITE CASTLE   Norman keep razed in 13th century when a new castle built on this site with great gatehouse. Fortifications are very strong and in good condition. On summit of hill 7 miles E of Abergavenny. In care of Dept of Environment, hours standard.

MONTGOMERYSHIRE

CAERSWS   Roman auxiliary fort covering about 5 acres, dating from 3rd century AD.

DOLFORWYN CASTLE   Remains of Welsh castle c.1273, 4½ miles NE of Newton. In care of Dept of Environment, not yet excavated and not yet open to public.

MONTGOMERY CASTLE   Remains of castle built 1223–7, under excavation. In care of Dept of Environment, open at any time.

OFFA'S DYKE   Formidable ditch and rampart dividing Welsh from Saxons, built between 757 and 796. Survives in places to height of 20 feet or so, with the ditch up to 12 feet deep. Best seen in grounds of Chirk Castle near Selattyn along the road from Knighton to Montgomery, and round Tidenham Chase outside Chepstow. Offa's Dyke Footpath in Monmouthshire follows the course of the wall for some miles, but there is little to see.

PEMBROKESHIRE

CAREW CASTLE   Originally founded soon after Norman Conquest, this castle dates mainly from the late 13th century. Notable for early windows of 16th century. Midway between Tenby and Pembroke.

CARN ENGYL LLE One of best preserved Iron Age forts in Wales, on height 1,138 feet called Carn Ingli, Nevern.

GARN FAWR Iron Age hill fort on highest point of Pen Caer peninsula, Strumble headland.

GOWER Peninsula running some 18 miles W from Swansea and having along it a series of small promontory Iron Age forts. Cil Ifor, $\frac{3}{4}$ mile E of Llanthidian is a good example, another with complex defence system is The Bulwark, on Llanmadog Hill.

LLAWHADEN CASTLE Early 14th century castle replacing earlier defences of timber and earth. Three miles NW of Narberth. In care of Dept of Environment, hours standard.

MANORBIER CASTLE Remains of castle built 1272–1325, 6 miles W of Tenby.

MILFORD HAVEN 16th century fort on westerly approaches to Milford Haven at Angle Bay, where also stands ruins of a peel tower. On Thorn Island is an old fort, probably of the Civil War period.

MOEL TRIGARN Iron Age fort on steep hill with inclined entrances.

PEMBROKE CASTLE Castle with parts dating from as early as c.1090. Surrounded on three sides by tidal waters and has a cylindrical keep and massive gatehouse.

ST DAVID'S PALACE Palace built between 1280 and 1350, protected by a curtain wall c.1300. Visible from many points. 16 miles W of Haverfordwest.

TENBY Gate and 6 towers of original medieval town defences, also parts of the walls, though much hidden by later building. Best seen from South Parade and White Lion Street. Dates from 13th century, strengthened 15th century and again at time of Armada.

RADNORSHIRE

CASTELL COLLEN Roman auxiliary fort covering some 5 acres, built in 1st century AD from earth and timber, rebuilt stone 2nd century. On private land and to be re-covered after excavation: doubtful if will be on view permanently.

4: Ireland

COUNTY ANTRIM

ANTRIM Well preserved round tower standing 93 feet high, one mile N of Antrim in the grounds of Steeple House. In Deerpark is a motte and bailey castle with stone-revetted ditches and in Ballyharvey Lower another castle of the same type.

ARMOY 10th century round tower by modern parish church, 6 miles S of Ballycastle.

BALLYPALADY Series of six Iron Age ring forts, 4 miles NE of Templepatrick.

CARRICKFERGUS CASTLE Original castle built end of 12th century, destroyed 1384 but subsequently rebuilt. The Norman keep survives in the NW corner. In the outer ward are gun platforms of the Tudor period. In State care, hours April to Sept, weekdays 10 to 1, 2 to 6, Sundays 2 to 6. Oct to March, weekdays 10 to 1, 2 to 4, Sundays 2 to 4.

CLOUGH CASTLE Motte and bailey castle of various dates, ending as a Planter's castle of c.1600. Destroyed by Cromwellians. Two miles WSW at Dundermot is a Norman motte.

DOONBOUGHT Iron Age fort, one mile SSE of Clough, reoccupied in medieval times.

DUNLUCE CASTLE 13th century castle with parts from 14 and 16th centuries. $2\frac{1}{2}$ miles WNW of Bushmills. In State care, hours April to Sept, weekdays 10 to 1, 2 to 6, Sundays 2 to 6. Oct to March, Saturdays 10 to 1, 2 to 4, Sundays 2 to 4.

FORESCORE FORT Oval ring fort of Iron Age, 3 miles E of Glenavy.

GREEN MOUND Small motte with earthwork, $1\frac{1}{2}$ miles ESE of Glenavy.

HARRYVILLE MOTTE Finest Anglo–Norman motte in Ulster, standing 40 feet high. Ballymena.

KNOCKAHOLET MOAT Remains of motte and bailey castle with motte in centre. 7 miles SSW of Armoy.

LOUGH NA CRANAGH Oval crannog with dry stone revetment over 5 feet above the water. 2 miles E of Ballycastle.

LOWER CLANNABOY CASTLE Remains of a castle and mansion which succeeded it, also of two motte and bailey earthworks on shore of Lough Neath. $2\frac{1}{2}$ miles through estate of Shane's Castle Park, S of Randalstown.

LYLE'S HILL Iron Age hill fort of stone faced ramparts, enclosing over 12 acres, on 753 foot hill two miles SSE of Templepatrick.

RATHMORE TRENCH Oval ring fort of the Iron Age with an Anglo–Norman motte built in the E end. Two miles E of Antrim.

TODD'S GROVE Large ring fort with double ramparts, $2\frac{1}{2}$ miles SSE of Lisburn.

COUNTY ARMAGH

ARMAGH Iron Age hill fort surrounding St Patrick's Protestant Cathedral.

CHARLEMONT FORT Remains of fort erected 1602 with earthworks of a star fort completed 1624 and extended in 1673. Finest example of 17th century artillery fortification in Ulster.

DANE'S CAST Rampart and ditch construction thought to have formed part of the defences of the old kingdom of Ulster. Best seen at Killyfaddy, Lisnadill, Latmacollum and Killycapple.

THE DORSEY Iron Age camp of 300 acres enclosed by earthen rampart and ditches.

LISLEITRIM FORT Iron Age ring fort with three ramparts and ditches. In Lisleitrim Lough is a large crannog.

JOHNSTON'S FEWS 16th century earthworks, later occupied in 17th century. 2½ miles S of Newton Hamilton.

NAVAN FORT Iron Age hill fort enclosing 18 acres with rampart and ditch, mentioned by Ptolemy in his 'Geography'. Nearby are traces of a ring fort.

COUNTY DOWN

ARDGLASS A collection of fine 14th to 16th century fortified houses: King's Castle, Margaret's Castle, Cowd Castle, Horn Castle, and Jordan's Castle.

AUDLEY'S CASTLE Well preserved 15th and 16th century castle, ½ mile NW of Audleystown. In the town itself is a small Plantation Castle c.1610.

BALLYMAGHERY CASTLE Motte and bailey castle with three concentric ditches, one mile ESE of Hilltown.

BALLYNAHINCH Small Iron Age hill fort, three miles SW. Three miles to the NNW is Magheraknock Fort, another hill fort of the same period.

BANGOR TOWER Tower house on the waterfront, built c.1637.

DUNDONALD MOTTE Motte standing to height of nearly 40 feet, probably raised c.1180. In Dundonald village on E side of Belfast.

DUNDRUM CASTLE Early motte and bailey castle with great keep c.1230 and gatehouse of c.1300. Important castle in Anglo-Norman attempt at conquest. Near village of same name on 200 foot high hill.

GREEN CASTLE Great keep of 14th century with gatehouse and curtain. Earlier castle represented by a motte nearby. Ruined by cannon in 1652.

HILLSBOROUGH FORT Star shaped artillery fort built during 1650s with arrow head bastions at each angle. Tower house erected c.1758.

KILLYLEAGH CASTLE Motte and bailey castle of Anglo-Norman times, replaced in 13th and 14th centuries by present castle. Severely damaged 1648, restored 1666 and again in mid 19th century.

LISNAGADE Centre for over a dozen Iron Age ring forts, the most important being at Lisnagade itself. Two miles E of Scarva.

MOYRY CASTLE Three storey square tower in one corner of a rectangular enclosure, built 1601 to secure Moyry Pass. Near Newry.

NARROW WATER CASTLE Tower and small enclosure of 1560, 2 miles NW of Warrenpoint on N shore of Carlingford Lough. In State care, hours April to Sept, weekdays 10 to 1, 2 to 6, Sundays 2 to 6. Oct to March, Saturdays 10 to 1, 2 to 4, Sundays 2 to 4.

PRETTY MARY'S FORT Fine example of multiple ramparted Iron Age ring fort in Aughnafosker, near Moira.

RATHFRYLAND Large Iron Age ring fort on hill 506 feet high.

STRANGFORD CASTLE 16th century fortified house, probably the best example in Ulster.

COUNTY FERMANAGH

DEVENISH 12th century round tower 81 feet high, one of finest in Ireland. Hours April to Sept, Mon to Sat 10 till 6, Sun 2 till 6. Oct to March, Sat and Sun only, 10 till sunset. Three miles NNW of Enniskillen.

ENNISKILLEN CASTLE Originally 15th century with keep's lower storeys incorporated in later building. Water Gate dates from c.1580. The Sconce, an earthwork to the SE in Broad Meadow, is an earthwork erected for the defence of the town at a later date. Fort Hill takes its name from the remains of a star fort built c.1689.

COUNTY GALWAY

DOOCAHER Great promontory Iron Age fort with massive stone rampart. 1½ miles W of Killeany, Inishmore, Aran Islands.

DOONCONOR Iron Age fort with great stone ramparts near centre of Inishmaan, Aran Islands.

DOONFARVAGH Iron Age ring fort of stone with terraced rampart, on Inishmaan, Aran Islands.

DUN AONGHUS Iron Age fort covering 11 acres with three concentric ramparts of dry stone and with an inner citadel. On edge of 300 foot cliff, ½ mile SW of Templenaneeve, Inishmore, Aran Islands.

DUN ONAGHT Large Iron Age ring fort with dry stone terraced ramparts, ½ mile SSE of village on Inishmore, Aran Islands.

FURMINA CASTLE 15th century tower set within an Iron Age ring fort on rocky hill S of the landing place on Inisheer, Aran Islands.

OGHIL Great Iron Age hill fort of dry stone masonry. N of Oghil village are the remains of another small ring fort and at close by Cowrugh village are the remains of a defaced but once large fort of stone.

COUNTY KILDARE

KNOCKAULIN Iron Age hill fort covering 20 acres with traces of ring forts within the ramparts. On 600 foot hill ¾ mile NW of Kilcullen.

COUNTY LONDONDERRY

BRACKFIELD CASTLE Square tower house of the 17th century built for the London Skinner's Company, with flanking towers at two corners.
CULMORE FORT Built in the 19th century to replace one of the 17th century and guarding the mouth of the Foyle, 5 miles NNE of Derry.
DUNGLADY FORT Iron Age fort with three rings of defences near village of Culnady, 5 miles SW of Kilrea.
GREENAN ELLY Iron Age hill fort, largely destroyed in 676. Remains comprise three rings of defences surrounding an inner citadel or ring fort of dry masonry, 77 feet in internal diameter and 17½ feet high. Five miles from Derry, on Greenan Mountain.
LONDONDERRY Medieval town walls encompassing the centre of the modern city were constructed in 1618. Most of the walls survive, together with bastions and gates.
MILLIGAN POINT Martello tower and old gun battery, guarding entrance to Lough Foyle, 2½ miles W of Coleraine.
MOUNT SANDEL FORT Motte measuring about 180 by 150 feet across the summit on a promontory outside Coleraine, overlooking the River Bann. Attributed to the Normans although legend states it was Dun-Da-Beann, the residence of an Irish hero.
ROUGH FORT Large Iron Age ring fort one mile W of Limavady.
ROUGH ISLAND An island in Lough Enagh, NE of Londonderry, having on it a crannog occupied from Neolithic times.
SALTER'S CASTLE Tower house or Plantation Castle built about 1619 by the London City Companies, with flanking towers at two corners.
WHITE FORT Polygonal ring fort of dry stone masonry in Cashel near Dungiven.

COUNTY MEATH

TARA A low hill one mile W of Dublin covered with ancient remains, including : Fort of the Synods, built between 1st and 3rd century AD in three stages : Fort of the Kings, an oval hill fort covering an area 950 by 800 feet : within this enclosure are The Royal Seat, a ring fort, and Cormac's House, a high, flat mound enclosed by two ramparts and ditches : S of this are the remains of Loigaire's Fort, an Iron Age ring fort. N of the Fort of Kings are The Sloping Trenches, two unusual earthworks. Half a mile S of Tara is a hill top with a multiple banked hill fort called Rath Maeve.

COUNTY ROSCOMMON

LOUGH GARA In the lough is an Iron Age crannog, thought to have held ten small huts. Near Boyle.

COUNTY TYRONE

BENBURB CASTLE Quadrangular enclosure with towers at each corner, built *c*.1615 above the river just south of the village and about 4 miles W of Moy.
DERRYWOONE CASTLE Early 17th century tower house on L plan about ½ mile NE of Baronscourt, near Newtownstewart.
HARRY AVERY CASTLE Interesting example of medieval castle, far from English influence. Flattened natural motte enclosed by curtain wall with at NE end a keep resembling a twin towered gatehouse. ¾ mile SW of Newtownstewart.
MACHUGH ISLAND Small island in Lough Catherine at Baronscourt, containing a crannog occupied from the Stone Age. A castle was built on the crannog consisting of a small tower house and barmkin and occupied up to 16th century.
MOUNT JOY CASTLE Remains of a square 'keep' with four projecting towers, built in 17th century inside a star fort of 1602. Captured 1641, burned down 1643. 4 miles ESE of Stewartstown.
ROUGHAM CASTLE Square tower house with round towers at the corners built in 1618. 2 miles SW of Stewartstown.

5: The Channel Islands

ALDERNEY

Immense fortifications constructed in the mid 19th century for the British Fleet, Fort Albert being the largest and most important part. Small garrison maintained until 1930, aided by the Militia of the island.

GUERNSEY

BELLE GRÉVE BAY Martello tower.
CASTLE CORNET Castle founded *c*.1204 on spur sheltering the harbour of St Peter Port. Important stronghold until Napoleonic Wars period ended.
FERMAIN BAY Martello tower.
IVY CASTLE Ruins of castle believed to date from 1031. Refortified in 17th century. On private land, but permission to visit from bungalow close by.
L'ANCRESSE BAY Five Martello towers along the bay.

PETIT BOT BAY Martello tower at entrance to a granite slipway, adapted by the Germans in World War 2.
SAINTS BAY Martello tower.
VAZON BAY Martello tower.

JERSEY

ELIZABETH CASTLE Mostly dating from 16th century with lower ward added 1626 and strengthened at outbreak of Civil War. On rock ¾ mile from shore of St Helier, reached by causeway at low tide. Open daily, normal hours.
FLIQUET BAY Telegraph tower, an old Martello tower.
FORT REGENT Mont de la Ville overlooking St Helier harbour has been the site of a castle for centuries; the present fortifications were built c.1806 and altered slightly by the Germans in World War 2.
GRÉVE DE LECQ Disused fort.
GROUVILLE BAY Six Martello towers and Mont Orgueil Castle.
MONT ORGUEIL CASTLE On a headland 310 feet up commanding the entire E coast of the island is a castle begun in the 10th century by the Dukes of Normandy and completed in the 13th century. Adapted for use by cannon later. Series of gateways are of great interest, 1st originally protected by a drawbridge, commanded by Harliston's Tower of 1470; 2nd early 13th century with drawbridge and portcullis; 3rd machicolation; 4th added 1593.
NEZ DU GUET Disused fort.
ST AUBINS BAY In addition to St Aubins Castle, Elizabeth Castle, Fort Regent, there are three Martello towers in this bay. St Aubins Castle was built by Henry VIII to protect the town from sea attacks, rebuilt 1742. Reached by a causeway at low tide.
ST BRELADES BAY Two Martello towers and the ruins of a battery.
ST CATHERINES BAY Three Martello towers, including one now known as Archirondel Tower, brightly painted and used as a landmark.
ST LAWRENCE German Military Underground Hospital constructed during World War 2 and now housing a museum of the German occupation. Open 10 until 6 weekdays.
ST PETERS BUNKER German underground bunker of World War 2 built to protect roads leading to the airport and W of the island. Open March to Oct only, 10 till 5.
ST OUENS BAY Three Martello towers, including La Rocca Tower which is ½ mile out at sea now.

World War 2 Fortifications

BERKSHIRE

READING Pill box in field beside junction of M4 and A4 between Reading and Theale.
THREEMILE CROSS Pill box to west of A33 from Reading, map ref 710 676.
Pill box west of this, at Lambwood Hill Common, map ref 703 673.
WOKINGHAM Pill box in church yard off A329 from Wokingham to Bracknell, map ref 815 688.
Pill box south-west of Wokingham, along B3349, at map ref 777 669.

BUCKINGHAMSHIRE

IVER Pill box of metal, igloo shaped, on south side of 1st bridge over railway line between Iver and Langley.

CAMBRIDGESHIRE

FEN DITTON Pill box in Fen Ditton, which is between the Newmarket and High Ditch roads.
WATERBEACH FEN Pill box at Joyce Farm.

DEVON

CROYDE Two pill boxes, to west and east of Croyde, off the Barnstable road.
DARTMOUTH Gun emplacement at Dartmouth Castle.
Pill box, west of Dartmouth at road junction on B3207 marked as Hemborough Post (The Sportsman's Arms), map ref SX 832 523.
DAWLISH WARREN Two pill boxes on a golf course near the peninsula by Dawlish Warren station.
TEIGNMOUTH Pill box on sea wall north of Teignmouth, where Exeter to Plymouth railway line nears the wall.
YELVERTON Gun emplacements on Yelverton Common.

DORSET

WAREHAM Pill box built into wall beneath the church where T. E. Lawrence is buried. Map ref SY 922 873.

DURHAM

HARTLEPOOL A number of ruined pill boxes along the sea front.

SOUTH HETTON Pill box off A182 to South Hetton, by junction with unclassified Haswell road to West.
SUNDERLAND Pill box in field off A690 Sunderland to Houghton-le-Spring road, by crossroads with Ryhope-Newbottle unclassified road.

ESSEX

BRADWELL-ON-SEA Two pill boxes by sea wall.
CANVEY ISLAND Gun emplacement on sea wall at The Lobster Smack.
Gun emplacement on sea wall behind Fielders Holiday Camp.
CHELMSFORD Six pill boxes in fields on either side of A130 from roundabout where A132 joins it from Great Baddow.
COALHOUSE POINT Two storied pill box on north bank of Thames, three miles east of Tilbury, map ref TQ 691 768.
ROCHFORD Pill box at side of Co-op on Rochford-Ashingdon road, at Golden crossroads one mile from Rochford.
SOUTHEND Pill box at side of railway line at Southend Airport between Warmers Bridge and the Anne Boleyn public house.
Pill box at Warmers Bridge.

GLOUCESTERSHIRE

BEACHLEY Two pill boxes on extreme end of Beachley peninsula, beside the Severn suspension bridge.

HAMPSHIRE

ISLE OF WIGHT Large gun emplacement at Puckpool Point between Ryde and Sea View. Large gun emplacement on Culver downs near the monument between Foreland and Sandown.
PORTSMOUTH Series of pill boxes between entrance to the harbour and Lee-on-Solent.
Series of World War 1 forts on Gosport peninsula.
(The forts are clearly marked on the Ordnance Survey 1 inch map, Sheet 180.)
SOUTH WONSTON A number of pill boxes south of here, in Worthy Down Camp.

KENT

APPLEDORE Several pill boxes along the Appledore and Military road from Rye.
CLIFFE Two pill boxes on south bank of Thames, $4\frac{1}{2}$ miles east of Gravesend, map refs TQ 713 755 and TQ 710 758.
FRANT Pill boxes and tank traps around Frant, near Tunbridge Wells.
HIGHAM Two pill boxes at Higham, 5 miles east of Gravesend, map refs TQ 726 733 and TQ 725 733.
SHORNEMEAD Two pill boxes on the sea wall on south bank of Thames, 3 miles east of Gravesend, map ref TQ 693 749.
WICKHAMBREUX Pill box on road to Canterbury leading from Wickhambreux, about 250 yards out on right hand side.

LANCASHIRE

COCKERHAM Pill box on east side of A588 north of village.
GARSTANG Pill box on bank of River Wrye.
HEYSHAM Gun emplacement on north side of road from Heysham village to Heysham harbour, incorporated in mock castle.
HORNBY Pill box on east bank of River Lune, on north-east side of Hornby-Gressingham road.
LIVERPOOL Pill box in Clarks Gardens on corner of Woolton Road and Springwood Avenue.
ST MICHAEL'S-ON-WRYE Pill box on bank of river.

LINCOLNSHIRE

CLEETHORPES World War 1 Fort Haile Sand, two miles south of the town, on sand flats.
Underground bunker at Suggits Lane railway crossing.
Tank traps at end of sea front promenade.
Pill box at north end of town, near golf links.
GRIMSBY Underground bunker beside Drewery Brothers fish factory on Grimsby dock estate. Underground bunker further along sea wall at old Admiralty slip.
HUMBERSTONE JITTIES Pill box on A1098 at Humberstone Jitties, south of Cleethorpes.
PITNEY LOCK Large underground bunker and gun emplacement at Pitney Lock, near Cleethorpes.
THEDDLETHORPE Two pill boxes along A1031 towards Mablethorpe from Grimsby, used for stores by RAF. (Area still used as bomb range.)

MIDDLESEX

ACTON Pill box by side of District Line (western direction) between LT train works.

CHISWICK Pill box on disused bridge across Southern Region railway line at back of LT works.
HAYES Pill box on top of factory outbuilding on south side of Western Region railway line between Hayes and West Drayton.
WEST DRAYTON Pill box at west end of coal depot by side of Western Region railway line outside West Drayton station.

NORFOLK

GORLESTON-ON-SEA Site of gun emplacement on cliffs, with underground works still intact.
GREAT YARMOUTH Pill box on A47 road out of Great Yarmouth.
Pill box on A12 from Great Yarmouth into Lowestoft.
Pill box on A143 from Great Yarmouth at St Olaves.

OXFORDSHIRE

UPPER HEYFORD Pill box near USAF base at Upper Heyford, near Oxford to Banbury canal, in angle formed by the A423 and B4031.

RUTLAND

WHISSENDINE Pill box in village, on east side half way down Teigh Lane.

SOMERSET

DUNSTER Two pill boxes off Minehead to Williton road, near Dunster Castle.
MINEHEAD Two pill boxes to east of Butlins Camp near Minehead, on edge of golf course overlooking sea.
TAUNTON Chain of pill boxes along Bridgwater-Taunton Canal in fields and near the railway line.

SUFFOLK

BELCHAMP OTTEN Pill box in field on edge of wood on road from Belchamp Otten to Sudbury, on Suffolk-Essex border.
BRADWELL Tank trap at Lound Waterworks near Bradwell.
FELIXSTOWE Series of five or six pill boxes on Landguard Point.
HOPTON Pill box at Hopton RAF radar station, south of Great Yarmouth.
OULTON Pill box on Somerleyton road from Oulton village.

SURREY

BISLEY Pill box on National Rifle Association ranges at Bisley Camp.
BOX HILL Pill box and gun emplacement on south side of Box Hill, across the River Mole, at map refs TQ 175 512 and TQ 175 511.
EPSOM Pill box east of railway station, facing the tracks on south side of main line to London. Map ref TQ 209 609.
Pill box in corner of field by junction of A240 and second class road just north of Epsom railway station at Drift Bridge, map ref TQ 230 602.
FARNHAM Pill box by Mill Bridge, off A287 south of Farnham by River Wey, map ref SU 868 445.
Gun emplacement off B3001 by Waverley Abbey, south-east of Farnham. Map ref SU 871 455.
GUILDFORD Pill box beside steep track on North Downs, north of Guildford-Dorking railway line, map ref TQ 115 490.
HORLEY Pill box just after a girder bridge over the main railway line past Horley, on the left going towards London.
REDHILL Pill box on Earlswood Common, south of Redhill, and on left side of main railway line going towards London.
TILFORD AREA Pill box near Somerset Bridge, map ref SU 922 439.
Pill box by Paulshott Farm, map ref SU 903 442.
Gun emplacement near Thundery Farm, map ref SU 902 439.
Two pill boxes by Tilford Bridge, map ref SU 874 435.
Pill box in Sheephatch School field, map ref SU 876 446.
Pill box by quarry at map ref SU 868 448.
Gun emplacement by Moor Park College, map ref SU 860 460.
Pill box by Moor Park College, in field, map ref SU 862 466.
Gun emplacement in garden at Moor Park College, map ref SU 862 465.
Gun emplacement near Moor Park Farm, map ref SU 861 473.

SUSSEX

BODIAM CASTLE Pill box in field by castle.
COOKSBRIDGE Pill box by railway line between Cooksbridge and Lewes, on right when travelling towards London.
LITTLEHAMPTON Pill box at junction of River Arun and east channel.

PETT LEVEL   Two storey gun emplacement on inland side of road, near Hastings.
RUSTINGTON   Pill box on sea wall, five miles west of Worthing.
RYE   A pill box on each side of the road from Rye towards Camber, near Monk Bretton Bridge.
SHOREHAM   Series of three or more pill boxes along south bank of River Adur by Shoreham airport.

WILTSHIRE

CODFORD   Pill box near railway station at Codford, near Warminster.
COLERNE   Pill box on village recreation ground.
Pill box on road between Colerne and the Shoe Inn, A420.
MARLBOROUGH   Pill box built into corner of a building halfway down the steep slope into the town, heading towards the town hall.
NORTON BAVANT   Pill box near Sutton Veny road into Norton Bavant, in field.
SUTTON VENY   Pill box on Sutton Veny-Longbridge Deverill road in a field, not far from an earth covered US Army supply dump.

YORKSHIRE

FILEY   Pill box on cliffs overlooking front.
HUBY   Pill box on top of hill in village of Huby, five miles north-east of Otley.
HULL   World War 1 Fort Bull Sand on sandbank south-west of Spurn Head lighthouse.
LEEDS   Gun emplacement on ACF weekend training camp east of Leeds.
Gun emplacement between Leeds and Pudsey.
OTLEY   Pill box in middle of a field, two miles north of Otley on moor road to Timble.

SCOTLAND : MIDLOTHIAN

EDINBURGH   Pill box overlooking railway embankment on shore of Forth in grounds of Challenger Lodge home for spastic children.

ULSTER : ANTRIM

PORTRUSH   Pill box on the East Strand in Portrush.

WALES
CARMARTHENSHIRE

CEFN SIDAN   Pill box on beach at Cefn Sidan, near Pembrey.
PENLLERGAER   Pill box on main Swansea-Carmarthen road, about three miles from Penllergaer crossroads.

GLAMORGAN

ABERCYNON   Pill box on side of the main road between Abercynon and Merthyr.
ABERTHAW   Several pill boxes and a line of dragon's teeth above the beach on the part of the coast known as The Leys at Aberthaw.
LLANTWIT MAJOR   Half a dozen pill boxes on the cliffs between Llantwit Major and St Donats.
PYLE   Pill box, fallen on to the beach, at Kenfig, near Pyle.

MONMOUTHSHIRE

USK   Two pill boxes on either side of the disused railway line 300 yards west of the A472 where it crosses the line.